Marketing for Parks, Recreation, and Leisure

Marketing for Parks, Recreation, and Leisure

Ellen L. O'Sullivan

Venture Publishing, Inc.
State College, PA

Cover Design: Sikorski Design
Production: Bonnie Godbey
Printing and Binding: BookCrafters, Chelsea, MI

Library of Congress Catalogue Card Number 91-65916
ISBN 0-910251-43-6

for Gary

Acknowledgements

Marketing for parks, recreation, and leisure programs and services is both an old and relatively new endeavor. Since our beginnings, practitioners have been striving to design programs and services to meet the needs of people. That process has been heightened by the growing diversity within people and their subsequent needs as well as escalating competition within the industry.

I am but a continual learner of the marketing process as it evolves within our profession and as such am grateful to those individuals who over the years have contributed to this learning process. While I am hesitant to list those individuals making such contributions for fear of overlooking someone, I feel the need to acknowledge my appreciation to the individuals named:

my parents, Gene and Janet Lupia, who both understood and supported my decision to study recreation and leisure;

the faculty at Cortland State, especially Dr. Harlan "Gold" Metcalf, who provided a solid foundation for my beginnings;

Dr. Harry E. Reynolds and my colleagues at the Longmeadow Massachusetts Parks and Recreation Department, who offered me the opportunity to learn and grow as a recreator during my eight years with them;

Dr. John Crompton, who pioneered marketing research and applications for our field;

Dr. Rod Warnick of the University of Massachusetts, and Clay Melnicke of the Ontario Ministry of Tourism and Recreation, who both so willingly shared information and resources over the years;

the National Recreation and Park Association–initially Bette Weseman and then Kathy Barlett of the Northeast office–who facilitated my involvement in marketing workshops and seminars;

my students, colleagues, and administrators at Southern Connecticut State University who supported my efforts in a myriad of ways;

Geoff Godbey and the people at Venture Publishing who facilitated this process; and

Wendy Rubin, executive director of the Connecticut Recreation and Parks Association, for her valued feedback during the review of early chapters.

I want to also acknowledge the contributions of several practitioners who have continued to be a source of learning for me–Pat Harden, U.S. Navy MWR Training Division; Margie Gruber, MWR Director at Brunswick, Maine Naval Air Station; Tom Dooley, Superintendent of Recreation in Wallingford, Connecticut; and Tom Wells from the Recreation Advisory Services for the State of North Carolina.

Finally, I wish to give a special thanks to the hundreds of park and recreation practitioners whom I've met over the past few years for sharing their marketing secrets, successes, and challenges.

Table of Contents

Introduction

It's the glow of achievement on the face of a six year-old as he dives into the deep end of the pool for the first time as well as the look of wonder in the faces of the children experiencing the magic of Disney World. It's a simple walk through the woods for a world-weary adult as well as the tremendous feeling of escape and relaxation brought about by vacationing at a remote resort. Park, recreation, and leisure pursuits encompass a vast array of experiences taking on different purposes and meanings for each participant. Those differences in purpose and meaning which make marketing such a vital phase of our operations at this time.

In the earliest stages of our development as a field, recreators strived to plan for and with people to meet their leisure needs and interests. This was marketing. In the ensuing years, marketing assumed a connotation more closely aligned with selling or promoting our parks, programs, and services

The leisure industry has come full circle. The ever-increasing variety of needs and interests inherent within the leisure experience, coupled with the escalating fragmentation of lifestyle groups and the rapid growth of competition, has reaffirmed the role of marketing within parks, recreation, and leisure.

Marketing is not just a group of highly-trained sales representatives. It is not just the publication of sophisticated promotional pieces. Marketing is the development of open spaces, recreation activities and leisure experiences carefully designed to reach out and attract specific groups of users by addressing their needs and interests.

Marketing for parks and recreation starts with people. It involves identifying and understanding subgroups of users. It consists of knowing and understanding these subgroups of users most completely and goes well beyond the usual focus upon age, gender, or income. Marketing addresses a myriad of questions. How do these people live, work, and play? What needs or benefits are they hoping to address through recreation participation?

For this industry, marketing consists of carefully considering decisions related to program and service elements within our control. It involves a concerted effort to select and include specific choices related to time, setting, personnel, price, and a host of variables associated with the design or construction of a park, program, experience, or service. Its purpose is to design and offer such programs and services that have been tailored to meet the needs of these subgroups we wish to attract to our organization.

Marketing for parks, recreation, and leisure involves the entire organization or delivery system, and should not be considered the responsibility of one department or person within that delivery system. Marketing is the orientation of a delivery system towards its user groups. The ongoing activities within that operation are designed to provide continued feedback and contact with patrons.

Yes, marketing is far more than selling or advertising. It involves an entire orientation toward increased knowledge and service of the user groups in a delivery system–not necessarily an easy task. The use of marketing within this industry relates to today's successes in terms of participation, and speaks to tomorrow's viability as delivery systems must continue to modify and adapt to meet the ever-evolving leisure needs and interests of the people we serve.

Chapter One

Marketing–The Process for Parks, Recreation, and Leisure

Common Concerns of Parks, Recreation, and Leisure Delivery Systems:

- The director of a small, municipal recreation department studies general marketing and wonders how to apply it to her department.

- A private swim club facing declining membership considers the role marketing may play in its future.

- A major theme park confronted with growing competition considers increasing the role of marketing within its organization.

- A large, urban fitness center feels confident that extensive advertising campaigns satisfy their marketing requirements.

Marketing–What It Is and Isn't

Marketing is a term used extensively in today's world. Mention the word marketing and it conjures up different images and meanings. To some people the term is synonymous with sales, and they envision a sales representative knocking on doors with a high-pressured sales pitch. To others, the term immediately suggests Madison Avenue and advertising agencies designing high-powered ads to sell products.

While both of these concepts, sales and advertising, are integral parts of the marketing process, they do not serve as accurate or complete definitions of marketing. Marketing is a far more complex and extensive process than these examples suggest. It consists of a myriad of different activities conducted as part of the ongoing operations of an organization. While there are a plethora of different definitions for the term, marketing is generally defined as *human activity directed towards satisfying needs and wants through exchange processes* (Kotler, 1980, p. 21).

As indicated by this definition, marketing is far more inclusive than solely being limited to sales or promotional techniques. The process of marketing consists of a host of activities designed to identify the needs and wants of potential consumers and to encourage these individuals to become involved in the exchange process. This exchange process may involve a simple monetary transaction as in payment of a registration fee or purchase of a travel package. When related to parks, recreation, and leisure, this exchange process may become more complex as leisure delivery systems attempt to encourage potential users to exchange discretionary time and money in exchange for participation in a recreation program or service.

As with any process, the concept of marketing has evolved over time. Marketing initially dealt specifically with the manufacture of products. This product orientation focused upon increasing outputs while reducing costs (Lefebvre and Flora, 1988, p. 301). Park, recreation, and leisure agencies practicing this orientation attempted to increase the range and number of programs and services while reducing the per capita expenditures associated with them. Programs and services were structured to be both basic and general with success related to the numbers of people involved or served.

Following this product-based era, marketing changed its focus to take on a sales orientation. This sales orientation was directed towards convincing consumers to purchase a particular product through the efforts of sales representatives or promotional campaigns. This stage of evolution of marketing is responsible for the image of advertising and marketing as being one and the same process. Commercial delivery systems created sales staffs to facilitate the purchase of their services by potential users. All types of delivery systems, including the public and nonprofit sectors, flooded their users with promotional materials.

A commonality shared by these two orientations, product and sales, was the emphasis upon the agency. These two orientations focused upon those programs and services the agency desired to provide for its users. This created a *push* relationship between the delivery system and the consumer (Lefebvre and Flora, 1988, p. 301). The organization created a program and then pushed that program at the consumer.

However, recent economic and societal factors have caused the process of marketing to evolve still further in response to changing times. Marketing is now perceived as having a customer or user-orientation. With this approach the focus of marketing is shifted and the aim of marketing is to investigate and understand consumers in order to design a product, program, or service specific to their needs or wants.

This is quite a different orientation from the initial approaches to marketing that addressed either the development of a product or the sale of that product. Those two orientations reflected an *internal* approach to marketing, since they addressed the needs of the organization as opposed to the needs and wants of the consumers. The customer or user orientation differs significantly from the other two orientations because it causes an organization to take an *external* approach and to look outward at the needs and interests of the user in an effort to *pull* them to the agency (Figure 1.1).

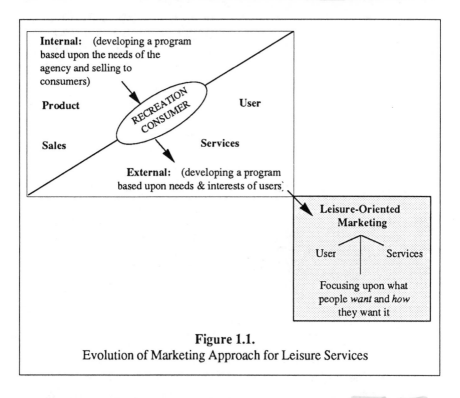

Figure 1.1.
Evolution of Marketing Approach for Leisure Services

Based upon the customer/user orientation, marketing for parks, recreation, and leisure has evolved even further to incorporate a services marketing approach. Whether running in a road race or taking the family to an amusement park, participation in recreational pursuits cannot be compared with the purchase of a box of cereal. Lovelock maintains that if users need to be physically present and must spend time while the service is performed, then their satisfaction will be influenced by services marketing (Lovelock, 1984, pp. 49-51). Since the vast majority of recreational and leisure pursuits meet the criteria outlined by Lovelock, the process of marketing for such organizations needs to be influenced and modified by this attention to the individual and his relationship with that service.

Marketing is a complex and creative process that can significantly impact upon an organization. Yes, it involves the design and creation of a program or service. It also requires the promotion of those programs and services to both current and potential customers. Although it incorporates some elements of both the product and sales orientations, the process has significantly evolved. Today marketing directs its attentions towards people. Who are they? What are their needs and interests? How do they want these needs and interests met? Marketing currently involves a host of activities employed to ascertain the needs and interests of consumers in order to design specific programs and services to facilitate this exchange process.

Why Marketing for Parks, Recreation, and Leisure?

Why construct a framework for marketing directed exclusively towards parks, recreation, and leisure? Why not just utilize concepts developed for organizations manufacturing products or delivering other types of services? While elements of general and services marketing are relevant for the marketing of leisure services, there are factors related to the leisure industry and to recreation participation patterns that require adaptations of these established concepts for parks, recreation, and leisure.

Recreation participation is not the same as purchasing a box of cereal. Since recreation participation involves consumption as opposed to just purchase, the marketing process needs to reflect that reality. Recreation consumption also differs from other forms of service patterns. One cannot equate participation in recreation activities with involvement with other service providers such as doctors, banks, insurance companies, or dry cleaning establishments. The exchange process differs, since one is attempting to motivate people to exchange discretionary time and money for participation in recreation programs and services.

Recreation is a basic human need but as such it is still a voluntary endeavor requiring the expenditures of discretionary time and money. How people choose to use their discretionary time and money and for what outcomes is a complex decision related to the individualized and specialized needs of the consumer. What is play to one person may be perceived as work by another. People seeking escape and relaxation are not seeking the same sort of activities as those desiring socialization and a sense of belonging. The variations among needs and wants to be satisfied along with time and money elements to be exchanged create a unique and complex marketing approach. These complexities are best addressed through a framework of marketing designed specifically for parks, recreation, and leisure.

These unique and complex choices related to recreational patterns play a significant role in the economy. Recreation consumption and subsequent expenditures are big business. The travel industry alone is estimated to be the second largest retail industry in the United States, second only to retail grocery operations. Recreation is no longer considered a nonessential or extra life pursuit. A recent study completed by the Roper Organization ("USA Snapshots," 1990) indicated that when people are asked to assess the importance of leisure and work in their lives, increasing numbers of Americans rank leisure as more important than work.

Since recreation and leisure may be of increasing importance to Americans, and because such activities are perceived as being pleasurable and attractive, it would on the surface appear as if marketing for such services were unnecessary. An overview of physical fitness levels in this country coupled with patterns of substance abuse indicate that while people may recognize the need for constructive use of leisure time, they are not necessarily capable of fulfilling these needs through actual participation. A marketing process developed specifically to target these consumers and better meet their needs is clearly necessary at this point in time. People have needs and wants that can be met through recreation experiences but appear to have difficulty exchanging time and money to resolve these needs in a positive manner.

A third area that clearly delineates the need for a marketing approach specifically related to parks and recreation is that of competition. This reference to competition differs from the kind of competition normally associated with most industries. When addressing competition within the leisure industry, such competition can be characterized as any competing use of time. The Edmonton Parks and Recreation Department (1988, ch. 6, p. 9) in Canada classifies competition as follows: desire, generic, service form, and enterprise (see Figure 1.2, p. 6).

Desire as a level of competition relates to needs people are seeking to satisfy in their discretionary time such as socializing as opposed to exercising. There are a plethora of needs people can seek to redress during leisure time, and the selection of one over another is indeed a matter of competition.

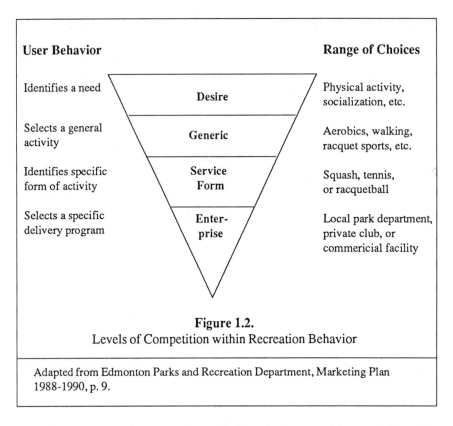

User Behavior		Range of Choices
Identifies a need	Desire	Physical activity, socialization, etc.
Selects a general activity	Generic	Aerobics, walking, racquet sports, etc.
Identifies specific form of activity	Service Form	Squash, tennis, or racquetball
Selects a specific delivery program	Enter-prise	Local park department, private club, or commericial facility

Figure 1.2.
Levels of Competition within Recreation Behavior

Adapted from Edmonton Parks and Recreation Department, Marketing Plan 1988-1990, p. 9.

Generic competitors are the second level of competition and gives rise to other vehicles for satisfying the identified need. If a person feels the need to socialize that person can choose to go to a bar, visit with friends, or attend a club meeting. Exercisers can also select from a variety of endeavors, such as walking, swimming, or racquet sports.

Once the individual has identified the need to be resolved and has made choices about the appropriate vehicle, competition continues to be a factor. This third level of competition is referred to as *service form*. If the person needing physical activity has decided upon racquet sports as a means for satisfying that need, there are several service form competitors from which to choose. Will the person select squash, tennis, or racquetball?

The selection of tennis as the service form now gives rise to enterprise competitors. *Enterprise* competitors refers to actual organizations offering the same form of services. This is generally what people refer to when they address competition. Will the would-be tennis player join a private club, rent time at a commercial tennis facility, or use the public courts in a nearby park?

Competition, when referring to recreation participation, is a complex process and cannot be limited to an examination of other organizations offering similar types of programs or services. These four levels of competitors clearly shape the marketing process for parks, recreation, and leisure.

Marketing is not just marketing. While concepts and elements inherent within a general marketing approach are applicable to parks and recreation, there are a number of factors which suggest that a framework or process of marketing adapted specifically for the leisure industries is appropriate.

Marketing for parks, recreation, and leisure needs to be developed with an external approach whereby the organization looks outside to identify the needs and wants of consumers. In addition to this consumer/user orientation, leisure marketing must incorporate elements of services marketing. Besides discovering *what* people need and want to do in their leisure time, one must also identify *how* they wish to participate.

Overview of the Process

The purpose of this chapter is to provide an overview of the marketing process for parks, recreation, and leisure delivery systems. Key concepts related to this process will be identified as well as a framework for understanding the interrelationship between these concepts that will be explored more fully in later chapters.

The very first element in this marketing process devised for parks, recreation, and leisure delivery systems is *people.* Leisure delivery systems have traditionally existed to meet the leisure needs and interests of people. This orientation and expertise provides such organizations with a head start in the marketing process. *The plan-with-people-as-opposed-to-for-people* approach that has provided a foundation for this movement will be an asset to an organization desiring to implement marketing into its system.

For marketing purposes, those people served by a recreation organization are referred to as *target markets.* Target markets are people desiring programs or services. This part of the process enables a delivery system to identify clusters or subgroups of users with similar needs and interests. Once identified, these target markets or subgroups of individuals then provide the basis upon which the organization can design and implement programs and services.

There are two steps within the target marketing process: identification and selection. Target markets are most often identified on the basis of common descriptors. The common descriptors appropriate for most park and recreation organizations are: leisure needs and interests, geographic, sociodemographic, behavioral, and synchrongraphic factors. Subgroups of users or potential users are identified on the basis of these descriptors.

Once these target markets or clusters of people with similar needs and interests have been identified, the organization proceeds to the second step of the process. This second phase of the target marketing process relates to the selection of target markets. Leisure delivery systems do not necessarily choose to select all target market groups identified.

While public departments or nonprofit organizations may select target markets on the basis of their organization's mission, private and commercial establishments would be more likely to focus upon one or several target markets that would be appropriate and profitable for them. For instance, an urban park district may select all people residing within a five-mile radius of a community center as its target market, while a resort in Florida might select upper-middle class, single adults from the northeast as its target market.

The identification and selection of target markets is usually the initial step in the marketing process and performs a critical function. Who are the recreation consumers? What do we know about them? How do they live, work, and play? What are their needs and interests? It is essential that leisure delivery systems conduct this phase of the process carefully, since it will be closely related to the effectiveness of the additional steps in the marketing process.

A marketing concept that is relevant to both target marketing and the entire marketing process is *positioning*. Positioning refers to the perception target market groups may have of an organization or of the programs or services offered by an organization. A travel agency specializing in European vacation packages needs to know how it is perceived by target market groups. Is the agency perceived as only booking European vacations and unable to arrange for a trip to Hawaii? Are its travel packages perceived as being fully structured, with little room for spontaneity? These perceptions can significantly influence relationships with current or potential target market groups.

The next step in the marketing process is the *manipulation* of the *marketing mix variables*. While the term marketing mix variables may not be a familiar one to people in this field, most recreators may already possess experience and expertise in this area. Marketing mix variables refer to those elements involved in the construction or design of a program or service. They are essentially tools and techniques utilized by park planners or recreation programmers expressed in marketing terms.

The general marketing process identifies the marketing mix variables as the *"four Ps" of marketing*. These "four Ps" of marketing actually refer to product, place, promotion, and price. This step in the process is referred to as manipulation of the marketing mix variables because within each of these categories are a number of factors that can be altered or changed in order to design programs and services specifically for certain target market groups.

The first "P" generally refers to a product but is better termed as *program/service* as it relates to leisure delivery systems. Two major factors within this area from a programming point of view actually relate to elements of program construction, area and form. Will the program being designed be a physical, social, cultural, mental activity? Will it be offered as a class, club, drop-in, or outreach? There are a whole series of important factors related to this "P." Additional elements such as name of the program or service and other benefits or amenities offered contribute to the manipulation of this marketing mix variable.

The second "P" of the marketing mix variables is *place*. A product-orientation marketing approach addresses this variable as place of production or place of purchase. This factor relates much differently for recreation and leisure delivery systems. When marketing for recreation, the place variable refers to a number of factors including the actual location of the program or service as well as accessibility to that location, availability of parking, time of day offered, length of time of the program as well as its duration. For parks and recreation, the second "P" of place is closely aligned to the program variable. Since recreation programs and services are consumed by the participant as opposed to being ordered by phone or purchased in a store, the factors related to location and time are of significant importance.

The third "P" of the marketing process is *price*. On the surface, this may appear to be a fairly straightforward marketing mix variable with which to deal. However, as related to participation in a recreation or leisure activity, the variable of price takes on more than one dimension. Naturally, it consists of the actual dollar amount to be charged for the program, but there are additional, nonmonetary costs of such participation that need to be addressed. Before taking up the game of golf, an individual may ponder whether the time can be found to play golf and whether or not it will be worth the effort to even try to learn the game. This is a particularly interesting dimension of the marketing mix to examine. Such parameters of price related to participation in recreation activities will be explored.

The fourth "P" of marketing is *promotion*. As mentioned previously this is an area of marketing that if often perceived as being the entire process. It is a critical element within the marketing mix variables since it involves communication with target market groups. However, it is just one of the variables to be addressed.

Promotion consists of communication. Delivery systems select methods of informing appropriate target markets of the existence of a program or service designed for them. There are actually two elements within this communication process, informing and persuading. Potential markets must know about the availability of the program or service and, just as importantly, they need to be persuaded that this program is worthy of exchanging their discretionary time and money.

A number of promotional options can be utilized within this variable, such as advertisements, publicity, sales promotion, and personal selling. These techniques will be examined in greater detail in an ensuing chapter.

An additional marketing concept with substantial impact upon these marketing mix variables is *program life cycle*. Program life cycle refers to the natural progression any program or service undergoes from the time it is first introduced to participants until such time that it is eliminated from the offerings. New programs and services may get off to a slow start with participation growing as people become more familiar with the program. Existing programs may begin to show a decline in popularity over time. This natural tendency of every program to have a life span of its own influences the "four Ps" of marketing. Much of the manipulation of these variables will be based upon strategies appropriate for each particular stage of the cycle.

Traditionally, marketing mix variables have consisted of the "four Ps": program, place, promotion, and price. However, these "Ps" of marketing need to be expanded to include the additional concerns of a service industry such as parks, recreation, and leisure. Lovelock (1984, pp. 49-64) maintains that if users need to be physically present and must spend time while the service is performed, their satisfaction will be influenced by interaction with service personnel, the nature of the service, and the character of other customers.

Since park, recreation, and leisure services are consumed and not just purchased, these peripheral factors need to be explored and included as part of the marketing mix. Peripheral factors, or other "Ps" to be addressed as marketing mix variables include: physical evidence, participants, process and procedures, public image, and political impact.

Physical evidence relates to the actual appearance of the facility or service center and can include such intangibles as mood and ambience. This dimension is considered to be increasing in importance as part of the marketing mix. Participants refer to those people involved in the consumption of the program or service. This particular marketing mix variable consists of two levels: other users involved in the same program or service, and personnel who come into contact with users. Another factor of great impact is process and procedures. This pertains to an organization's rules and regulations related to registration, membership, attendance, and participation. Variations within process and procedures can result in ease and enjoyment of participation on the part of the users.

The two remaining "Ps" of these additional marketing mix variables are public image and political impact. Both of these factors are largely perceptual on the part of target market groups. Public image relates closely to the concept of positioning mentioned previously and influences participation by potential target market groups. A fitness center that is perceived as being socially oriented will attract a different target market than a similar center that is perceived as having serious training and exercise programs. Political impact also is a perceptual factor. Once thought to be solely the concern of public delivery systems, this factor now crosses all boundaries. Organizations today are judged by both users and nonusers in relationship to how they conduct business. This is an area that has become of growing importance.

The marketing mix variables form essentially the basis of an agency's existence as a leisure delivery system. They collectively represent the programs and services offered by the organization and as such are highly visible evidence of the recreator's involvement in the marketing process.

All components of the marketing process for parks, recreation, and leisure need to address and incorporate the concepts established for *services marketing*. Since the leisure industry is a part of the more generic service field, these elements need to be incorporated into the marketing process. Lovelock (1984, pp. 49-64) identified six characteristics of the services industries that affect the way marketing is undertaken and applied. These six characteristics with implications for park, recreation, and leisure delivery systems are as follows:

1. Nature of the service act
2. Relationship of organization with customers
3. Room for customization or specialization on part of the service provider

4. Nature of the demand for services
5. Method of service delivery
6. Attributes of the service

Each of these characteristics needs to be addressed by individual park, recreation, and leisure delivery systems. Many of these characteristics vary based upon the delivery system involved in the marketing process.

An analysis of the six characteristics for specific delivery systems would enable them to more effectively and appropriately manipulate elements of the marketing mix variables. For instance, the nature of the service act can be either tangible or intangible. Working out at a fitness club involves tangible action on the part of the user, while attending a theatre production involves activity directed more at the mental involvement of the user. The service act may or may not be directed at the primary consumer. Summer camp programs may be designed primarily for working parents as opposed to their children.

An additional characteristic, the relationship between the organization and the customer, may also vary from one delivery system to another. Relationships may be formal or informal as well as service being continuous or discrete. Are participants members of the community center or casual users of park property? Are participants continually involved with the organization on a year-round basis, or do they only purchase season ski passes for the winter months?

Another characteristic requiring examination is the extent of customization or specialization in the service delivery. This is often related to the user-staff ratio. Treatments at a health spa would naturally allow for a high level of customization while attendance at a large, outdoor special event open to the general public would not allow for that type of specialization.

The nature of the demand for the service is an additional characteristic that varies based upon the delivery system. There are a number of issues to be addressed within this characteristic, such as the extent of supply and demand fluctuations over time and the ability of the delivery system to meet demand during peak time periods. Weekend tee times at golf courses during the summer months reflect peak demand with long waiting times or lists. Due to the seasonal nature of many recreational pursuits, this is often a factor for our industry.

The method involved in the delivery of the service often varies based upon the organization. Do participants have to come to the organization to receive the service and if so, is there only one location available for this service? Does the organization bring the services to the customer, or are transactions limited to some form of electronic communication? Does a municipal park and recreation department have tennis lessons available at just one site or at several locations? Personal fitness trainers differ from health clubs, since they generally bring their services to the home or office of their clients.

Recreation marketers also need to analyze the characteristics of the service product. Services often consist of two components as perceived by users: equipment/facility attributes and people-based attributes. The range of these preferences can be from low to high. Do people join private country clubs or swim clubs because of the potential interaction with current members, or are they attracted to the facilities these clubs are able to provide?

The impact of services marketing is critical to understanding and utilizing the marketing process for parks, recreation, and leisure delivery systems. Growing competition among recreation providers coupled with increased public demand for customization, personalization, and specialization make this concept one of great importance to recreators.

The final component of the marketing process for leisure delivery systems is *strategic marketing planning*. The utilization of strategic marketing planning by many organizations is largely responsible for the elevation of marketing to a management function within recreation and leisure delivery systems. Strategic marketing planning focuses upon *doing the right thing* as opposed to the "doing things right" that is often the focus of more traditional planning approaches.

The strategic marketing planning process involves essentially three components: environmental scanning, market assessment, and organizational inventory. Due to its substantial focus upon the changing needs and interests of people, which is key to the success of recreation delivery systems, this is a particularly effective part of the marketing process.

The environmental scanning portion of this process involves identifying opportunities and threats existing in the environment or outside of the organization. Such factors as economic considerations, legal/political issues, sociodemographics, and technology are examined to identify trends serving as either opportunities or threats for the organization. The second step in this process is the market assessment. The market assessment examines current, past, and future characteristics of user groups on a number of different factors such as psychographics and service expectations. The third component of this process is the organizational inventory that compels the delivery system to objectively and accurately compile a listing of its strengths and weaknesses.

The eventual outcome of strategic marketing planning is the identification of strengths, weaknesses, opportunities, and threats for the delivery system. This determination can then be translated into an action-oriented strategy for maintaining profitability or viability in the future.

One essential component of the marketing process, *market research*, is not included as part of the ongoing process detailed in Figure 1.3. Market research is not a discrete or separate part of the process of marketing, but rather, it is an integral and ongoing function of the entire process. Market research is of equal importance in all phases of the marketing process.

Target marketing could not occur if substantial information was not available related to current or potential target market groups. It would be difficult to accurately make decisions when manipulating marketing mix variables if information was not available related to the wide variety of factors inherent within this part of the process. Conducting strategic marketing planning without the benefit of market research would reduce the effort to an exercise in sheer conjecture.

Market research is an essential part of marketing. It is necessary for the implementation of marketing by park, recreation, and leisure delivery systems. There are essentially three categories of information necessary for market research: internal, standardized, and specialized research information. An overview of the creation of a marketing information systems (MIS) within a leisure delivery system, as well as specific techniques to be utilized, are explored in an ensuing chapter.

This marketing process for parks, recreation, and leisure is not a static concept. All components of the process are interrelated with one another, with findings or decisions in one area influencing other components within the process. It is an ongoing process encompassing activities within the delivery system on a daily basis, as opposed to an annual activity to be conducted by the organization.

Marketing for parks, recreation, and leisure is an inherent part of any such operation. Identifying the needs and wants of consumer groups and creating programs and services to meet these needs reflects the real mission of leisure delivery systems.

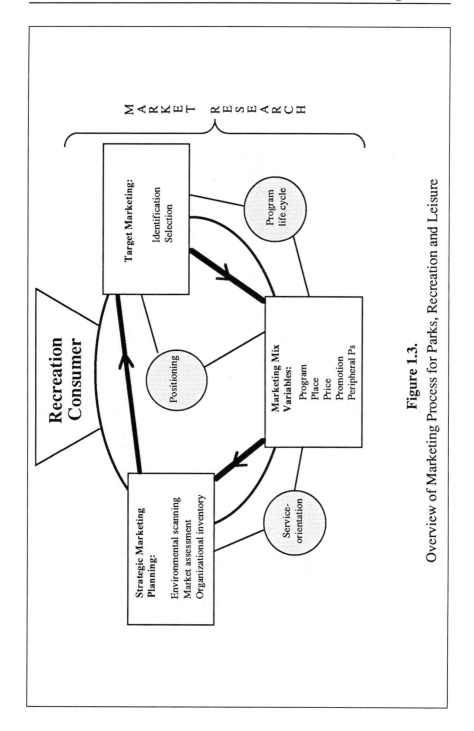

Figure 1.3.

Overview of Marketing Process for Parks, Recreation and Leisure

Summary

Marketing is a process that has been extensively used by industries in this country in recent times. As a process, it has evolved from its original intent with a product orientation focusing upon cost-efficient manufacture of products to be sold to consumers. It has also changed since the onset of the sales orientation attempting to sell or push these products onto consumers. Today, marketing has evolved to embrace a consumer/user orientation that focuses outward from the organization and attempts to identify the needs and wants of consumers. This current approach to marketing recognizes societal and economic changes, which makes attention to the customer the key to an organization's success.

The marketing process for parks, recreation, and leisure delivery systems incorporates this current consumer/user approach as well as a services marketing orientation, addressing not only what consumers want, but also how they want to consume services. Due to the nature of recreation participation, it is necessary that marketing for leisure delivery systems incorporate general and services marketing approaches. However, it is critical to the success and continued viability of such delivery systems that they undertake a marketing process specifically adapted to address the uniqueness of leisure services delivery.

The marketing process for parks, recreation, and leisure consists of a number of basic components such as target marketing, manipulation of marketing mix variables, and strategic marketing planning. These essential components of the marketing process are significantly influenced by marketing concepts such as positioning, program life cycle, and services marketing. The components of the marketing process as well as critical concepts are all dependent upon market research. Market research is related to all phases of the process and significantly shapes decisions and choices to be made.

The purpose of this chapter was to provide an overview of essential components of the marketing process for parks, recreation, and leisure while also addressing critical concepts related to this process. Ensuing chapters will examine each of these components, concepts, and elements in greater depth in order to enable recreators to successfully introduce and implement this process into their delivery systems.

Suggested Activities

1. Select several leisure delivery systems and attempt to identify the marketing orientation used by these different organizations.

2. Select one commonly purchased household product and compare this purchase and usage process with participation in a recreation activity.

3. Identify a specific leisure delivery system and examine the activities undertaken by this organization as it relates to the marketing process.

4. For a specific delivery system, examine the four different levels of competition for this agency. Suggest strategies for addressing these examples of competition.

5. Analyze a specific recreation program or service on the basis of the six characteristics outlined by Lovelock.

References

Edmonton Parks and Recreation Department. *Marketing Plan 1988-1990*. (p. 9). Edmonton, Alberta, Canada.

Kotler, P., (1980). *Marketing Management: Analysis, Planning, and Control,* (4th ed.) Englewood Cliffs, NJ: Prentice-Hall.

Lefebvre, R. G. and Flora, J. E. (1989). Social Marketing and Public Health Intervention, *Health Education Quarterly, 15*(3) (p. 301).

Lovelock, C. H., (1984). *Services Marketing.* Englewood Cliffs, NJ: Prentice-Hall.

USA Snapshots, *(1990, March 7). USA Today* (p. D1).

Chapter Two

Target Marketing

Common Concerns for Parks, Recreation, and Leisure Delivery Systems

- A YMCA located in urban area of the northeast wonders how to survive as former members move to suburbs.

- A large county park district in British Columbia, Canada identifies an underutilized park facility in a remote area of county and wonders how to increase usage of that area.

- A resort located in the southeastern portion of the United States speculates as to whom will occupy rooms during the off-season.

- A program director for Morale Welfare and Recreation wonders why it seems as if it's the same group of people who always seem to sign up for programs.

Target Marketing: Its Role and Purpose for Parks, Recreation, and Leisure

The answers to these areas of concern shared by many park, recreation, and leisure delivery systems can be addressed through an understanding and utilization of target marketing. The concept of target marketing is a central component upon which the marketing process builds. Target markets are people, and the understanding of people is a key to the success of leisure organizations.

A common approach shared by programmers and managers in leisure delivery systems is to design programs and services for the majority of the users or to focus upon the average user. Attempting to construct programs and services for everybody usually results in the attraction of a group of "somebodies" to the program or service. There is no one program that will meet the needs of everyone.

Target marketing is the conscious and purposeful identification of sub-groups or clusters of "somebodies." This process of target marketing enables the leisure organization to design services and construct programs specifically to meet the needs of these subgroups, its target markets.

Crompton and Lamb (1986) refer to target marketing as a key marketing concept and define the target market as "a relatively homogeneous group of people who have relatively similar service preferences with whom an agency seeks to exchange." In the past, many leisure delivery systems have instinctively designed a program or service for a group of people and then attempted to attract those people to that particular program or service. Target marketing takes a reverse approach to this process by providing for the identification and analysis of groups of people, and then for the creation and design of programs or services for those particular target markets.

Target marketing starts with people. One begins the process by identifying clusters of users or potential users who have similar needs and interests. Following the identification of these clusters or market segments, you then select specific subgroups or market segments for whom you wish to schedule programs or provide services. Target market decisions can be the most important decisions an organization makes because it is upon these decisions that all other choices–including time, location, fees, promotion, and policies–will be determined.

The process of target marketing is two-fold. It first addresses the issue of who these subgroups or segments of the population are who share similar leisure needs and interests. It then allows the delivery system to purposefully select those market segments, specific groups of "somebodies" that the organization they wishes to attract to its park, program, resort, or facility.

Common Market Descriptors

If the first step in the process is to identify market segments, then what factors require examination for this purpose? There are a number of descriptors that may be utilized when attempting to isolate market segments. In order to apply this process to parks and recreation, the following descriptors should be considered: (a) leisure needs and/or interests, (b) geographic location, (c) sociodemographics, (d) behavioral factors, and (e) synchronographics (see Figure 2.1).

Although there are five different descriptors of target marketing, an organization is likely to look at these descriptors in conjunction with one

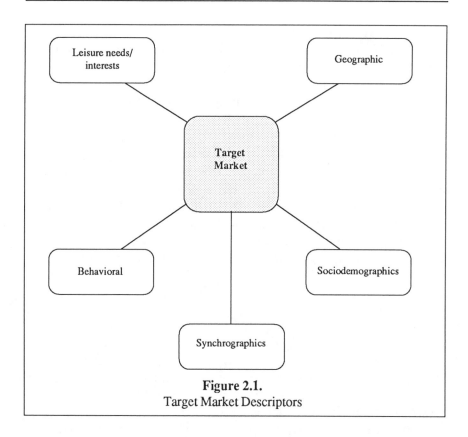

Figure 2.1.
Target Market Descriptors

another. There are relationships and commonalities among the descriptors and *full utilization* of *all descriptors* enables a more *complete identification* of the target market to be developed.

Leisure Needs/Interests as a Descriptor

People elect to participate in recreation activities, programs, or experiences for different reasons. These motivational reasons can be divided into two categories: needs and interests. Individuals may have different leisure interests as revealed by the myriad of recreation activities outlined by Edginton, Compton, and Hanson (1980, pp. 97-98) which include a variety of activities within the general categories of the arts, physical activities, hobbies, outdoor recreation, mental and literary activities, self-improvement activities, social activities, volunteer service, and travel.

Any one of these categories of recreational activities can include an array of different activities–the arts encompass fine arts, crafts, music, dance, drama; physical activities include individual, dual, and team sports as well as games and fitness pursuits. This indicates to recreators that interest in a specific recreational activity can lead to the identification of possible market segments.

However, recreation or leisure interest is just one aspect of this descriptor. People are also attracted to various recreation activities or experiences on the basis of their needs. Crompton (1983) illustrates this point when discussing golfers as a market segment. Initially, we could assume that golfers are individuals who share the interest of golf as a recreational activity. However, Crompton points out that the needs fulfilled by different groups of golfers through this interest in golf may vary, and could include escape from family, socialization, and exercise or physical fitness (1983, p.12). On the basis of this, it is apparent that leisure needs should be addressed as a target market descriptor as well (see Figure 2.2, p. 23).

People possess a variety of different needs upon which they seek out and select various recreational activities. These needs may be reflective of an individual's stage in the life cycle, type of employment, or individual personality or preference. After examining theories of human needs, Tillman developed a list of ten needs as meaningful for explaining participation in recreation activities. The identified needs included escape/relaxation, physical or mental activity, dominance, socialization or sense of belonging, creativity, recognition, service to others, security, and need for new experience.

The interest in the activity itself is often not a complete picture of a market segment. The interest in a specific activity when coupled with the need for participation provides for a more in-depth and effective manner of identifying market segments. The combination of these two factors helps to explain why some individuals prefer sports over the arts, and further delineates differences between people who select jogging over aerobic classes or oil painting classes over attendance at the opening night of an art exhibit.

Resorts targeting people with an interest in travel need to consider the attraction to travel as well. Attracting individuals who desire travel for escape and relaxation would be quite different from attracting those who look to travel to address the need for socialization. It would be as inappropriate to lump together these two different types of travelers as it would be to plan a family tournament for those golfers who use the sport as a means of escaping family.

This descriptor represents a natural starting point for identifying potential target markets. Information related to peoples' leisure interests can be easily secured through leisure interest surveys. However, the recreator still needs to address the need or motivational factor inherent within this interest in order to more fully identify market segments.

Leisure Needs/Interests Related Factors	Considerations
Interests: various recreation interests usually revealed through participation in the specific activity, i. e., golf, reading, etc.	Arts: art, music, dance, drama Physical Activity: sports, games, athletics, or physical fitness Hobbies Outdoor recreation Mental and literary activities Self-improvement Social activities Volunteer service Travel
Needs: reasons for seeking out or selecting specific recreation activities	Escape/relaxation Physical/mental activity dominance/security Socialization/belonging New experience Creativity Recognition Service to others

Figure 2.2.
Leisure Needs/Interests as Target Market Descriptor

Source: Adapted from Edginton, Compton, and Hanson. *Recreation and Leisure Programming: A Guide for the Professional.* Philadelphia: Saunders College, 1980. pp. 97-98 and Tillman, Albert. *The Program Book for the Recreation Professionals.* Palo Alto, CA: Mayfield Publishing Company, 1973. p. 29.

Geographic Location as Market Descriptor

The geographic descriptor for target marketing addresses a number of questions important to recreators. Who are these groups of "somebodies"? *Where do they live, work, and play?*

Use of this descriptor is common and relates to how an organization or agency defines its catchment area, the geographic radius or area from which possible participants may elect to utilize a program or service. This definition may appear to be fairly obvious for public parks and recreation departments whose mission is to meet the needs of all its residents within given city, county, or state boundaries. However, redefinition of these boundaries may be required, for example, to examine whether or not an urban center should include those individuals who work in their city as part of their population, or whether or not a state park system views visitors from neighboring states as part of its target market as well.

The most commonly utilized geographic descriptor involved in this process is the place of physical residence, where people actually live in relationship to the leisure delivery system. Categories for subdivision related to this factor may be neighborhood, town, city, county, district, state, region, or even country. Based upon the nature of the delivery system and its mission, one might expect to find one or more of these dimensions as likely subgroups.

In this era of commuting with sizable portions of the American population working in locales outside of their area residence, place of employment as well as travel time and distance may well be a suitable factor to utilize in the identification of market segments. Many urban YMCAs as well as commercial health clubs have identified as their target markets individuals who commute into their city to work or pass by their facility on their way to work. The place of employment as well as travel time and distance can be utilized as a mechanism to identify subsegments of markets. Highway overcrowding and heavily utilized traffic patterns may work for or against a delivery system depending upon the actual location of the program or service and how this factor is utilized in the identification process.

The impact of the variation between place of residence and place of employment upon delivery systems is substantial and needs to be recognized. Recreation and leisure delivery organizations located in and around large metropolitan areas can design hours of operation and scheduling of services to respond effectively to the problems of "rush hour." Some organizations offer early morning hours or programs as well as after-work times and encourage prospective participants to make better use of their time by exercising or learning oil painting as an alternative to sitting in rush hour traffic. The revised schedules of these delivery systems score points for reducing stress and improving quality of life as well.

Other leisure delivery systems make schedule changes on the basis of travel time and distance as well. There are suburban park and recreation delivery systems who recognize that a substantial portion of their population spend the majority of their work week away from their place of residence, either at work or commuting. Rather than continue to schedule programs during the day or during weeknights, organizations such as the county park districts within commuting distance of Washington, DC often shift the delivery of their programs and services to the weekends when residents are more likely to be spending time in their area and stress the convenience of not having to drive long distances to recreate.

Accessibility is another factor to be addressed under this heading of geographic descriptors; it refers to ease of access for members of a target population. The urban YMCA whose members have moved to the suburb no longer find the urban Y an easily accessible location. Many YMCAs have addressed this issue by either developing outreach programs in suburban communities by renting space for programs, or in some cases by building branch YMCAs in these newly identified catchment areas.

Ease of access is an important consideration. Recreation delivery systems developing after-school programs for children with working parents as alternatives for sending children home to an unsupervised home need to take into consideration the ease of access of these programs. After-school activities offered in or near schools or with transportation included may make a substantial difference to the success of these programs.

Accessibility can take into account a whole host of factors. It can include the inconvenience of traffic patterns during the scheduled time of an activity or the participants' sense of the remoteness of the area or facility. This can work for or against an organization based upon the target market. The park district in Canada that identified an underutilized park may find that the park area is considered desirable by potential users, but that these same people may be unable to provide their own transportation to the facility. Parks personnel would then need to identify people who have their own cars as a potential target market.

A remote tourist resort that requires air transportation by a small carrier followed by additional ground transportation may make the most of its inaccessibility by targeting segments of the travel market that are attracted to this remoteness by a need and desire to escape from the rest of the world.

Club Meds are generally located away from the well-developed sections of resort locations. This remoteness reinforces the desire on the part of market segments looking for that "antidote to civilization" which such organizations include in their advertising campaigns.

Accessibility and its relationship to identifying potential target markets may be based upon both real and perceived barriers. Many airlines and tourist attractions are making a special effort to promote their accessibility for the physically disabled. However, barriers related to accessibility are tangible. Potential target markets may perceive the location of a facility as being inaccessible based upon their perception of safety in a particular area or at a particular time of the day. While perceptions are not necessarily based upon fact, they are quite real in the minds of potential target markets and should be addressed in this process.

The geographic descriptor provides organizations with a mechanism for providing a framework in the identification process. Certain factors inherent within this descriptor may assume greater importance over others based upon the organization's definition of the catchment area (Figure 2.3).

Related Factors	Considerations
Place of residence	Neighborhood, town, city, county, district, state, region, or country
Place of employment	Hours spent within or outside of your catchment area
	Possible impact of commuting
Accessibility	Physical proximity of your organization
	Traffic patterns and travel time
	Ease of access-walk, ride, drive
	Physical access for special populations
	Perception of safety or desirability of location

Figure 2.3.
Geographic Descriptor as Related to Target Market

Source: Adapted from Crompton, John. "Selecting Target Markets-A Key to Effective Marketing," Journal of Park and Recreation Administration. Vol. I, No. 1, Summer 1983. p. 14.

Role of Sociodemographics as a Target Market Descriptor

There are a myriad of factors included within the descriptor labeled socio-demographics. According to Crompton and Lamb (1986, p. 121), this set of descriptors are used more frequently than other descriptors because of ease of access to this type of information and due to the relationship between these factors and service preferences and needs. Kotler (1980, p. 199) includes the following factors within this descriptor: age, gender, income, education, occupation, stage in the family life cycle and size of family, religion, race, nationality, and social class.

These factors are easily utilized by leisure professionals who are accustomed to developing profiles of groups of people in order to design park areas, facilities, or programs. Recreators have already made extensive use of these factors previously, as evidenced by tot lots designed for preschoolers, drop-in center activities for senior citizens, or adult swim hours.

Chubb and Chubb (1981, p. 201) believe that age and stage in the life cycle relate to an individual's physical, mental, intellectual, and social abilities to participate in recreation as well as the individual perception of the primary value of recreation and needs to be fulfilled through recreational experiences.

Age-related characteristics impact not only upon an individual's physical capability for acquiring a skill or participating in an activity, but also upon motivational factors inherent within that particular life cycle stage. While recreators generally do an outstanding job of establishing target markets for such groups as preschoolers, teens, and senior citizens, they often lump adults together into one target market. The motivational factors for adult participation in leisure are strongly influenced by individual's stage in the life cycle. Osgood and Howe (1984) address this concept more fully and provide recreators interested in further segmenting this profitable target market of adults with valuable insight and information.

Two other factors within this descriptor are often addressed in conjunction with one another, marital status and stage in the family life cycle. In recent years, the options within the heading of marital status have expanded. Some of the options are: single, divorced, widowed, single head of household, married with no children, married with young children, married with grown children, and stable significant-other relationships.

Marital status and stage in the family life cycle become increasingly more complex with the addition of other related factors such as two-income families, couples having children at a later age, the role of reconstituted families, and the rise of alternative relationships. Key elements reflected in

	Young Adulthood (age 20-35)	Mid-Life (age 35-55)	Late Life (age 55 →)
Selected Activities	Vigorous physical recreation (m) Entertainment, spectator sports Home-centered and family-oriented activities Going to bars (m) Courting, dating Outdoor recreation	Spectating, home-centered activities Organizations, clubs visiting Reading, radio, shopping Entertainment, TV Volunteering, new experiences Relaxing, bars, restaurants Civic/community-centered activities Work-related activities	Contemplation, introspection, life review Group participation, travel, socializing Relaxation, meditation Spectator sports, TV watching Reading, gardening, resting Fishing, walking, picnics, sightseeing Handicrafts, church-related activities
Values	Success (m) Career (m), upward mobility (m) Home and family (f)	Career, success, productivity Performance, family, community	Family
Motivations and Meanings	Extrinsic achievement, accomplishment Competence, arousal, power Affiliation, social bonding (f) Relationship building and strengthening Excitement and adventure Social role-related Instrumental (m), expressive (f) Novelty Autonomy Prestige, status, identity Sensual transcendence Fun	Extrinsic arousal, novelty Achievement Productivity, creative expansion Retain health and vigor Recuperation (compensation from work) Order, continuity Service Status, prestige Role-related Change from work, escape Instrumental	Intrinsic arousal, personal satisfaction Pleasure, creativity Peace, comfort, security Association, socializing, affiliation Self-esteem, integration Retain health, maintain social functioning Passing and structuring time Service to others Unconditional Expressive

Key
m = males especially involved
f = females especially involved

Figure 2.4.
General Leisure Patterns Over the Traditional Adult Life Course

Source: Osgood, Nancy J. and Howe, Christine Z. "Psychological Aspects of Leisure: A Life Cycle Development Perspective," Society and Leisure, 7, no. 1, 1984 from Howe, Christine Z. and Carpenter, Gaylene M. Programming Leisure Experiences: A Cyclical Approach. Englewood Cliffs, NJ: Prentice-Hall, 1985. p. 27.

these combinations relate to availability or lack of availability of time, money, and other people with whom to recreate. The needs of each group are also a key factor when translated into interests.

Singles, whether divorced, widowed, or never married, generally have more time available for recreation and sometimes more available funds to pursue such activities. This commonality would not carry over to single heads of households. The members of this growing segment of our society often have limited time and money available for recreation due to the need to assume multiple roles within the family unit. A commonality many of the individuals in this group might share would be the need for social interaction.

Married with no children or "DINKS" (double income no kids) present still a different potential target market group. Often these individuals have more discretionary time and money with which to pursue recreation. This subgroup could also include alternative lifestyle groups who may be involved in a stable relationship with no children. These groups make excellent target markets for private and commercial recreation delivery systems.

Married with children is a subgroup with still additional factors impacting upon their delineation as a target market. Recreators need to go beyond the initial label of identification and determine the stage in the family life cycle (young children, teens, empty nest) and whether or not this is a two-income family. The answers to these questions influence amount of discretionary time and money as well as degree of commitment or time for recreation pursuits with children based upon the age or continuing presence of children.

The age of potential target markets is also relevant in another way. The age of an individual reveals the period of time in which the person grew up and the subsequent development of attitudes towards recreation and leisure. Adults reaching retirement at this point in time have a fleeting recall of the Depression; they worked and raised children during the post-World War II era, when the unofficial motto was "hard work pays off." This value system related to their era may affect their view of recreation.

The attitudes of this group can also be contrasted with those of their children, the baby boomers who grew up with little league, summer camp, and art lessons. This group of individuals perceives recreation as their right as opposed to a reward for hard work and will approach leisure pursuits differently.

Chubb and Chubb (1981) identify gender as a factor related to recreational needs and interests. However, they point out that this factor becomes more related to age of the individual than actual leisure needs and interests (p. 132). Based upon the changing attitudes of our society related to gender roles, one sees the impact of this factor diminish. As girls grow up playing little league and high school hockey and as men assume more child-rearing responsibility, the needs and interests based upon gender will continue to blur. This category may become more age-related than anything else. For instance, individuals who attended high school in the age of gender-segregated physical education classes may have an entirely different attitude about joining a coed fitness club than the age group that follows.

It should be noted that the factors of occupation, education, and income when presented in Figure 2.5 are addressed collectively. The interrelatedness of these three factors makes it appropriate to address them in this manner, and determinants of social class are often based upon the combination of these three factors. Higher income levels are often associated with higher levels of education and occupation types. Social class not only impacts upon the obvious, such as amount of discretionary dollars to expend upon recreation, but also relates to types of activities selected as well as a preference for active versus passive participation. The examination of psychographics as a target market descriptor will explore this interrelationship and subsequent impact upon leisure patterns more completely.

Recreators should not overlook the nature of an individual's work as an important factor when differentiating target markets. The level of socialization as well as the amount of energy expended during the workday may relate to a person's preference for recreation activities. As the employment patterns in this country continue to shift from industrial to service and technology, a change in the types of activities required as "recreative" experiences may follow.

A final category of factors included within the sociodemographic descriptor is religion/ethnicity. Religious affiliations continue to be an important factor in this country, and the time and effort related to these affiliations varies as it does with most group memberships. The amount of restrictions placed upon use of leisure time and selection of recreation activities may also vary based upon the affiliation.

Racial and ethnic membership is also a factor included in this category. Chubb and Chubb (1981) believe that ethnic/racial membership impacts upon people in three basic ways: available opportunities (economic and educational), physical attributes, and traditions related to national or cultural heritage (pp. 208-211). These factors relate to determination of target market groups, especially at it relates to appropriate activities, scheduling of those activities, and interest in special events and cultural programs.

Related Factors	Considerations
Age (stage in the life cycle)	Physical, mental, intellectual, and social abilities
	Values and attitudes towards play, recreation, and leisure
	Needs and interests
Gender	Societal norms and expectations
	Needs and interests
Income/occupation/education	Attitudes towards leisure
	Participation rates
	Cost of activities
	Activity Preferences
	Skill and exposure levels
	Participation preferences
Marital status (stage in family life cycle)	Time availability
	Significant others
	Socialization needs
Ethnicity/religious affiliations	Values and opportunities
	Customs and traditions

Figure 2.5.
Sociodemographic Factors as Target Market Descriptor

Source: Adapted from Kotler, Phillip. *Marketing Management: Analysis, Planning, and Control, 4th ed.* Englewood Cliffs, NJ: Prentice-Hall, 1980. p. 199.

The Behavioral Descriptor

Behavioral characteristics can be defined as "the distinctive mode or orientation an individual or group has towards life representing the way in which *people choose to spend their time and money*" (Howard and Crompton, 1980, p. 352). On the basis of this definition, the importance of this descriptor for target marketing in leisure services becomes more apparent since participation in a recreation activity involves choices for the use of individuals' discretionary time and money. After all, participation in recreation is a behavior.

Behavioral characteristics related to an examination of target market identification and selection for parks, recreation, and leisure include: *usage status, level of ability, level of specialization, and lifestyle (psychographics)* (Crompton, 1983, p. 17) (see Figure 2.6, p. 35).

Usage Status

Usage status refers to the varying levels of participation by an individual or group as it relates to their involvement (or lack of the same) with an organization's programs or services. Kotler (1980, p. 203) addresses user status by segmenting markets into nonusers, ex-users, potential users, first-time users, and regular users of a product, program, or service.

Usage status will determine how an organization chooses to design programs and services as well as techniques for communicating with these current or potential user groups. The strategies for such design and communication would vary based upon the user's former, current, or nonuse of your program or service.

Target markets can be further delineated on the basis of usage level. It is suggested that markets can be segmented into light, medium, and heavy users of programs and services and that there may well be different common geographic or sociodemographic factors which describe these three different groups (Kotler, 1980, p. 203).

When analyzing target markets in this manner, many recreation delivery systems may discover that it is indeed that same group of people who seem to participate in the majority of their programs or services. This is not a group to be taken for granted. It is imperative that a more complete profile of this group be developed to aid in the continued participation by this group. Although this group, designated as heavy users, often represents a small percentage of the overall user profile, this group may account for a substantial portion of the participation or revenue generated by the agency. The "20-80" rule of marketing applies in this situation, where it is suggested that 20 percent of an organization's participants may account for 80 percent of the usage.

Marketing objectives and strategies can be developed on the basis of an examination of usage status. If a resort was to develop a profile of regular users of their facilities, that information could be used not only to ensure their continued usage but also to develop profiles of nonusers. By examining similarities and differences among the two groups, different marketing strategies could be developed. An amusement park or a community recreation department could establish a profile of its heavy users and utilize that profile as a mechanism for discriminating between the heavy users and the light user group as a method of increasing usage by the light user group.

Skill and Specialization Levels

While skill and specialization levels are utilized in a general approach to marketing, these descriptors are particularly appropriate for recreation participation. Skill level designations are commonly utilized by public departments and nonprofit delivery systems when devising a structure for any learning activity, whether it be needlepoint or racquetball. It is common for such classes offered to be designated for beginner, intermediate, or advanced levels. Skill and ability levels have become so important that it is not unusual to see fitness classes advertised in such a manner as well.

Level of specialization has a slightly different connotation and can be closely associated with benefits sought. Specialization in a particular activity can be visualized on a continuum of interest from a general or recreational approach up to a highly specialized involvement in the activity.

Envision the differences between individuals who utilize public parks or open space for a pleasant, enjoyable walk through the woods with individuals who utilize this same space for the purposes of identifying species of bird and wildlife. Level of specialization substantially impacts upon levels of skills to be acquired as well as willingness to expend resources upon this activity. For instance, the individual who skis on an occasional weekend or two over the course of the winter and the diehard, serious skier are quite likely to expend different amounts of money on ski equipment.

Benefits Sought

This factor serves as a means to subsegment groups of users on the basis of their motivation for participating in a particular activity. It is closely related to some of the factors described in the needs/interest descriptor. People may choose to participate in the same recreational activity, while their reasons for selecting this particular activity maybe quite different. Similar to the example of the golfers cited earlier, people may appear on the surface to be similar on the basis of their common interest in an activity but the reasons for participating may be quite different.

Imagine the challenge for a tour operator who organizes a bus trip for senior citizens to visit a nearby region of interest. Seated on that bus may be people who seem similar in their attraction to a moderately-priced, secure type of getaway. In reality there may be people whose reasons for taking the trip are quite different, varying from the history buffs to the picture-takers, the shoppers, the nature lovers, and the socializers. Attempting to plan an excursion where each subgroup has its motivations accommodated fully is virtually impossible. This is a good example of the role target marketing plays in the improved delivery of recreation and leisure pursuits. There is no average user. There is no one trip for everybody. Park, recreation and leisure organizations are really in the business of designing programs and services for specific groups of "somebodies."

Loyalty Status

Loyalty status refers to the degree to which a participant or user feels an allegiance to a program, service or organization. This sense of allegiance can range from individuals having no feelings of loyalty to an organization to feelings of incontestable regard. There are people who will change health clubs annually to save a few dollars on the fee or to receive a complimentary sweatshirt, while there are those who wouldn't consider venturing to a new service provider solely on the basis of a price or incentive consideration.

A recent study examining consumer loyalty in municipal parks revealed low to moderate levels of loyalty to these organizations (Howard, Edginton and Selin, 1980, p. 352). The study found that low income participants, once attracted to public park and recreation departments, demonstrate a high degree of loyalty. This suggests a marketing opportunity for public agencies to focus efforts on initial attracton of this demographic group.

Since repeat participation accounts for a substantial portion of the usage rates for many recreation organizations, it is worthwhile to identify program or service factors related to such loyalty and to include as part of a marketing plan the conscious attempt to enhance such factors.

Readiness Stage

An individual's readiness stage to participate in a recreation activity is actually a continuum divided into four stages: awareness of the activity, knowledge of the activity, interest in the activity, and intent to participate in the activity. This reflects the actual progression people experience related to a leisure activity and accounts for participation levels. Newly introduced activities such as ski-surfing begin with low levels of participation. It takes

Related Factors	Considerations
Usage status	Potential, 1st time, or regular user; nonusers or exusers
Usage rate	Light, medium or heavy
Skill level	Beginner, intermediate or advanced
Specialization	Continuum from general recreation to high level
Benefits sought	Wide array ranging from tangibles such as price or ease of access to nontangibles such as escape or status
Loyalty status	None, moderate, strong
Readiness stage	Levels of awareness, knowledge, interest and intent
Psychographics	Need-driven, inner or outer directed, integrated

Figure 2.6.
Behavioral Factors as Target Market Descriptors

Source: Adapted from Kotler, Phillip. Marketing Mangement: Analysis, Planning, and Control, 4th ed. Englewood Cliffs, NJ: Prentice-Hall, 1980. p. 199.

time for people to become initially aware of an activity until the time they decide they'd like to try the activity. This pattern is more thoroughly explored in the section on program life cycle.

Health clubs and self-improvement programs take natural advantage of this factor. The beginning of a new calendar year laden with New Year's resolutions is usually the time for promotions encouraging people to put into action their intent to lose weight, take up exercise, or learn to make better use of their time.

An awareness of the readiness continuum enables marketers to manage participation levels and develop programs and promotions based upon this progression. It should be noted that changes in lifestyle or stages of development may precipitate changes in this readiness progression.

Psychographics

Until the 1970s, market research was dominated by segmenting markets demographically. "People research" or "psychographics" has now taken its place as a form of market research that is critical to understanding user preference and participation patterns. A commonly accepted system for this "people research" is VALS (values, attitudes, and lifestyles), developed by the Stanford Research Institute (SRI) (Atlas, 1984, p. 50).

This research conducted by SRI resulted in the categorization of nine American lifestyles. On the basis of these lifestyle profiles, recreators can better understand how peoples' values influence their behavioral patterns. Although there has not been a substantial amount of research directed specifically to recreation, the information uncovered through VALS can enhance the target marketing of recreation and leisure delivery systems.

VALS identified four categories of groups that described the values, attitudes, and behaviors of Americans and nine lifestyles related to those groupings. The four categories with related lifestyle designations (Atlas, 1980, pp. 49-58) are as follows:

Need-Driven: 11 percent of the population; Survivors and Sustainers

Inner-Directed: 19 percent of the population; I Am Me, Experientials, and Socially Conscious

Outer-Directed: 68 percent of the population; Belongers, Emulators and Achievers

Integrated: 2 percent of the population combination of Inner- and Outer-Directed

On the basis of these categorizations, understanding of leisure behavior can be greatly enhanced. The Need-Driven category refers to those individuals who for the most part are outside of the American mainstream and consider themselves unlikely participants in the American dream (see Figure 2.7). This category consists of two lifestyles–Survivors and Sustainers. Both of these groups tend to be the least well-off members of our society, with lower incomes and less education than Americans in general (Mitchell, 1983, pp. 65-69). The focus of their behavior is on maintaining their day-to-day existence.

The Outer-Directed group is the most sizeable group in our society. This categoy refers to people who tend to conduct themselves on the basis of what other people will think (see Figure 2.8, p. 39). They tend to create ways of life and leisure that are geared to more visible, tangible, and materialistic expressions. This category can be further divided into three lifestyle groups: Belongers, Achievers, and Emulators. Belongers cherish

Survivors (4%)	Needs	Activities
Poorest and oldest of all groups Least educated-maybe single	Not self-confident or happy Conservative Thinks being part of a group is important	Depends upon TV Absent from physical pursuits Little menial, cultural, intellectual activities
Sustainers (7%)	**Needs**	**Activities**
Younger, many employed part-time Children at home High level of divorce, separation	Unhappy group; feels left out Values status and group membership Little satisfaction from work, friends	Likes hedonistic, exciting activities Substantial TV viewing, bowling, clubs, amusement parks

Figure 2.7.
Need-Driven

Source: Adapted from Mitchell, Arnold. The Nine American Lifestyles.
New York: Macmillian Publishing, 1983. pp. 65-83.

our long-standing institutions and traditions and want very much to "fit in" to life rather than stand out in anyway. Achievers are a well-educated and prosperous group who are fairly traditional but willing and able to try new things that interest them. Emulators are the youngest of this category. They are a socially-inclined lifestyle group who tend to copy the patterns of others. They emulate achievers who they desire to be someday (Mitchell, 1983, pp. 65-69).

The Inner-Directed VALS category is demographically younger than the other categories and consists of individuals whose lifestyles are more self-expressive and individualistic (see Figure 2.9, p. 40). They derive their sense of self and subsequent behavior from within themselves rather than from outside forces. While they currently represent only 19 percent of the population, they should be of interest to the field of recreation due to their levels of discretionary income and SRI's prediction that this group will reach 60 percent during the 1990s.

The Inner-Directed category consists of three lifestyles: I Am Me's, Experientials, and the Socially Conscious. The "I Am Me's" tend to be young, single, and lead a unique and highly expressive lifestyle with high levels of participation in active sports, creative endeavors, and traveling. The Experientials are a prosperous, well-educated group who derive substantial satisfaction from nonwork activities and have a strong outdoor orientation. The Socially Conscious are similar demographically to the Experientials, but are much more aware and active in social issues.

The Integrated group represents the VALS ideal, and it is estimated that they compose only two percent of the American population. This lifestyle is described as a balance between inner- and outer-directedness. They can be pictured as both movers and makers, observers and creators (Mitchell, 1983, p. 23). VALS researchers admit that they currently have little specific data regarding this small lifestyle group.

The differences in these lifestyle groups go far beyond a general demographic description of each category. This system enables recreators to subsegment markets on the basis of behavioral preferences. For instance, although Belongers and the Socially Conscious may possess many similarities in age, education, and income, it is their differences that will determine their leisure behavior. While Belongers may attend the opening night of an art exhibit, the Socially Conscious will participate more frequently in cultural events and are likely to avoid opening night festivities. Emulators and I Am Me's are similar in age and income, and both like to go out and socialize. However, Emulators are drawn to activities that have already been done by others while I Am Me's are drawn to new and unusual pursuits.

Belongers (38%)	Needs	Activities
White, married female	Derives satisfaction from family and friends	Family is most important
Large, aging group bit removed from action	Groups are important	Prefers to stay home
Lives in towns, not cities or suburbs	Content-clings to status-quo	Low in vigorous activities, cultural pursuits, adult learning and travel

Emulators (10%)	Needs	Activities
More males than females	Would rather go out than stay in	Favors pool, bowling, dancing, fast food, stereos, alcohol
Many singles and minorities	Low job satisfaction	
High school grads; employed full-time	Bit of a swinger	Socially inclined without resources
Prefer city life	Needs to conform; copies others	Seeks out status activities
Underrepresented in professions		

Achievers (20%)	Needs	Activities
Many middle-aged men	Well-adjusted and self-confident	Likes traditional activities
Well-educated; 20% self-employed	Conservative	Little involvement with arts; enjoys TV
50% live in suburbs	Families are important	Likes golf, cultural events, adult education
	Don't feel left out	

Figure 2.8.
Outer-Directed

Source: Adapted from Mitchell, Arnold. The Nine American Lifestyles.
New York: Macmillian Publishing, 1983. pp. 84-111.

I am me (3%)	Needs	Activities
Young, single, many students Many white, males Raised comfortably Live in cities	Prefers going out to staying home Feels best is ahead, but feels left out Unique, highly-expressive	Shuns at-home activities Owns lots of recreation equipment High levels of active sports, outdoor and creative activities as well as travelling
Experientials (5%)	**Needs**	**Activities**
Prosperous, well-educated, liberal Prefers part-time work and cities Many single	Very inner-directed Doesn't rely on group or status Tries anything once	Little TV; into self-learning High levels of camping, backpacking, swimming, snow skiing, racquet sports, travel
Socially-Conscious (11%)	**Needs**	**Activities**
Liberal, affluent and well-educated Professional/technical employment	Self-confident and independent Little need for status or group membership	Participates in arts, cultural events, reading, travel and educational TV Active in healthy, outdoor sports-cycling, jogging, etc.

Figure 2.9.
Inner-Directed

Source: Adapted from Mitchell, Arnold. The Nine American Lifestyles.
New York: Macmillian Publishing, 1983. pp. 112-145.

Psychographics and the research conducted by SRI can be most useful for marketers of parks, recreation, and leisure as a means to go beyond the usual demographics to identify and attract nonusers and potential users on the basis of the values and attitudes that guide their leisure choices. The information secured by addressing psychographics is more than just helpful. Its insights can have great impact. For example, a VALS buyer survey commissioned by Recreational Equipment, Inc., an outdoor equipment retailer in Seattle, revealed that between 48 percent and 50 percent of its customers were designated as Socially Conscious. The retailer then designed its catalogs to feature models who resembled this group with beards and slightly longer hair (Atlas, 1984, p. 56).

Synchronographics as Target Market Descriptor

Synchronographics is a relatively new descriptor in the target marketing process. The designation of this factor is fueled by the increasing importance of time-related factors within our society. Time, use of time, and availability of time combine to bring this factor into the process.

Since opportunities for participation in recreation and leisure are related to the availability of discretionary time, this factor holds significance for parks, recreation, and leisure. It was originally projected that by the 1980s, Americans would have a significant reduction in the work week accompanied by dramatic increases in leisure time. However, a recent Louis Harris poll reveals that hours worked by Americans have increased by 20 percent since 1973 and that the amount of leisure time has decreased by 32 percent (Hall, 1988). The increase in the number of salaried employees working well over 40 hours, the increase in time spent commuting, and the time crunch experienced by dual-income couples as they struggle to manage careers, children, and household have all contributed to this downward plunge in available time for leisure.

Synchronographics is a crucial factor in this process. All factors related to time segmentation combine to impact upon target marketing. Synchronographic factors can include the following:

- Time of Day
- Time of Year
- Day of Week
- Length of Time
- Seasonal Considerations

Target markets can be selected or eliminated from consideration by an organization based upon the scheduling of its programs or services.

Synchronographics can be used as a marketing advantage for the organization as well. Scheduling activities targeting singles for Sunday afternoons or evenings has worked well for some delivery systems. The travel industry has addressed this factor by packaging weekend trips and getaways designed to attract dual-career couples who can no longer afford the time for the traditional two-week vacation. The Learning Annex, a national company offering short-term learning and recreational activities in major cities, has created a myriad of successful programs scheduled for one or two evenings or one weekend, rather than the 8- or 10-week commitment required by many recreation organizations. Resorts have had success by specifically targeting groups of people available and interested in visiting their facility in the "off-season" time periods.

Synchronographics may be relatively new to this process, but its impact merits consideration. Time considerations are a natural link with recreation and leisure services. The role of this factor will become more critical as organizations project future markets based upon shifts in this time availability. The aging of the American population and the impact of retirement upon discretionary time make this factor worth considering.

Summary

Target marketing represents the most natural starting point for the marketing process for parks, recreation, and leisure. Target marketing focuses upon the identification of subsegments of potential users of leisure services. The purpose of this process is to better meet the needs of users by developing programs and services that address the specific needs and interests of similar groups of users.

Target markets can be identified and described using the following descriptors: needs and interests, geographic, sociodemographics, behavioral, and synchronographics. Each of these descriptors include a myriad of factors that can enhance the leisure delivery system's understanding and subsequent identification of appropriate, potential target markets for the organization.

Application of target marketing enables the recreator to plan programs and services to meet the needs and interests of a specific group of "somebodies" rather than attempting to attract everyone to the same park, program, facility, or service.

Suggested Activities

1. Develop a list of several facilities, programs, or services offered by a recreation delivery system. Describe current users as well as nonusers of these facilities or programs.

2. Select three or four current target market groups identified in the previous activity and analyze these groups using the five target market descriptors overviewed in this chapter.

3. For any two of the target markets utilized in the previous exercise, compile a list of sources of information for analyzing the target market descriptors. Be sure to include sources of information currently being used as well as other information readily available. Develop plans for making better use of this information and strategies for securing descriptor information presently not available.

4. Select two or three similar programs. facilities, or services offered by different delivery systems and identify similarities and differences of the target markets for these programs, facilities, or services.

5. For your specific recreation delivery system, identify which of the target market descriptors appear to be most critical for describing your target markets. Be sure to include factors inherent within these descriptors which are of most use to your organization. Develop a systemized approach for incorporating this information into your marketing plan.

References

Atlas, J. (1984 October). Beyond Demographics, *The Atlantic Monthly.*

Chubb, M. and Chubb, H. R. (1981). *One Third of Our Time? An Introduction to Recreation Behavior and Resources* (p. 201). New York, NY: John Wiley and Sons.

Crompton, J. (1983, Summer). "Selecting Target Markets–A Key to Effective Marketing. *Journal of Park and Recreation Administration. (1).*

Crompton, J. L., and Lamb, C. W., Jr. (1986). *Marketing Government and Social Services.* New York, NY: John Wiley & Sons.

Edginton, C., Compton, D., and Hanson. (1980). *Recreation and Leisure Programming: A Guide for the Professional.* Philadelphia, PA: Saunders College.

Hall, T. (1988, January 2) Why All Those People Feel They Never Have Any Time, *New York Times.*

Howard, D. R., and Crompton, J. L. (1980). *Financing, Managing and Marketing Recreation and Park Resources* (p. 352). Dubuque, IA: Wm. C. Brown Company.

Howard, D. R., Edginton, C. R., and Selin, S. W. (Winter 1988). Determinants of Program Loyalty. *Journal of Park and Recreation Administration.* 6(4) (pp. 41-51).

Kotler, P. (1980). *Marketing Management: Analysis, Planning, and Control (4th ed.).* Englewood Cliffs, NJ: Prentice-Hall.

Mitchell, A. (1983). *The Nine American Lifestyles.* (pp. 65-69). New York, NY: Macmillan Publishing.

Osgood, N. J., and Howe, C. Z. (1984). Psychological Aspects of Leisure: A Life Cycle Development Perspective. *Society and Leisure,* 7,(1). Howe, Christine Z. and Carpenter, Gaylene M. *Programming Leisure Experiences.* Englewood Cliffs, NJ: Prentice-Hall, 1985. (p. 27).

Tillman, A. *The Program Book for Recreation Professionals.* Palo Alto, CA: Mayfield Publishing Company. (1973).

Chapter Three

Target Market Strategies

Common Concerns for Parks, Recreation, and Leisure Delivery Systems

- A community recreation department is planning a Spring Festival and contemplates types of benefits they can offer potential user groups

- An entrepreneur in the Pacific Northwest is opening a gymnastics school and speculates over the role of competition related to target marketing

- A suburban YMCA is opening a fitness center to generate additional revenues and debates targeting current users as opposed to new target market groups

- A marketing director at a dude ranch has tracked geographic and demographic descriptors of visitors and deliberates the role of lifestyle clusters in future strategies

Target Marketing—Selection and Strategies

While understanding target marketing is a first step towards developing a marketing orientation for parks and recreation, it is only the beginning of this process. Recreators must select specific target market segments that may be profitable or appropriate for their organization and then develop strategies for attracting these selected market segments to their programs and services.

The process of selecting specific target market segments and then developing marketing strategies for those selected groups consists of the following four phases: (a) establishing criteria for selection; (b) exploring alternatives for selection; (c) developing market clusters; (d) selecting actual target market strategies. An overview of this process is presented in Figure 3.1.

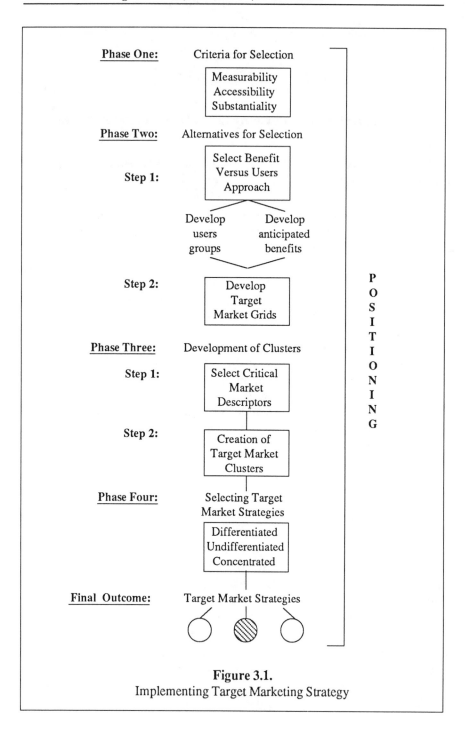

Figure 3.1.
Implementing Target Marketing Strategy

Criteria for Selection of Target Markets

Kotler (1982) specifies three criteria for the selection of viable target market segments. He believes potential target markets must exhibit the following characteristics: measurability, accessibility, and substantiality (p. 228).

Measurability refers to how easily the recreator is able to ascertain the size of the potential target market as well as information related to amounts of discretionary time and money or other related information of importance. In some cases, demographic or geographic information is quite easily accessed while information related to needs, psychographics, or stage of readiness is often more difficult to obtain.

For example, program specialists or marketing personnel employed in military recreation would easily be able to measure their target markets, since the number of military personnel at an installation as well as specifics regarding their rank, age, and family/marital status would be readily available to them. Marketing personnel associated with a resort would face a greater challenge. Membership in their target market is not defined by place of employment or assignment to a specific location. The task of measuring target markets for a resort would consist of effectively delineating potential target markets by geographic and lifestyle factors appropriate for that particular resort. Such questions as "Where do these people reside?" and "What benefits do they seek in vacation travel?" would be issues requiring attention.

A second criterion for the selection of target market groups is *accessibility*. The programs and services offered by the leisure delivery system must be accessible (and attractive) to the proposed target market. This accessibility could consist of a number of factors including location, timing, or affordability of the program or service developed or modified for this target market segment. For example, many public and nonprofit leisure delivery systems have difficulty designing accessible (attractive) programs for teenagers. Commercial recreation offerings that are usually housed in facilities not associated with schools or other "child-like" activities are often better able to access this target market group.

In addition, this criterion also refers to the actual ability of the leisure delivery system to contact and communicate effectively with this potential market. The recreation coordinator in a corporate setting is able to contact and communicate with the target market because the target market is clearly defined as employees of that corporation and they can be reached through corporate newsletters or departmental bulletin boards. The marketing director for the resort mentioned earlier faces a much more complex approach when attempting to contact his target market because they do not necessarily live or work within the immediate radius of the resort.

The final consideration is *substantiality*. This criterion, which refers to the size of the target market, may mean different things to different agencies. If an organization is going to develop or modify programs and services for a specific target market segment, then that target market must be large enough to make this venture worthwhile. The value of this venture may mean that there are enough people to generate economic profitability for a commercial venture, or it may be interpreted as a group which is sizeable in terms of importance or need within the public or nonprofit sectors.

For instance, a community recreation department may deem that a group of "at-risk" youth are substantial enough to warrant their selection as a target market while the actual number of these teens may be quite small. Their selection as a target market is based upon the perceived "size" of the social need rather than the actual size of the target population. The reverse is true in the commercial sector. A health club would never consider opening a facility in an area where there was not a sizeable number of their potential target market within easy access of their proposed location.

Alternatives for Selection

Once the recreator has examined the criteria for selection of the target markets, the next concern is deciding which type of approach to utilize when visualizing the target markets. The first step in this phase relates to making just that type of decision.

Crompton and Lamb (1986) suggest that when selecting target markets, one can either initiate the process by identifying potential *benefits being sought* by user groups or by identifying *potential user groups* and then categorizing similarities of benefits sought (p. 116). The outcome of either approach is essentially the same.

Utilizing the benefit alternative, the leisure delivery system would examine types of benefits being provided by a specific program or service; it would then identify groups of individuals who might be seeking that benefit, and delineate them on the basis of geographic, demographic, or behavioral descriptors. The second approach would be implemented by identifying potential clusters of users on the basis of target market descriptors and then attempting to identify common benefits they may be seeking from a particular recreation activity.

For instance, let's assume that the New York State Department of Tourism wishes to implement the benefit approach to segmentation. New York is a large state geographically with great diversity in tourism attractions. The Department of Tourism might segment their state on the basis of benefits being sought by potential tourists. Possible benefits could include such things as enjoying nature, exploring history, or participating in cultural events. This serves as a starting point for developing target markets. The second step using this approach would be an attempt to identify common target market descriptors for those people interested in history, culture, or the outdoors.

On the basis of this alternative for target market strategy, the State of New York could then begin to market its attractions. Potential tourists interested in plays and museums might receive information regarding the attractions of New York City, while those people looking to escape and experience nature would be forwarded promotional materials on the hiking and camping opportunities of the Adirondack Mountains.

The approach utilized by an organization depends upon the nature of the organization and may vary based upon its mission, current conditions, or relationship to its target market. For example, the Morale, Welfare, and Recreation Division of the U. S. Navy has as its mission the provision of recreational outlets for members of the Navy community. Its mission is clear and the target market is established. Its recreators might approach target marketing by more clearly defining potential groups on the basis of common market descriptors and then anticipating benefits desired by these groups and modifying programs and services accordingly.

Possible target market groups for the Navy MWR Division might include the following: single sailors ages 18 to 24, married sailors ages 20 to 35, married sailors over 35, single sailors over 35, spouses, and retirees. Having identified the potential user groups, marketers in this setting could then hypothesize possible recreational benefits being sought by these user groups ranging from physical activity to escape and relaxation.

While the outcome of either strategy results in the development or refinement of programs, facilities, or services to meet the needs of the identified target market, the selection of the strategy is a key one. A marketer needs to determine which approach will most effectively meet the needs of the organization.

A resort may use a user group approach to target marketing during its peak season. The resort may begin by developing a list of types of people who may be interested in coming to the resort, such as singles or dual-career couples. During its off-season, the same resort may wish to use a benefits approach to target marketing in an attempt to boost occupancy rates. The benefit that could be offered at this time would be reduced rates and uncrowded conditions. The resort then identify potential user groups such as retirees or families with limited vacation funds as potential target markets for this off-season period.

One mechanism that assists the recreation marketer in the appropriate selection of an alternative for target market selection is the construction of a grid. This grid approach enables the recreator to choose an appropriate approach for a marketing strategy.

The grid allows the recreator to visually demonstrate the choices of a *benefits* or a *user* approach to target marketing. Which of these two alternatives is appropriate for one's own delivery system? Is it best to identify potential benefits the organization can offer, such as was the case with the New York State Department of Tourism, or is it more beneficial to delineate potential user groups as was appropriate for the Navy MWR?

Examples of grid approaches for both of these organizations based upon their selection of a benefits approach versus a user group approach is illustrated in Figure 3.2.

Tourism Agency-Benefits Approach				
Benefits	**Singles**	**Adults**	**Families**	**Sr. Citizens**
Nature			√	√
History		√	√	√
Culture		√		
Escape	√			

MWR-Navy: User Group Approach			
User Groups	**Fitness**	**Socialization**	**Relaxation**
Young, single sailors		√	
Young, married sailors			√
Married sailors over 35	√		
Single sailors over 35	√	√	
Spouses		√	

Figure 3.2.
Grid Approaches

Developing Target Market Clusters

The *third phase* for developing a target marketing plan is the *development* of target market clusters. Target market clusters are groupings of target market descriptors which more clearly and fully describe potential user groups.

The *first step* is to select *critical market descriptors*. The five common target market descriptors (geographic, leisure needs and interests, socio-demographics, behavioral, and synchronographics) consist of a large number of related factors. The role of the recreator is to identify and select those related factors that are most important to the organization when attempting to best describe their target markets.

How does one decide just which target market descriptors are most critical to the success of their organization? The answer can be best addressed by recalling the mission and current or projected needs of the organization as well as the facilities, programs, or services being provided.

A community parks and recreation department has as its mission serving all people within its geographic location. Therefore, when planning a Fourth of July special event, the planners would not expand upon the geographic descriptor, but focus on creating target market clusters on the basis of sociodemographic factors. On the other hand, a commercial fitness center cognizant of the critical nature of the proximity of people to its facility might focus on geographic factors as the basis for developing the target market clusters.

Regardless of the alternative one chooses to utilize, a complete definition of target markets enables the recreator to better understand and anticipate the specific needs and requirements of these groups. This completeness of definition will eventually lead to the creation and modification of facilities, programs, and services that seem to be exclusively designed for that target market group.

Several approaches are currently being introduced as mechanisms to address the development of market clusters. One such mechanism is geographic information systems (GIS). As the name implies, the focus of this computerized approach is upon geographic factors. The initial and most customary use of the GIS program has related to land planning and development. It has recently been utilized by recreation organizations to provide a valuable link between where people live and certain other market descriptors.

There are essentially two component parts to this computerized program: spatial data (i.e., maps, geographic factors) and a data base that allows attribute information similar to census data to be overlaid with the spatial information. Various computer programs allow for the selection of geographic parameters including governmental areas such as states and counties, as well as statistical areas such as regions of the United States, standard consolidated statistical areas (SCSA), neighborhoods, and zip codes. Types of information available through the use of this program include age breakdown, income and education levels, employment patterns, and travel time to work to name a few.

The GIS system allows an organization to select specific marketing characteristics such as age, occupation, marital status, and income and to locate pockets of these potential target markets for the organization. Although this technology is rather new, it is becoming more available and is being utilized extensively in park planning operations.

Another approach to cluster marketing is *Prizm Potential Rating Index for Zip Markets*. Created by Jonathan Robbins in 1974, this popular target marketing system matches zip codes with census data and consumer surveys (Weiss, 1988, p. xii). Robbins essentially utilized his research, the census data, and a computer to sort the nation's 36,000 zip codes into 40 "lifestyle" clusters. Robbins' corporation, the Alexandria, VA–based Claritas, enables its corporate clients to get the complete picture of their target market by incorporating such factors as household density, type of community, ethnic makeup of the neighborhood, and type of family, along with age, education, and employment levels.

Claritas has given nicknames to each of the 40 clusters identified. For example, "Gray Power" describes a group of consumers older then 65 who live without children in multifamily housing in suburban communities, and who had worked in white collar jobs. "Norma Rae-ville" describes neighborhoods of consumers between the ages of 18 and 54 who live with their families in smaller towns, work in blue collar jobs, and have attended some high school (Advanced Analysis, 1987).

This type of cluster target marketing enables clients of Claritas and other such marketing firms to deal with the changing makeup of American society. The information gathered by such marketing firms provides clients with information regarding purchasing behavior which includes everything from cars to frozen dinners to TV viewing habits, to which clusters prefer Coke® over Pepsi®.

Other marketing companies have developed clusters that are similar to those established by Claritas. Claritas' Prizm system divides Americans into twelve different social groupings and assigns nicknames to the forty clusters identified within these social groups.[6] The social groups and nicknames for the 40 clusters along with percentages of existence in U.S. households are illustrated in Figure 3.3.

Essentially, this advanced analysis marries demographics to psychographics. Information secured from computerized programs such as GIS and Prizm enables businesses in this country to better identify and target profitable markets for their organization. This information can lead to the creation of new products, programs, and services or the modification of existing programs. It also serves as direction for both how and where one promotes the services of one's organization.

Recreation delivery systems can utilize the "clustering" technique to their advantage. One option would be to utilize the GIS system, which is becoming increasingly more available. A second option would be to incorporate a "lifestyle cluster" system for one's organization. Commercial delivery systems may utilize the services of a marketing agency for this purpose. Public and nonprofit organizations can tap into state technical assistance offices who possess GIS capability or utilize components of the lifestyle quiz found in the appendix of Weiss' book *The Clustering of America* (1988). This book may be of value and interest to anyone needing a more in-depth picture of the clustering approach, and it provides valuable information about values, attitudes, and behavior patterns of various lifestyle clusters.

Phase Four: Target Market Strategies

The final phase of this process is the selection and development of target market strategies for the market clusters you've created for your organization. Your market clusters have been identified and developed to provide a more in depth understanding of the people you intend to target as users of your products, programs, or services. The recreation organization needs to then consider its marketing strategy for each of these clusters.

There are three different target market strategies from which a recreation delivery system could select. Kotler identifies these three strategies as differentiated, undifferentiated, and concentrated.[7] The selection of one of

America's Forty Neighborhood Types		
Cluster	Thumbnail Description	Percent U. S. Households
Blue blood estates	America's wealthiest neighborhoods include suburban homes and one in ten millionaires	1.1
Money and brains	Posh big-city enclaves of townhouses, condos and apartments	0.9
Furs and station wagons	New money in metropolitan bedroom suburbs	3.2
Urban gold coast	Upscale urban high-rise districts	0.5
Pools and patios	Older, upper-middle class, suburban communities	3.4
Two more rungs	Comfortable multi-ethnic suburbs	0.7
Young influentials	Yuppie, fringe-city condo and apartment developments	2.9
Young suburbia	Child-rearing, outlying suburbs	5.3
God's country	Upscale frontier boomtowns	2.7
Blue-chip blues	The wealthiest blue-collar suburbs	6.0
Bohemian mix	Inner-city bohemian enclaves à la Greenwich Village	1.1
Levittown, U. S. A.	Aging, post-World War II tract subdivisions	3.1
Gray power	Upper-middle-class retirement communities	2.9
Black enterprise	Predominantly black, middle-and upper-middle-class neighborhoods	0.8
New beginnings	Fringe-city areas of singles complexes, garden apartments and trim bungalows	4.3
Blue-collar nursery	Middle-class, child-rearing towns	2.2
New homesteaders	Ex-urban boom towns of young, midscale families	4.2
New melting pot	New immigrant neighborhoods, primarily in the (nation's) port cities	0.9
Towns and gowns	America's college towns	1.2
Rank and file	Older, blue collar, industrial suburbs	1.4
Middle America	Midscale, midsize towns	3.2

Figure 3.3.
America's Forty Neighborhood Types

America's Forty Neighborhood Types (continued)		
Cluster	**Thumbnail Description**	**Percent U. S. Households**
Old Yankee rows	Working-class rowhouse districts	1.6
Coalburg and corntown	Small towns based on light industry and farming	2.0
Shotguns and pickups	Crossroads villages serving the nation's lumber and breadbasket needs	1.9
Golden ponds	Rustic cottage communities located near the coasts, in the mountains or alongside lakes	5.2
Agri-business	Small towns surrounded by large-scale farms and ranches	2.1
Emergent minorities	Predominantly black, working-class, city neighborhoods	1.7
Single city blues	Downscale, urban, singles districts	3.3
Mines and mills	Struggling steeltowns and mining villages	2.8
Back-country folks	Remote, downscale, farm towns	3.4
Norma Rae-ville	Lower-middle-class milltowns and industrial suburbs, primarily in the South	2.3
Smalltown downtown	Inner-city districts of small industrial cities	2.5
Grain belt	The nation's most sparsely populated rural communities	1.3
Heavy industry	Lower-working-class districts in the nation's older industrial cities	2.8
Share croppers	Primarily southern hamlets devoted to farming and light industry	4.0
Downtown dixie style	Aging, predominantly black neighborhoods, typically in southern cities	3.4
Hispanic mix	America's Hispanic barrios	1.9
Tobacco roads	Predominantly black farm communities throughout the South	1.2
Hard scrabble	The nation's poorest rural settlements	1.5
Public assistance	America's inner-city ghettos	3.1

Figure 3.3. (continued)
America's Forty Neighborhood Types

Household percentages are based on 1987 census block groups and estimated to the closest 0.1 percent. Source: PRIZM (Census Demography), Claritas Corp., 1987.

these three strategies is based upon the degree of homogenity found within your target market; the mission and needs of your organization; and the nature and type of competition.

The three strategies provide a range of choices for addressing target market selection. The three approaches consist of the following:

Undifferentiated: Address your target market as one, large group with similar needs and interests

Differentiated: Perceive your target markets as consisting of several distinct market segments with varying needs and interests

Concentrated: Single out and select one narrow market segment and concentrate your focus upon that group

Based upon the mission of your organization and the nature of the competition, a recreation delivery system may select one or more of these approaches. Public parks and recreation departments due to their mandate may decide upon an undifferentiated target market strategy to provide services for their entire community, county, or district. Resorts in the Carolinas, Georgia, and Florida may select a concentrated approach and narrow their market to include winter visitors from New York, New Jersey, and Connecticut. They may further delineate this approach by concentrating on one small segment of the population such as families with small children or adult golfers depending upon the nature of their facilities. Another term for this concentrated marketing strategy is niche. The agency may choose to concentrate all its efforts on one niche or small segment of the entire market.

Recreation delivery systems are not limited to the selection of just one marketing strategy. For instance, if a public delivery system was planning a 4th of July Festival, they may select an undifferentiated approach while simultaneously utilizing a differentiated approach for summer workshops and a concentrated strategy for summer day camps. Figure 3.4 provides an overview of the utilization of these three strategies.

Target market strategies essentially reflect how your organization chooses to view the people you serve or wish to attract to your facility, programs, or services. Do you visualize them as one large group of participants? Do you see them as one small group of users who have specific needs and interests which match the services and mission of your delivery system? Do you perceive your target market as consisting of several, distinct market segments who possess different characteristics and needs? The importance

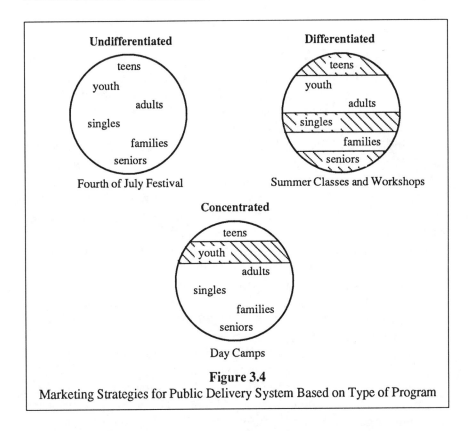

Figure 3.4
Marketing Strategies for Public Delivery System Based on Type of Program

of this perception of target market and your eventual selection of target market segments and strategies will serve as a basis for developing and adapting the marketing mix variables. An overview of the marketing mix variables and their implementation for parks, recreation, and leisure are discussed in ensuing chapters.

Final Outcome: Target Markets

The organization has now reached the point where it has clearly and specifically identified its target market(s). The number of target markets and the homogenity of these markets will vary for each organization. This serves as the framework for the organization. It now shifts its role and attention to the creation, modification, or delivery of programs and services which meet the needs of its identified target markets and reflect the strategy as devised by the organization.

Positioning

Positioning is a concept central to all phases of the marketing process which is especially critical in its relationships to target marketing. Ries and Trout refer to positioning as "the battle for your mind" and cite the virtual bombardment of American society with media, new products, and advertising overload as three of the basic factors which necessitate the need for positioning.[8]   They illustrate the need to battle for the consumers' mind by citing $200 per year per capita consumption of advertising in America; the presence of over 10,000 individual products available in supermarkets; and the recent entry of newcomers such as doctors, lawyers, hospitals, and governments into the advertising fray as underlying factors contributing to this growing phenomena of over-communication.[9]

Given these conditions, it becomes increasingly difficult for marketers in any field or sector to reach out and grab the attention and interest of the people whom they are trying to attract. Recreation and leisure delivery systems are experiencing the same types of explosions of competition for the discretionary dollar and the promotion and media madness which is now associated with all segments of our society.

The days of one "family-type" vacation destination are over. The time has past when there was only one option available for people who wanted to swim, play tennis, or exercise. Gone also is the reliance upon the "one-size fits all" park, program or service which could be promoted simply by informing the general public of your existence through a flyer brought home by school kids or posters in the grocery stores.

As the competition grows for the leisure providers so do the number and variety of leisure pursuits and outlets for participants. As the level of communication and advertising grows in our society so does the challenge of breaking through and getting the attention and interest of those you choose to attract to your delivery system.

The concept of positioning refers to the perception people have of your leisure delivery system. This perception is critical to the marketing process. You need to ascertain how your target markets perceive your agency, its programs and services, and how this perception relates to their needs and interests.

Common "Positioning" Factors

There are a number of fairly common perceptions or positions which are often held by recreation and leisure delivery systems. Some general categories of positions held by parks, recreation, and leisure organizations are as follows: season of year, type of participants, types of programs/services, price, and market position.

Many public park and recreation departments have often had to deal with overcoming the "seasonal perception" of their organizations. Residents and taxpayers often mistakenly positioned these agencies as being "summer" only. Similarly, ski resorts needing to maintain profitability by generating revenue on a year-round basis have had to fight the public's perception that ski resorts function only in the winter.

The types of people who utilize the services of a particular recreation delivery system is also another positioning factor. For many years, the YMCAs were for young, Christian men. Even after they opened their doors to females, adults, and the general public, they were often perceived as being for "boys only." You will note that the YMCAs are seldom referred to by their full acronym anymore having repositioned themselves as the "Y".

Types of programs, activities, and services are also another area of market positioning. Ys are often associated with swimming pools and fitness programs. Some community recreation departments are often associated with team sports and leagues. Sometimes an area can come to be associated with a particular activity similar to the way that people tend to think of golf when they hear Myrtle Beach, South Carolina mentioned.

Different recreation delivery systems can be perceived by potential users in terms of pricing differentials. People come to expect that public parks and nonprofit organizations should provide services that are free or of low-cost. They anticipate that private or commercial recreation opportunities will be more expensive. Often, this pricing perception determines where people think they should participate or where they can afford to participate or where they would like others to think they can afford to participate.

An additional category of perception refers to market position. In this instance, market position refers to the public's perception of your organization in relationship to your competitors. For instance, Disney World in Florida would be considered the market "leader" when people think of taking their family on a trip to that part of the country. Busch Gardens in nearby Tampa might be considered a market "challenger" in this instance. They would like to challenge Disney World for its hold on this market and manage to convince tourists to make a visit to their amusement area as well. The Kennedy Space Center in Florida might be considered as having a "niche" position. It certainly is an attraction for families visiting Florida, but attracts a much smaller number of visitors who may differ from those attracted to Disney World and Busch Gardens.

Positioning is critical to the success of recreation and leisure delivery system to ensure their viability by attracting target markets to their organization. The position held by their organization is a major determinant in reaching selected target markets. Community recreation departments can't expect to attract adults to their fall and winter programs if they are perceived as being providers of children's activities offered primarily in the summer. Ys would find it difficult to enroll adult women in their aerobic classes if they had continued to be perceived as a place for young men.

Positioning Reflects People (Target Markets)

The position of your organization should reflect the needs and interests of the people who you serve or the people you wish to attract. Reis and Trout refer to positioning as a concept which sparked a revolution in advertising but the role and importance of positioning actually starts with the selection of target markets.

The position of your organization should reflect the needs and interests of your target markets to facilitate their perception of your organization as the recreation delivery system designed for them. Since people change, it means that position needs to change over time as well.

An excellent example of positioning change over time and its importance and relationship to changes in target markets is Club Med. Club Med, the worldwide resort organization with villages in semi-remote locations around the world, advertises itself as the "antidote for civilization." It holds a perception in the mind of consumers as being located in desirable beach areas around the world filled with a plethora of active recreation activities. In the 70s, if you mentioned Club Med, people would conjure up an image of attractive single people playing and romping on the beaches. During the 80s, many of the Club Meds added "camp programs" for children so that their singles target markets of the 70s could return with their young families in the 80s and still find their newly revised version of an antidote to civilization. Recent advertisements for Club Meds still feature the "anti-dote to civilization" slogan accompanied by beaches but they do so differently. Rather than seeing young people running around and participat-ing nonstop, you see a more mature individual who is floating in the water watching the world go by rather than racing nonstop from one active physical activity to another. The aging of the baby boomers, one of the initial target markets for Club Meds, have caused Club Med to once again modify their position to continue to attract people whose maturing has caused them to rethink their idea of the perfect vacation.

People change, and as people change, recreation organizations need to change their market positions as well in order to continue to address the needs of their target markets and continue to attract participants to their facilities or programs.

Incorporating Market Position

In order to incorporate this important concept into the ongoing operation of your organization, there are essentially three steps you need to undertake: identification of position of your agency; examination of relationship of position to your target markets; and the identification of the position of your competition (if appropriate).

How does a recreator determine the position of his organization? This assessment can be completed quite easily and efficiently by constructing a positioning plot. A positioning plot consists of a vertical and horizontal axis which reflect two important positioning factors which are critical to your agency.

For example, a community recreation center concerned that its position may be that of a "summer-based organization primarily serving children" may select season and age of participants as the two positioning factors they feel are critical to their organization. The selection of the two factors to be examined is based upon the organization's mission and marketing goals at the time. Several position plots can be done utilizing various positioning factors which enables an organization to look at its position in a variety of approaches.

After examining population projections through GIS, the neighbor-hood recreation center discovers that the population or potential target market groups in their area are maturing and that future projections reveal an increase in the number of adults especially females. They may wish to examine their current position in light of this information. They would begin by selecting two positioning factors to be used in this process. Since the maturing of the population is one critical factor they may select age as one of their factors. After a perusal of their current programs offered, they notice that programs could be broken down into two categories physical activities and nonphysical activities which they choose as their second factor.

They then begin to place on the positioning plot where each of their current programs, activities, or services would fall on this plot. The outcome of this process is illustrated in Figure 3.5.

A preliminary perusal of this positioning plot for the community center reveals a potential target market member reading their brochure would perceive it as an organization providing primarily physical activities for children. This analysis would provide a basis for consideration when planning for the projected population changes for their neighborhood. They clearly need to begin to "reposition" themselves as a community center serving adults and senior citizens with a variety of activities. Females who may not be attracted to the structured physical activities currently being offered may be selected as a new target market group.

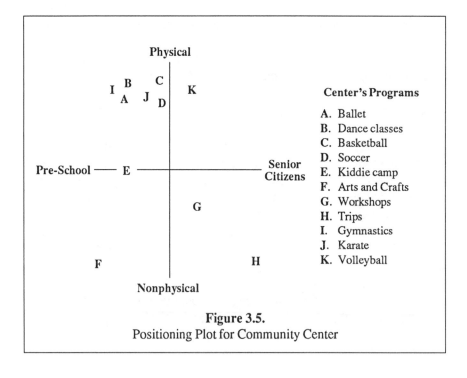

Figure 3.5.
Positioning Plot for Community Center

There are other uses for the positioning plot as well. That same community center could select two other factors and then analyze its position in relationship to a different set of circumstances. The community center could also plot the "position of its competition" within that neighborhood as well.

Assuming that there was a Y located in that same neighborhood, the community center could expand upon the information secured in their positioning plot by graphing the programs which the Y offers which may or may not be in competition with them. The placement of the Y's programs onto this plot are illustrated in Figure 3.6.

An examination of the community center's position in light of the programs offered by the nearby Y reveals that they are not currently direct competitors. The Y offers a variety of physical activity programs for adults as opposed to children, as is the case with the community center. However, in light of the information regarding the population aging in that neighborhood, it would appear as if the Y could seriously threaten the community center as the population ages and adults continue to participate in Y physical activity programs. In this instance, the community center is able to identify a possible threat of competition using the positioning plot. However, the

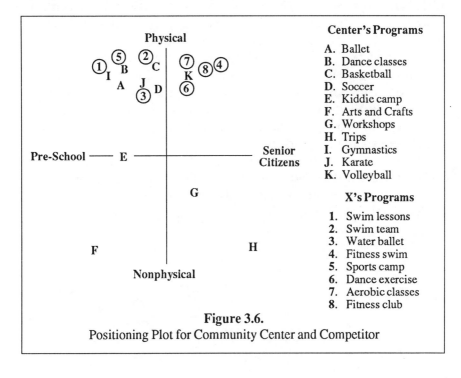

Figure 3.6.
Positioning Plot for Community Center and Competitor

positioning plot involving their competition reveals some opportunities for the community center as well. The local Y virtually offers nothing in the way of nonphysical programs and activities. This information could suggest that the community center may wish to maintain its current position of physical activities for children while beginning to shift its emphasis to nonphysical activities for adults.

Positioning is a critical part of the marketing process and can be utilized in a variety of ways. In the public and nonprofit sectors, such a positioning plot could be used cooperatively in an attempt to avoid duplication of services and facilitate meeting the vast variety of needs of many residents. In the commercial sector, it can assist a recreation delivery system in uncovering a competitive edge for their organization to enable them to set themselves apart from their competition or to reveal strategies for attacking them directly.

Positioning and Its Relationship to Target Marketing

There are some marketers who consider positioning a concept which is related only to advertising and promotion. While positioning is a critical factor in the development of a promotional strategy, its value and importance is closely related to the entire marketing process.

Positioning relates to the perception potential or current target markets may have of your organization and its programs and services. Therefore, it is important to consider this factor in the development of target marketing strategies. In addition, your organization's position can be modified by choices and decisions you make about the programs and services you plan and offer to your target markets.

An understanding and appreciation of positioning and its relevance to decisions which will be made as organizations modify and manipulate these elements of the marketing mix may make the difference between the short- and long-range success of that delivery system.

Summary

Understanding the concept of target marketing is essential for marketing parks, recreation, and leisure delivery systems. Recreators need to apply the concept specifically to their organization by identifying and selecting specific target market segments which are profitable or viable for their delivery systems.

This process of identifying and selecting target market segments involves four phases: establishing criteria for selection; deciding upon alternatives for selection; developing target market clusters; and selecting target market strategies. The outcome of this process enables a recreation delivery system to subsequently modify current programs or services or to develop services to attract these appropriate and profitable target markets to their doors.

Closely integrated with the identification and selection of target market segments is the concept of positioning. Positioning refers to the perception people have of a recreation delivery system and can enhance or detract from the effectiveness of target marketing strategies.

Suggested Activities

1. Select three current programs or services of a recreation delivery system and attempt to identify target market strategies utilized. Suggest how changes in these strategies would impact upon the organization.

2. Review a brochure or flyer from a delivery system. Select two important positioning descriptors and plot the market position of the organization on the basis of these factors. Do the same for its competitors.

3. For a new program or service under consideration, undertake the target market selection process on the basis of benefits. Redo using a user group approach. Compare and contrast results.

4. Identify the less popular programs and services being provided by a recreation delivery system. Explore possible changes in target market strategies to enhance the viability of these programs or services.

Footnotes

[1] Kotler, Philip. Marketing for Nonprofit Organizations, 2nd ed. Englewood Cliffs, NJ: Prentice-Hall, 1982, p. 228.

[2] Crompton, John L. and Lamb, Charles W. Jr. Marketing Government and Social Services. New York, NY: John Wiley & Sons, 1986. p. 116.

[3] Weiss, Michael J. The Clustering of America. New York, NY: Tilden Books, 1988. p. xii.

[4] "Advanced Analysis Marries Demographics and Attitudes," The Hartford Courant, September 7, 1987, pp. 15-16.

[5] Ibid.

[6] Ibid.

[7] Kotler, Philip. Marketing Management: Analysis, Planning, and Control, 4th ed. Englewood Cliffs, NJ: Prentice-Hall, 1980, pp. 206-209.

[8] Reis, Al and Trout, Jack. Positioning: The Battle for Your Mind. New York, NY: Warner Books, 1982, pp. 16-19.

[9] Ibid.

Chapter Four

Marketing Mix Variables–
The First Two Ps: Program and Place

Common Concerns for Parks, Recreation, and Leisure Delivery Systems

- A community recreation director scheduling activities for senior citizens deliberates between offering activities at multiple locations once a week versus activities twice per week at fewer locations.

- A MWR director examining program attendance records questions the cancellation of programs that had waiting lists just six months ago.

- A once popular resort seems to have fallen out of favor recently and considers marketing strategies to revitalize its operation.

- The fitness director at a Y reads that it's the augmented product that provides the competitive edge in today's environments and speculates as to what this means for the facility.

There are essentially four "Ps" of marketing, which are referred to as the marketing mix variables. The four "Ps" are product or program, place, price, and promotion. When applying the first "P" to parks, recreation, and leisure delivery systems, it is necessary to perceive this "P" as being any *product, program, or service* that an organization chooses to offer its target market to satisfy a determined need of that market. An examination of the marketing mix variable referred to as product or program is a natural starting point, since recreators generally consider various programs or service options first in meeting the needs of their target markets.

Due to the critical interrelationship between the product/program/ service and various place factors such as location and schedule, the second P of the marketing mix variables, *place*, is examined in conjunction with the product/program/service variable.

Three Dimensions of a Product/Program/Service

Any program or service consists of a variety of factors. Kotler (1980) defines a product as "anything that can be offered to a market for attention, acquisition, use, or consumption including physical objects, services, personalities, places, organizations and ideas and refers to these factors inherent within any program or service as being a "bundle of benefits" (p. 351).

For instance, a neighborhood park is more than just a park. It is perceived on the basis of the attributes or bundle of benefits present within that park, such as jogging trails, picnic tables, or a tot play area. The same would be true for a commercial fitness center. The fitness center is viewed by the target market in its entirety, which may or may not include such things as equipment, classes, and shower facilities.

Kotler (1982) maintains that there are three dimensions to every product: the *core* product, the *tangible* product, and the *augmented* product (pp. 291-292). The *core* product refers to the most fundamental level of the program or service which the user is seeking. The core product focuses upon the *primary benefit* being sought by the potential consumer and addresses questions such as, "What is the participant really looking for from a recreational experience?" or "What need is this individual attempting to satisfy through involvement with this service?"

When analyzing use of a park, the recreator needs to identify the primary benefit users seek when visiting the park. This identification of the primary benefit, whether it be exercise or communing with nature, would be the core portion of the product being offered.

The second dimension is the *tangible* product. Every core product, program, or service is made available to the target market in some tangible form that includes the following five categories: *styling, features, quality, packaging,* and *brand name* (Kotler, 1982, pp. 291-292).

Styling refers to the distinct "feel" that a program or product has about it. Much of the current competition within recreation and leisure services relates to styling. People may select a commercial fitness center over a fitness workout room in a local community center due to the attractiveness of the room or the appearance of the staff as opposed to the actual core product of exercise.

An additional component of the tangible product is referred to as *features.* These features can consist of components that can be added or deleted from a core product. When visiting a park, the availability of paddle boat rentals or a food concession are examples of two such features that could be added or deleted from the core product. The fitness center also has a host of features that could be included within its operation such as showers, fresh towels, babysitting, exercise classes, or a juice bar. Features are important components of the tangible product because they more clearly delineate the target market's use of the program or service on the basis of additional benefits they seek.

Another factor related to the tangible portion of a product is *quality*. Quality has become the buzzword of the 1990s in the service industry. Quality of a product, program, or service plays an increasingly important role in recreation delivery systems, but it is important to remember that quality is based upon individual perception. This perception can include an extensive array of factors ranging from phone etiquette to cleanliness of the facility.

Quality can vary based upon the benefits being sought by different target markets. Recreational golfers may not be especially concerned with turf maintenance when playing their occasional round of golf. However, this perception of quality would be uppermost in the minds of serious golfers. Parents looking for a safe and secure experience for their children may question at some length the qualifications of the instructors in a preschool movement class. When selecting an exercise program for themselves, those same adults may not even think to ask about the certification of the fitness instructor.

The *packaging* of a product is also important. How is the product packaged? Does the park have clearly marked jogging trails so it appears suitable for that activity? Does the fitness center have thoroughly vacuumed carpeting for floor exercises, well-ventilated rooms filled with an assortment of modern exercise equipment? All of these factors compose the packaging of a product.

The final component of the tangible product is *brand name*. This refers to a name or symbol representing the organization. This name or symbol needs to clearly define the organization related to the product or service offered and simultaneously differentiate the agency from its competitors.

Disney is a perfect example of positive use of a name and a symbol. Disney stands for quality, family entertainment. Its latest products such as the movie studio and lagoon park in Florida are related to this perception of family entertainment. At the same time, the Disney name and its symbol, Mickey Mouse, set it apart from products or services offered by its competitors. An organization's name, reputation, logo, or symbol are all part of this tangible portion of its products and services.

The *augmented* product is the third level of every product. The augmented product is any and all additional services or benefits offered to the target market that go beyond the core and tangible levels. Kotler (1982) identifies such things as installation, delivery, credit terms, warranty, and after-sales service as factors related to the augmented product (p. 296). While these factors are essential when purchasing a piece of recreation equipment and are related to the policies and procedures of the organization, they do not fully address the possible factors related to a program or service.

The creation and delivery of a recreation program or service is quite different from selling a product because programs and services are more intangible than tangible. Programs and services are consumed, not owned, so there will be additional factors included in this picture of the augmented product when it comes to dealing with recreation programs and services.

These added or augmented features may include such things as whether the organization allows payment by cash, check, or credit card, and what its policies are regarding cancellation of sessions or membership. These are policies and procedures that correspond with the consumption of a service as opposed to the purchase of a product. Due to the nature of a program or service being consumed by the user, the role of participants, which includes an organization's personnel as well as fellow participants, is also impacted upon in this factor. (See Figure 4.1).

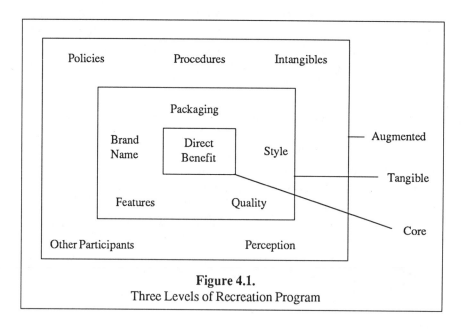

Figure 4.1.
Three Levels of Recreation Program

Role of Secondary Benefit(s)

These added intangible features composing the augmented product are often referred to as the "real competition" in parks, recreation, and leisure and relate essentially to the *secondary benefit(s)* being sought by users of one's programs and services.

Secondary benefits are key to the success of parks, recreation, and leisure. The decision to participate in a recreational activity or with a specific delivery system is not made in one dimension. People who enroll in an exercise program or join a fitness center do so because the primary benefit being sought is physical activity and fitness. If they simply wanted to exercise and get in shape, what would prohibit them from doing so on their own? This is where the concept of secondary benefit comes into play.

If an individual is unsure as to how to go about getting in shape, then the person may be looking for expertise and instruction. If individuals feel they won't stick to a program on their own, they may be seeking a group experience to utilize competition or socialization as a motivator. They may, in addition to exercise, be looking for a place to meet new people or acquire the status associated with being a club member.

A recreator needs to take into consideration the possible secondary benefits being sought by a target market when constructing a program or service. These benefits, which are often related to the augmented or "intangible" portion of the product, may be more difficult to ascertain but can make the difference when attempting to reach and attract specific target markets to one's delivery system.

Components of Product Mix

Prior to developing or modifying a set of programs and services to be offered for a target market, an analysis of current offerings by an organization or by that of its competition if venturing into a new area should be analyzed. The combination of all products and services offered by the organization to its target markets is referred to as the *product mix.*

Product mix can be further broken down into product line and product item. Kotler (1982) defines *product line* as "groups of products within a product mix that are closely related because they function in a similar manner, are available to the same consumers, or are marketed through similar outlets" and refers to *product item* as "a distinct unit within a product line that is distinguishable by size, appearance, price, or some other factor" (p. 289).

Product Lines ➡ ⬇	Physical Activities	The Arts	Aquatics
Entry-Level	Beginner tennis classes	Learn-to-draw classes	Swimming lessons
Skill Improvement	Soccer clinic	Painting workshop	Lifesaving classes
Unstructured	Open gym	Photography workroom	Free swim
Competitive	Softball leagues	Art contest	Swim team
Special Event	New games festival	Art in the park	Water ballet show

Figure 4.2.
Program Analysis for Community Recreation Department

Before undertaking modification of current programs or services or the creation of new programs, it is helpful to analyze the product mix through the use of a grid. The grid developed in Figure 4.2 has been constructed to illustrate the product mix, product lines, and several product items offered by a community recreation department. This grid analyzes the product mix according to various program areas and illustrates the product lines through forms of programs or services currently being offered.

A recreation delivery system can also be described by analyzing its product mix in terms of its length, width, and depth. In this instance, the product *length* refers to the number of product lines within the mix. The *width* assesses the variety of product lines within the mix and the *depth* reflect the actual number of offerings for each of these product items.

The length, width, and depth of the product line of a resort are illustrated in Figure 4.3. In this instance, the product mix was identified in three areas: sports, lessons, and special events, with the width of these product lines listing the specific facilities or activities related to these product lines. The numbers listed beside each of these specific activities reflect the number areas or facilities present at this resort or the number of times each activity is offered during a 1-week period in the season.

Resort	← Product Mix Length →		
	Sports	Lessons	Spec. Events
↑ Product Line Width ↓	Golf course (2) Driving range (1) Tennis courts (12) Pools (2)	Tennis (15) Scuba (3) Yoga (5) Aerobics (5)	Tennis tourney (1) Boat tour (2) Dance contest (1)

Figure 4.3.
Resort Analysis by Length, Width, and Depth of Product Line

This particular type of product analysis is of use to recreators in a number of ways. When considering modification of current programs and services, this serves as a starting point for determining program balance and variety in relationship to one's target market. When interested in introducing a new program or service, it can serve as a mechanism for establishing how the new program would integrate with current offerings as well as ascertaining its relationship to the competition. The use of this type of analysis is also helpful in compiling a more complete picture of an organization's position as it relates to its perception by the target market.

Impact of Program Life Cycle

Product or program life cycle is a concept that greatly impacts upon this first P of the marketing mix variables. When examining activities and programs, it sometimes appears as if some program go on forever while others lose popularity in a relatively short time span. Each program and activity has its own life cycle or stages of development. Living things have their own stages of growth and development with each stage of development marked by certain characteristics. The same is true for for recreation products, programs, or services.

The program life cycle concept is a powerful mechanism to be utilized by the recreator. It enables the recreator to examine programs and services in a different framework to respond more effectively to the changes that occur outside of the organization and to plan for the most efficient use of resources.

The life cycle for recreation programs creates a path that is indicative of users' acceptance and rate of participation from the time a program was initiated until the program is no longer offered. Recreation programs generally go through five different stages of the life cycle as follows: *introduction, take-off, maturation, saturation,* and *decline* (Howard and Crompton, 1980, p. 378). Each stage of the life cycle has various characteristics that are particular to that stage. Each stage is also marked by various marketing activities that need to be undertaken by recreators to address those characteristics (see Figure 4.4, p. 78).

The first stage in the recreation program life cycle is *introduction.* Introduction is that stage when the program, service, or activity is first introduced into the product mix offered by a recreation delivery system. Generally, it is characterized by a small number of participants due to the relative newness of the program itself or the lack of awareness among consumers that the organization is offering such a program. Naturally, this low level of participation means that there will be little or no profitability at this stage.

There are a number of activities which the recreator could undertake when a program is in the introductory stage. The program might need to be modified to address any oversights often involved with the creation of a new program or to accommodate feedback from the initial participants. At this stage, there needs to be heavy emphasis placed upon promotion of the program to build awareness and acceptance among target market groups. The recreator must find ways to encourage people to give this program a try; techniques such as introductory offers, price discounts, and premium giveaways are often used at this stage.

The second stage in the program life cycle is termed *take-off.* The take-off stage is characterized by a rapid growth in the number of participants. This is a stage when one can anticipate a sharp increase in revenues and when the recreator needs to focus upon the continued management of this program. Promotion is no longer a major focus in this stage since word-of-mouth from participants usually generates awareness and acceptance of this program. However, from a marketing viewpoint, the recreator now needs to begin creating user loyalty. The recreator must maintain the high quality of this program or service in order to assure that current users continue to participate in the program as offered by the delivery system.

It is difficult to anticipate the length of time involved with these first two stages of introduction and take-off. Howard and Crompton (1980, p. 379) believe that the length of these stages will vary based upon the following factors:

(a) newness of the program,
(b) its complexity in terms of level of skill required for participation,
(c) cost of required equipment,
(d) presence of other agencies offering substitute/similar programs,
(e) ease of participation,
(f) degree of promotion undertaken and visibility achieved by the program, and
(g) the extent to which it is compatible with other programs offered.

An analysis of the aforementioned factors will assist the recreator in predicting the duration of these two stages.

The next stage in the program life cycle is called *maturity*. During this stage of the life cycle, the number of participants continues to increase but that increase is at a slower rate than during the take-off stage. Since there is high awareness of this program by users, it is generally a stage which is marked by the entry of competitors offering the same type of program.

The reduced rate of new participants into the program accompanied by outside competition signals the time for a different marketing strategy. The recreator must now begin to generate ideas and strategies that are designed to maintain user loyalty and interest. It may be time to make improvements or modifications within the program or to look for new target markets who may be interested in this program.

During the *saturation* stage which comes next in the program life cycle, there are virtually no new participants enrolling in the program and the recreator becomes dependent upon repeat participation. The program has reached its peak period of success in terms of participation. During the maturity stage it experienced competition from outside the organization; outside competition will continue in this stage, but now internal competition is also a factor as participants become susceptible to new programs or activities. If recreation is to be a *recreative* experience, then continued participation in the same program often becomes routine rather than recreative and participants begin to look around for other programs or activities both within and outside of the organization to fulfill this need.

The final stage in the program life cycle is *decline*. This stage is characterized by a decline in the number of participants as they begin to become involved with other seemingly more attractive programs and activities. This stage is an inevitable part of the life cycle and consists of several scenarios that may reflect this stage.

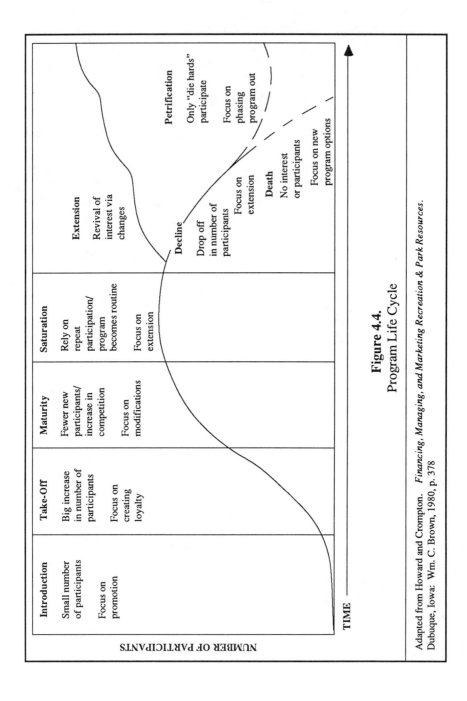

Figure 4.4.
Program Life Cycle

Adapted from Howard and Crompton.   *Financing, Managing, and Marketing Recreation & Park Resources.*
Dubuque, Iowa: Wm. C. Brown, 1980, p. 378

There are three different scenarios that may occur at this juncture: petrification, death, or extension. *Petrification* consists of a few "die hards" who continue to remain involved with this program. Recreators need to examine the resources inherent with maintaining a program given the situation. Another alternative in this stage is *death*. In this instance, the recreation organization ceases to continue offering this program or service. A third alternative which is much more desirable for the recreator to undertake, is extension. *Extension* refers to techniques and strategies that can be employed by the recreator to "extend" the life cycle of the program.

Strategies for Extending the Program Life Cycle

While it is imperative for recreation delivery systems to create new programs and services for their target markets, it is far more common for delivery systems to employ *extension* strategies which *revitalize* and *reinvent* their current offerings. In reality, there are very few truly new or innovative programs or activities. Most of these programs and activities are examples of products or programs that were modified in some way to provide them with a new life, thus recreating the life cycle.

Racquetball is essentially a modification of squash that was introduced to a user group accustomed to playing tennis. Yo-Yos™ and Hula Hoops™ are not new products. They are simply reintroduced periodically to a new group of users who were previously unfamiliar with their existence. Just as there are a plethora of names associated with aerobic classes, there is virtually no such thing as a completely new product or program.

The strategies that are being employed here are market extension strategies (see Figures 4.5 and 4.6). The strategy options which recreators have available to them for recreating and revitalizing programs are as follows: *market penetration, market development, reformulation, market extension, replacement, diversification,* or *demarketing* (Crompton, 1983, pp. 62-63).

These strategies are particularly appropriate for parks and recreation because they involve essentially two elements: programs and people. All of the aforementioned strategies include building a marketing strategy around present target markets or new target markets and combining one of those strategies with current or modified programs.

Market penetration consists of a strategy that includes devising methods to encourage the present target market to participate more frequently in current programs. The recreator devises methods to provide an incentive

Markets	Programs and Services			
	New Programs or Services	Modification of Existing Programs or Services	Existing Programs or Services	Retrenchment/ Termination of Existing Programs or Services
Existing Participants/ Members/ Clients	REPLACEMENT AND EXTENSION STRATEGIES (replace with improved version or increase range of programs)	REFORMULATION STRATEGIES (modify to improve program for current participants)	MARKET PENETRATION STRATEGIES (generate greater participant support and loyalty)	DEMARKETING STRATEGIES (change elements of marketing mix to discourage user participation OR discontinue the program)
New Participants/ Members/ Clients	DIVERSIFICATION STRATEGIES (new programs to new target markets)	MARKET EXTENSION STRATEGIES (modify program to attract new users)	MARKET DEVELOPMENT STRATEGIES (find new target markets for existing programs)	
Stage in Program Life Cycle	DECLINE/ INTRODUCTION	MATURITY/ SATURATION	SATURATION/ DECLINE	PETRIFICATION

Figure 4.5.
Marketing Strategies

Adapted from Crompton, John L. "Formulating New Directions with Strategic Marketing Planning," *Parks and Recreation,* July 1983, p. 62-63.

for current program attendees to enroll in more sessions or to utilize the facilities more frequently. For instance, one could offer a sales promotion allowing people enrolled in dance lessons an additional discount for signing up for more than one class. This strategy attempts to generate greater participation and thus higher revenues through increased participation. The market penetration strategy is appropriate at the onset of the saturation stage.

Market development consists of taking an existing program which is most likely in saturation or the early decline stage and promoting that program to a new target market. For instance, initially, aerobics classes were almost exclusively composed of female participants, but market development strategies involved offering this same program for men, children, or senior citizens.

Another set of strategies, *reformulation and extension,* involve the modification of existing programs and services. With the reformulation strategy you modify or improve the program for current participants and with the extension strategy you make similar changes to attract new users. The purpose of both of these strategies is to breathe renewed life into programs which are in maturity or saturation. You could modify, improve, or renew an existing program for current participants by making changes in leadership, content, or types of benefits. One might attract new users by making small modifications such as changing the time, location, or price. For instance, changing an ongoing cooking class from Wednesday mornings to Sunday afternoons may attract an entirely new target market. Such a change would be an example of use of the extension strategy.

The extension strategy is closely related to the replacement strategy. The *replacement* strategy involves replacing existing programs with an improved or different version of the program or increasing the range of programs to assure the continued participation of current users. Aerobics is an excellent example of the use of this type of strategy. There are now several different names being associated with aerobics as well as a wider range of programs addressing different age and ability levels.

Diversification is yet another strategy in this category which involves the introduction of new programs. However, this time the focus is upon changes and expansion in the programs or services to attract new user groups. Creating a noncompetitive or recreation league may begin to attract people who were not previously interested or involved in your highly competitive adult athletic leagues. This would be a fairly simple application of this strategy.

In some cases, diversification can mean making substantial changes in your organization. When Disney World developed Epcot Center a few years ago, it created an entirely new product to attract other target market groups such as families without young children and older adults.

Either of these strategies, replacement or diversification, would be used by the recreator when existing programs and services are in the decline stage. These are strategies that are employed to extend the life cycle of existing programs and add renewed life to these options so they can begin the life cycle process over again, entering introduction and take-off.

Demarketing is the final strategy to be considered. This strategy involves making changes in the program to discourage continued participation by those "die hard" users. Appropriate for a program in the petrification stage, the ultimate outcome is the demise of these programs to make better use of the organization's resources to serve larger numbers of participants.

Program: Aerobics Classes
Organization: YMCA
Stage in Cycle: (re)introduction
Goal: to offset decreasing participation and maintain user base
Strategy: replacement–modify existing programs and increase range of activity options by adding watercise and low impact aerobics

Program: Adult Volleyball
Organization: Community Recreation Department
Stage in Cycle: Saturation
Goal: to modify program to attract new user groups
Strategy: extension–change name of program to "coed" and offer on Friday night or Sunday afternoon to attract singles

Program: Evening Participation in Park Activities
Organization: Amusement Park
Stage in Cycle: Decline
Goal: to develop new programs and activities to attract new user groups
Strategy: diversification–offer concert series twice a month to bring adults to your facility

---

Figure 4.6.
Implementation Examples of Marketing Strategies

The concept of program life cycle has many implications for recreation managers, marketers, and programmers. An understanding and utilization of the concept enables the recreation delivery system to pre-plan programs through the tracking of current programs and services. It also supports a proactive approach for adding, modifying, and eliminating programs.

This process can be integrated into the ongoing operation of a recreation delivery system quite efficiently by the use of a tracking and strategy system similar to the one shown in Figure 4.7.

Results obtained from these data can assist the recreator by pre-planning action to be taken on existing programs and services to facilitate a proactive marketing management approach.

Name of Program	Participation Rates *				Stage in Cycle	Specific Strategies to be Employed
	1	2	3	4		

* Refers to the number of times particular program has been offered; maybe once a year or every ten weeks

Figure 4.7.
Program Life Cycle Worksheet

Incorporating Marketing Mix Variables: The Program/Product/ Service

These concepts related to program, product or service, the first "P" of marketing, need to be integrated into the ongoing planning process of the recreation delivery system. There are essentially three phases of such an integrated process:

(a) propose program/product/service,
(b) consider target marketing and program factors, and
(c) make program/service decisions.

The completion of these three steps results in the creation of a program/ service description.

How does one get started? One begins in the same way one would normally progress when dealing with an idea for a new program. Generally, the recreator either has the beginnings of an idea for a new program or the change in an existing one, or perceives the need to create a product or service for a specific target market. Sometimes this phase of the process appears to happen simultaneously. In any event, both the idea for a program and the suggestion of a target market should be addressed in the proposal of a new program or service.

Once one has the idea for a new program, product or service, one must then incorporate pertinent factors related to target marketing and elements of the program/service variables. There is a strong connection between these two categories, and it is imperative to consider them in conjunction with one another.

There are a number of factors to be considered related to target marketing. Who is the proposed target market? Which of the key market descriptors (geographic, demographic, behavioral, etc.) are most important in this instance? What are the dimensions of the target market? Will the program be designed for all members of the target market or will the program be constructed within certain parameters? What target marketing strategy will be employed with this program? Will it be undifferentiated, differentiated, or concentrated? These are just a few of the questions the recreator should address before proceeding with this phase of the process.

It is also important to consider certain program factors or concepts such as type and extent of competition, stage in the program life cycle, relationship to current product mix, and impact of positioning. The marketer will want to ask: Who are my competitors for this type of program and/or with this specific target market? What is the stage of the life cycle of this proposed program? Will this stage impact upon marketing strategies and elements of the product mix? How does the proposed program fit with existing product lines? Will this relationship help or hinder the introduction and acceptance of this program? What about our organization's positioning profile in relationship to this type of program and this target market?

The answers to these and other questions pertinent to the recreation delivery system may cause the recreator to modify or redirect the proposed program at this juncture. It may provide the recreator with a new perspective or framework upon which to make additional program decisions.

Having focused upon some key target marketing questions and the potential impact of some pertinent program concepts, the recreator is now able to make certain decisions regarding the first marketing mix variable, program. These decisions include determination of program area, program form, and name, as well as a more complete description of the core, tangible, and augmented levels of the actual program.

This phase of the process which involves product/program decisions, is referred to as *manipulation of marketing mix variables*. Choices made in this phase of the process will significantly impact upon the success of the program and its acceptance by the target market. What will the program be called? Will the same name be used for two versions of the program offered to two different target markets? Does the name of the program reflect both the primary and secondary benefits desired by each targeted group? Is the area of the program appropriately defined? What's the difference between basketball and volleyball as a physical activity choice to the target market? What about the form that has been selected for the program area? There are vast differences between forms of recreation programs. Classes speak of acquiring a new skill. Workshops refer to the same thing, but usually in an abbreviated time period. Consider the differences between tournaments and leagues, clubs and drop-ins. The selection and manipulation of the program form can often be one of the most critical decisions the recreator can make.

It is recommended that such program decisions be made by identifying both the primary and secondary benefits being sought by the target market groups. The impact of the two levels of benefit may influence choices the recreator makes regarding elements of the program/service mix.

Whether the program is an entirely new one for the organization or for the target market or whether the program is designed for more than one target market or is considered active, physical, or passive, the process of incorporating these elements into the market mix manipulation would be the same.

An overview of activities associated with the incorporation of these elements with manipulation of the marketing mix are presented in Figure 4.8.

Case Study: Newtown Wants a New Summer Look

At the first department meeting of the new year, the recreation staff of the Newtown Parks and Recreation Department decided that their joint New Year's resolution would be the creation of a new look for their upcoming summer season. The department had traditionally offered playground programs at various locations throughout the community for children of all ages. Dropping attendance over the past few summers coupled with some changes in the community served as additional impetus for the staff to undertake the creation and development of a new summer program.

They decided to propose a package of structured, recreational programs for the youngsters of their community. Upon reviewing key target market factors, it was decided that three different target markets existed: children ages 3 to 5; children ages 6 to 10; and youngsters 11 to 14. They also

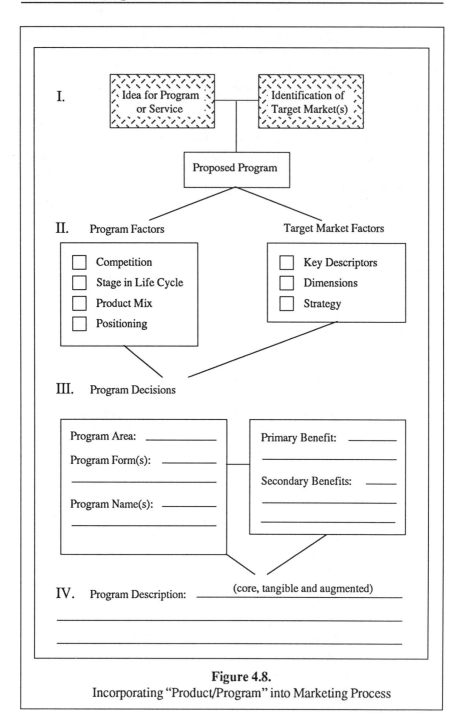

Figure 4.8.
Incorporating "Product/Program" into Marketing Process

believed that geographic location in terms of neighborhood was an important consideration. The staff also considered the impact of parents as an equally critical target market group for the two younger age groups. They decided that they would utilize a differentiated strategy for the structured program for the two younger age groups and would implement a concentrated approach for the youngsters age 11 to 14 on the basis of more specialized areas of interest.

When discussing the various aspects of the program factors, it was determined that the traditional summer playgrounds were in a decline stage of program life cycle and that steps needed to be taken to provide for the extension of this program. This reinforced their decision to go with a more structured summer program.

It was determined that the existence of successful camp programs run by the local Y and two other private organizations constituted the competition for the new program. The existence of structured, recreational programs for children in the community suggested that such programs would be in the maturity stage of the program life cycle.

A review of the product mix line and the positioning of the organization also boded well for the proposed change. The proposed summer programs were compatible with existing product lines and the organization's position was currently well-established as summer play for children. However, the position did not address structured, closely supervised situations as proposed in the new summer programs.

Prior to making decisions regarding elements of the product/program mix, the group decided to review and refine the primary and secondary benefits desired by the target markets. Having correctly identified parents as the "real" target market for these programs, especially the ones for the two younger age groups, they subsegmented the parents into two different groups–those looking for play and recreation for their children and those whose primary consideration was satisfactory supervision and care of their children during working hours.

Therefore, the department decided to create two programs for preschoolers: a structured morning program called Playscape and a structured full-day program called PlayDay. The levels of each of these programs would differ. Playscape would focus upon and emphasize quality interaction and socialization among children, while PlayDay would stress staff competency and quality in relationship to full-day care of children.

When working on the development of the summer program for teens and preteens, the staff had to shift their focus from parents as the target markets to the teens themselves. In this instance, the name of the program was especially critical. This age groups wants no part of playing or going to camp because they don't want to be perceived as children. The recreation staff decided upon a program entitled Summer Thing and from within the Summer Thing menu, teens could select from attending two-week programs in the following specialization areas: the arts, sports, nature, computers, and out-trips.

The recreation staff then went to work on various aspects of this new summer program. Plans and strategies went through several revisions as they developed the programs. For instance, the Summer Thing programs had little competition related to the arts and out-trips but had substantial competition in the areas of sports and nature. They determined that the life cycle for their programs for the younger children was different than that for the teens, since their current market position reflected summer programs for children, not teens.

It took time. It took effort. It took brainstorming. However, the Newtown Recreation Department staff had made an initial start at revamping their summer recreational offerings. Their next step would be to address the additional marketing mix variables.

The product/program/service variable is only one marketing mix variable that needs to be addressed. However, it represents the most natural starting point for the creation or modification of existing programs and services. The decisions that are made in conjunction with this first "P" represent only a portion of the elements of the marketing mix variables. When hearing of a particular recreation program or service of interest, the next concern of users is: "Where and when will this program be offered?" Since this is the case, it is only natural that recreators next move to manipulating the second market mix variable, place.

The Second Marketing Mix Variable: Place (Scheduling)

The second "P" of the marketing mix variables is termed *place*. A more definitive term for this particular "P" would be *scheduling*. Since the marketing concept was originally developed around the creation of a product, the place variable referred to the place of manufacture and channels for distribution of the product, such as wholesalers and retailers.

However, park, recreation, and leisure delivery systems rarely create products that are simply purchased and taken home. They are more likely to be involved in providing programs and services. These programs and services differ substantially from the purchase of a product, since participants in recreation programs *consume* rather than just purchase. Often the manufacture of the service takes place simultaneously with this consumption, in contrast to the case of an assembly line in a distant factory.

Due to these differences between product marketing and service marketing, the place variable needs to be addressed quite differently in recreation and leisure settings. In the recreation setting, the place variable refers to a variety of factors such as physical *location,* the *area* or *facility* itself, as well as a variety of related marketing factors. Many of these place considerations are closely tied to the first marketing mix variable, program/ service, and discussion of one should not take place without the inclusion of the second (see Figure 4.9).

Location

Where will the program or service actually be offered? This is a critical marketing mix decision that will influence response and acceptance of the proposed program. Crompton and Lamb (1986, p. 197) cite location, accessibility of location, and visibility of location as key factors related to this variable.

One important element of the designation of a location for the program or service is *accessibility.* This can refer to both *real* and *perceived* accessibility. Accessibility can refer to ease of access as it relates to travel time or actual distance. Fitness clubs often target working adults as their clients

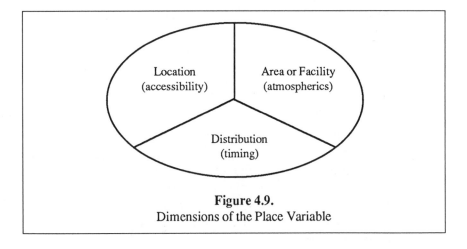

Figure 4.9.
Dimensions of the Place Variable

and prefer a location in close proximity to heavily trafficked, commuter routes. YMCAs who service both adults and children might prefer to be close to well-traveled traffic patterns but not located on a busy thoroughfare due to the potential danger for children coming and going from their facility. Parks designed for heavy use in active recreational pursuits would be appropriately located in a highly populated area, while a park designed for preservation and highly specialized, or passive usage might benefit from a more remote location.

Access can include a variety of components, including access by special population groups. With the aging of the population accompanied by recent trends of greater community integration of disability group members, this is an important consideration.

Parking is another feature relative to accessibility. This is a critical consideration when planning a special event that will attract large numbers of people, but it also impacts upon programs of lesser magnitude. The advent of shopping malls with their acres of plentiful, free parking has changed the way Americans perceive parking. The plethora of cars circling a fitness club waiting for a parking spot close to the facility so they don't have to walk suggests such a change in this perception.

Access to a location can also include users' perceptions. If parents perceive that it is unsafe for their children to walk on their own to participate in an after-school activity offered by an organization, they may not enroll them in that program. A community center with teens hanging around the building may serve as a deterrent to participation by older adults. Beginner tennis lessons offered at a racquet club might be perceived as being too threatening or embarrassing a location for the total novice. People may make heavy use of a park in the daytime yet feel unable or unwilling to use it in the evenings. Perception of the location may be an important factor related to the development of marketing mix variables.

Area/Facility

The second component of the place variable is the actual *area* or *facility* where the program or service is being offered. Kotler (1982) mentions that the *atmospherics* of an area or facility will become increasingly more important in the future. Atmospherics is defined as "the conscious design-ing of space to create or reinforce specific effects on buyers" (pp. 325-326). The suitability and perception of an area or facility are currently an important consideration.

How is an aerobics class at a local community center different from one held at the commercial fitness club down the street? One of the key differences is the atmospherics to which Kotler refers. Such atmospherics are closely aligned with the tangible and augmented levels of a program or service. Such physical factors as the presence or lack of air conditioning, carpeting, spacious room(s) with mirrors, adequate privacy, and availability of lockers and showers may be the difference. The commercial fitness club may *look and feel* more like an appropriate and attractive place to exercise.

Campsites are another example of the close relationship between the two marketing mix variables, program and place. Use of a campsite for one night or one week is a service that is heavily impacted upon by place variables. The core product might be a campsite but the tangible and augmented levels of the product would relate to location and the actual features of the facility. Location may be a key factor related to the selection of a particular campground. The one-night camper would be looking for a campsite within close driving distance from home. Others might select a campsite because it is located in close proximity to a tourist attraction they intend to visit. The physical attributes of the campgrounds would then come into play. Different target markets would be looking for different physical features ranging from a private, primitive campsite for tenting to a fully developed site that featured hot showers and a swimming pool.

When constructing a program or service, the recreator needs to ask some key questions regarding location. Is the proposed location convenient and easily accessible for my target market? Will the target market perceive the location as being safe, attractive, and appropriate for them? Does the area or facility have a look that makes the proposed program look suitable for it? How are the atmospherics?

Distribution

A third component of this place variable is *distribution,* which includes such things as number of locations and timing of offerings. When applied to leisure delivery systems, distribution impacts upon a number of marketing mix decisions. Such things as single versus multiple locations for a program or service, frequency and timing of the offerings, and subsequent differentiation between the same or similar programs on the basis of the aforementioned factors need to be addressed.

Organizations such as many YMCAs or a resort, which are dependent upon one area or facility, are faced with what Crompton and Lamb refer to as distributional uncontrollability (1986, pp. 177-178). Organizations with greater options related to either ownership or access to multiple areas and facilities have marketing mix decisions to make in this area.

However, most all leisure delivery systems have numerous decisions to make because distribution refers to both number of locations and frequency with which a particular program or service is offered. The intensity of distribution or the number of times and locations one offers a program or service can range from exclusive to intensive (Crompton and Lamb, 1986, pp. 193-194). An *exclusive* distribution would consist of offering a program at *one* location only, while *selective* distribution would include *multiple* times or locations for a program or service, and an *intensive* distribution would involve scheduling *many* different times and locations.

The Newtown Recreation Department mentioned earlier most likely offered numerous locations for its traditional playground, an intensive distribution approach. A fitness center with only one location would be an example of an exclusive distribution approach, while a chain of such facilities with three or four clubs within a geographic area would be considered a selective distribution approach.

The intensity of one's distribution approach may be based upon a number of factors including: the mission of the organization, availability of resources, popularity or need for the program/service, and differentiation of target market groups. A private swim club has no problem with an exclusive distribution approach, while a public parks and recreation department may struggle over whether or not it must or can afford to offer every program in every neighborhood. If a program or activity is particularly popular as in the take-off stage of the life cycle, then an intensive plan might be appropriate. Applying that approach to a program in the late saturation stage of the life cycle would likely result in the cancellation of a number of those programs offered at multiple times and locations.

The Timing Factor

An additional component of the distribution factor is that of timing. *Timing* can refer to a multitude of variables including: *time* of day, *day* of the week, *season* of the year, *length* of time, and *frequency* of offerings. What time do you offer the program? Do you offer it once a week or three times a week?

Do you only offer this program in the winter? Should you offer the service for 10 weeks or fifteen? Do you offer the same program in different time slots?

The list of questions a recreator needs to address around this issue are innumerable and quite important. People participate in recreation activities during their leisure time, so it is *critical* to the success of a program that the recreator *identify* the *correct time* of day, week, month, or year as well as the amount of time that people are either willing or able to expend upon this activity.

Some of these "time" questions are addressed for us. An organization can't offer cross-country skiing in the continental United States in August, and doesn't offer programs for children during the day when they are in school. However, many of these timing issues are not so clear and require extensive thought and study on the part of the recreator.

While we've practiced variations of timing patterns based upon when our target markets have been working or in school, some timing factors are relatively new for our consideration. People now play soccer and tennis on a year-round basis rather than just in its appropriate "season." Ski areas and beach resorts now utilize a year-round approach to attracting people to their establishments.

How we utilize *time* as an element of the marketing mix is becoming increasingly more important as it relates to length of time and frequency. Consider the revitalized summer program being developed by the Newtown Recreation Department. A three-day-a-week program for preschoolers would appeal to mothers who do not work outside of the home but would prove too complicated for most working parents. A camp program scheduled to run from 10 a.m. to 4 p.m. might not be as attractive to working parents, who perhaps need a program that is more compatible with their working schedule.

Adults whose work schedules are subject to change might be attracted to a fitness center where aerobic classes were offered on the hour as opposed to three times a day. Some people might be willing to participate in a softball tournament scheduled for a long weekend but not be able to make the commitment to a softball league that stretches over a 20-week season.

There are critical questions related to this marketing mix variable. How much time do people have available for recreation and leisure? When is that time? How can manipulation of this marketing mix variable by the organization contribute to or detract from participation by one's target market(s)? How can changes in this factor serve as a better delineation of one target market over another?

The element of time is critical and closely related to the initial marketing mix variable, program/service. Time variable decisions made by an organization can serve as either an incentive or a deterrent to participation by target markets. These decisions should be made after careful examination of the needs and lifestyle patterns of the target markets. Timing decisions should reflect the patterns and preferences of these individuals while creating rather than curtailing participation options for them.

Summary

The first two "Ps" of the market mix, product/program and place, are key components of the overall marketing strategy for any park, recreation, or leisure delivery system. An identification of the three dimensions of the product/program–core, tangible, and augmented–enables recreators to better manipulate this variable to attract specific target markets.

Further analysis of product/program/service offerings by mix, line, and item provides additional insights into target market segmentation. The inclusion of the program life cycle concept enables the recreator to develop proactive strategies for the marketing management of its delivery system.

The second "P," place, is closely aligned with the product/program variable. The place variable consists of a variety of factors including physical location, the area or facility, and the distribution and timing factors related to the development of a product or program.

Since these two factors are so closely linked to one another as it relates to target marketing, it is suggested that these two "Ps" of the marketing mix be examined in conjunction with one another.

Suggested Activities

1. Select two similar program/services offered by different delivery systems. Compare and contrast each program on the basis of the three levels of the product/program.

2. Select one leisure delivery system and analyze its offerings on the basis of program mix, line, and item.

3. For this previously selected organization, select a product/program line and graphically depict the length, width, and depth of such a line.

4. Identify program attendance or participation patterns for a recreation delivery system over the past two years or seasons. On the basis of this information, identify stage(s) in the life cycle and suggest appropriate marketing strategies.

5. Assume you've been asked to develop a new program for two different target markets. Brainstorm how the program area, form, and name could be manipulated to attract the two different groups.

6. Select three different leisure delivery systems in your area and identify similarities and differences among them on the basis of place factors. Be sure to include distribution as well.

References

Crompton, J. L. *Parks and Recreation.* (July 1983) "Formulating New Directions with Strategic Marketing Planning" pp. 62-63.

Crompton, J. L. and Lamb, C. W., Jr. (1986). *Marketing Government and Social Services.* New York, NY: John Wiley & Sons.

Howard, D. R. and Crompton, J. L. (1980). *Financing, Managing and Marketing Recreation and Park Resources.* (p. 378) Dubuque, IA: Wm. C. Brown.

Kotler, P. (1980). *Marketing Management: Analysis, Planning, and Control (4th ed.)* (p. 351) Englewood Cliffs, NJ: Prentice-Hall.

Kotler, P. (1982). *Marketing for Nonprofit Organizations (2nd ed.)* Englewood Cliffs, NJ: Prentice-Hall.

Chapter Five

Pricing–The Third P of the Marketing Mix Variables

Common Concerns for Parks, Recreation, and Leisure Delivery Systems

- A large county park system is concerned because low-cost camp-sites are under-utilized by residents.

- An urban YMCA struggles with pricing policies, attempting to provide access for economically disadvantaged youth while generating revenue through adult fitness programs.

- An MWR operation is concerned with elasticity of demand consequences related to pricing increases mandated for club operations.

- A health club considers offering a "2 for 1" promotion to improve cash flow during the non-peak months of July and August.

Pricing

The third marketing mix variable is *price*. There was a time when this element of the marketing mix was usually addressed towards the end of the process and often without consulting those members of the organization who had prepared the product or program. It was almost as if price existed outside the realm of the marketing mix variables.

This is not currently the situation. The element of price is very much a part of the marketing mix and has a strong relationship to various decisions made. This marketing mix variable impacts upon levels of the program or service offered as well as place considerations such as location, timing, and frequency.

Upon initial perusal, it would appear as if this marketing mix variable is solely concerned with money and the generation of revenue, but in reality it is much more complex than just dollars and cents. All recreation delivery systems, whether they be public, nonprofit, private, or commercial, must make marketing mix decisions regarding price. Some of the factors that need to be examined to gain a more complete understanding this marketing mix variable include: the nature of pricing, pricing objectives, pricing strategies, and the psychological aspects of pricing.

The Dimensions of Price

Every product, program, or service has its price (see Figure 5.1). That price may vary from free to thousands of dollars and may be referred to by a variety of terms including membership dues, tuition, assessments, fares, or admission fees, to cite just a few. However, price can go far beyond the dollars and cents that people exchange in order to participate.

Price consists of two separate levels–*monetary* and *nonmonetary* (Crompton and Lamb, 1986, p. 316). The most obvious level of pricing related to a recreation program or service is the monetary level. This level refers to the *actual dollar amount* the consumer must exchange in order to participate in this program or take part in this service. There are two different types of prices involved in this monetary level–direct and indirect.

The *direct* price is the amount of money the leisure delivery system is charging the user for the program or service. How much will it cost to enroll in gymnastics lessons? What is the annual membership fee of the health club?

However, this dollar figure does not represent the complete price. It is necessary to take into consideration the *indirect price* as well. The indirect price consists of those additional expenditures related to the participation or consumption of the program or service. The cost of transportation, required

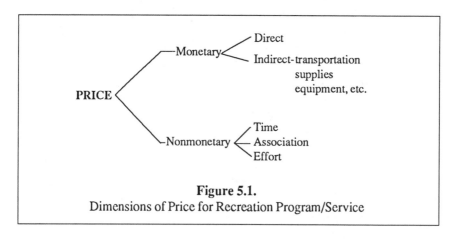

Figure 5.1.
Dimensions of Price for Recreation Program/Service

supplies or equipment, or clothing are examples of indirect costs associated with such participation. Depending upon the type of activity or the situation, the indirect price of a program or service can range from minimal to substantial.

Nonmonetary Price

At marketing's inception, marketers were only concerned with the actual cost or price of the product being developed and sold. As marketing evolved, pricing took on added dimensions and with the advent of service marketing, the role and impact of the nonmonetary price began to receive near equal attention with that of the monetary level.

Purchase of a product consists of a unilateral exchange. The purchaser is exchanging a specific dollar amount for a product which the purchaser then takes home. Participation in a recreational activity or program does not consist of just one level. Participation is related to a variety of exchange dimensions that go far beyond the initial exchange of a dollar amount.

There are three additional segments related to the pricing of a program or service: time, association, and effort. Recreation participation requires use of discretionary time and money. While the discretionary money relates to the monetary price, there are also significant factors directed towards the discretionary time portion of the equation that relate to nonparticipation time, association, and effort.

Crompton and Lamb (1986) refer to the opportunity cost of time and specify three related categories: travel time, waiting time, and consumption time (p. 316). Golf is a recreational activity that would rank high on the scale for time. Due to the land requirements for golf courses, they are usually located outside of heavily trafficked areas, which necessitates the expenditure of travel time. Once at the golf course, with frequently overcrowded conditions, the golfer often has to wait for a tee time, which is an additional time expense. Golf is often perceived as an expensive sport due to the cost of equipment and membership or greens fees, but in actuality, when examined in relationship to its nonmonetary costs, the expense of golf climbs even further.

An additional category included in the nonmonetary cost of a recreation program refers to effort. How much effort on the part of the participant is involved in the participation in the activity? Does the activity require a great deal of time and effort to acquire the specific skill involved? Is it relatively easy to access needed information to participate in this program? Are there hassles involved in participating in this activity that may mitigate the value received from actual participation? Participation in any program or activity requires effort on the part of the user. Recreation delivery systems need to consider these effort factors when developing programs and services for particular target market groups and to also identify strategies that can be adopted by the organization to reduce this cost of participation to its user groups.

The association costs implies the social nature of recreation behavior that occurs in a public setting. This factor can refer to the price paid for being associated either with a specific program or with people enrolled in a program. It may be too embarrassing for an adult to take swimming lessons in a public pool. It may be threatening or unpleasant for individuals to participate in a program with people who they don't know, or who may make them feel uncomfortable in some way.

Begin to consider the potential impact that social and nonmonetary costs may have upon an organization's programs and activities. Is it too much effort for people to leave their homes on winter evenings after dinner? Is it too time consuming for parents to bring children to a gymnastics class that meets three times a week? Is it too harried for an individual to leave work exactly on time and fight the traffic to participate in a scheduled aerobics class? Social and nonmonetary costs are real and can raise or lower the price of exchange for the recreation user.

Pricing Objectives

It would be an oversimplification if the establishment of a price were perceived to be solely for the generation of revenue. The objectives of pricing can relate to the mission or current needs of the organization. What are the political implications associated with the mission of the organization as well as philosophy and policies related to pricing? What are the current objectives of the organization in terms of resource allocation and usage patterns?

Public, nonprofit, private, and commercial delivery systems all have different missions, and these missions often translate into pricing objectives. Public organizations may offer programs at no charge or at a nominal charge to comply with their mission of providing opportunities for recreational activities to all members of the community. Political considerations may require a sliding scale for different population groups as well as rates for residents and nonresidents. The commercial recreation delivery system will have as its pricing objective the generation of revenue in excess of cost to provide for a percentage of profit. However, this same commercial establishment may sponsor a special event for disabled users at no charge as a public relations gesture.

Mission is not the only factor that affects the pricing objectives of an organization. The current conditions, both external to the organization and within the organization, are factors. Economic factors such as the local unemployment rate or rate of inflation may play a role in pricing objectives. Participation rates and patterns along with cash flow and stage in the program life cycle all combine to play a part in influencing pricing objectives within an organization.

Before an organization can conceive of prices for its product, programs, or services, it needs to determine what objectives it wants to achieve. Kotler (1982) outlines four different pricing objectives: surplus maximization, cost recovery, usage maximization, and market disincentivization (pp. 305-309).

These four different objectives achieve different ends for the organization and influence price as well. *Surplus maximization* refers to a situation where the organization establishes its prices for the purpose of generating a surplus of revenue. While one would normally associate this pricing objective with commercial recreation organizations, it is often used selectively in the public and nonprofit sectors to generate surplus revenues to offset the costs of providing recreation opportunities for groups of participants who may not be able to afford such participation.

Cost recovery as a pricing objective establishes a certain ratio that can range from a modest percentage to full recovery of the actual cost of providing the program or service. A YMCA may wish to recover only the cost of swimming aids used in its youth swimming lessons while electing to recover 100 percent of the cost for a more specialized program for adults such as scuba diving.

A third pricing objective is *usage maximization.* When utilizing this approach to pricing objectives, the recreation delivery system desires to establish the price in such a manner that it encourages participation by a large number of people. Generally, in this situation a low price is used. Public and nonprofit organizations may select this approach to encourage sizeable numbers of people to participate in a worthwhile program such as youth fitness. Commercial recreation organizations can utilize this approach on the premise that lowering the price attracts a larger user group and that profit can be generated by increased usage.

The final pricing objective is referred to as *market disincentivization*. The purpose underlying this objective is to discourage people from participating in a particular program or service. There maybe a variety of reasons why an organization would choose this approach. If demand for the program exceeds facility or personnel capacity, the agency could increase the price to cut down on participation. If the program was in the petrification stage, the agency might increase the price in an attempt to encourage those last few "die hard" participants to give it up.

The initial step in determining the price of a recreation program or service should include the establishment of a pricing objective. All recreation delivery systems need to establish pricing objectives regardless of their mission, and the pricing objectives should be reviewed regularly in light of current situational analysis.

It is important to note that agencies can have more than one pricing objective. The same objective does not need to dictate to all programs and for all people. A resort may utilize usage maximization during its off-season periods. Public departments may offer their youth programs with usage maximization as their objective based upon their perception of the mission of their organization, while utilizing a cost recovery approach for adults.

Pricing Strategies

How does a recreation delivery system go about establishing a price for its programs and services? Certainly, the initial step would be deciding upon its pricing objectives for the particular program as mentioned previously, but pricing strategies are generally taken into consideration as well. There are essentially three different approaches that can be used as pricing strategies: *cost-oriented, demand-oriented,* and *competition-oriented.* All of these pricing strategies are used in conjunction with the pricing objectives of the delivery system. The selection of the specific strategy is based upon the situational and philosophical considerations of the recreation organization.

Oftentimes the price of a program or service is determined on the basis of what "everyone else" is charging. This is referred to as a *competition-oriented* strategy. In this instance, the recreation delivery system identifies other recreation organizations offering the same or very similar programs or services, whom it determines to be potential competitors. The recreator compiles a list of fees that are currently being charged for this program or service and determines their price on the basis of what the competitors are charging.

If a recreation delivery systems decides to utilize this pricing strategy, it has three different options from which to select. The organization can establish the price for this program as being the same, higher, or lower in relationship to its competitors. When contemplating a pricing decision using this strategy, it is necessary for the marketer to reexamine the three levels of the product or program. In this instance, the core program and primary benefit would be the same so it is the differences in the tangible or augmented levels of the program that will determine the organization's pricing strategy. Recreation services offered in the private or commercial recreation sectors are often able to charge a higher price than many public or nonprofit delivery systems based upon the additional services and benefits they are able to offer, as well as intangibles such as styling and prestige that make the program or service worth more to the customer.

Another pricing strategy is the *demand-oriented* approach. When using this approach, the recreator asks what members of the target market would be willing to pay for a specific program or service. This particular pricing strategy is quite user-oriented and attempts to price a program/service on the basis of the users' perception of value as well as their ability to pay this price.

This pricing strategy often results in the creation of different prices for different groups of people for the same or similar programs or services. Sometimes prices for programs vary based upon the target markets. Often price differentials are extended to include senior citizen discounts or youth rates. Another reason for use of price differentials relates to time. In this instance, time can refer to time of day, day of the week, or even the season of the year. Tennis and racquetball clubs establish different rates for play at peak and off-peak time periods, with the discounted price meant to encourage people to play during the off-peak days or times. Resorts generally reduce prices during the off-season period to attract guests to their facilities.

Place is still another variable that can reflect pricing differentials. This is often used in entertainment and sports arenas, where proximity to the stage or playing field is reflected in the price of the admission fee. Place is also used in resorts where rooms on the ocean, with an ocean view, and with no water view are priced accordingly. Sometimes, public park and recreation departments may have a different fee structure for people desiring a park pass for one park as opposed to all parks within their jurisdiction.

Naturally, the actual product and the "bundles of benefits" within the product could result in pricing differentials. A program or service consisting of just the basics as opposed to one where there are a number of features can have an added impact upon the price.

The last pricing strategy is *cost-oriented*. Using this approach, the price of a program or service is established in relationship to the actual cost of providing the program or service. Use of this strategy does not imply that the price of the program or service is the cost of providing it, but that the cost is taken into consideration when establishing the price.

Recreation organizations may choose to determine cost in a variety of manners. Four commonly utilized approaches are average cost, variable cost, partial overhead, and cost-plus pricing. Average cost pricing includes all fixed and variable costs of a program divided by the total number of users, while variable cost pricing includes only the variable costs and no fixed costs. Partial overhead pricing covers all variable costs and some fixed costs (National Park Service). Variable costs are related to the actual number of participants in a program, while fixed costs do not vary based upon participation.

A public park and recreation department may have a pricing policy which dictates that the price of specialized programs will be based upon the variable costs of that program. A YMCA may determine its program prices to reflect partial overhead pricing and include all variable costs and some fixed costs in the price. A private swim club would most likely use the average cost pricing approach, covering both fixed and variable costs in its annual membership fee, while a commercial establishment would utilize this same approach plus add a suitable percentage for profit to the fee or price of services.

Many recreation delivery systems actually utilize a portion of all three strategies in arriving upon the prices of their programs and services. The cost-oriented strategy is generally a starting point for the organization (see Figure 5.2). After looking at the actual cost of providing such a program, recreators often review the prices for similar programs being offered by other organizations, thus incorporating a competition-oriented strategy. The program price may be modified after the examination of the competition's prices and the demand-orientation may come into play as the recreation organization develops additional strata of prices for certain groups of people or during certain periods of time.

Impact of Elasticity of Demand

A concept critical to the successful implementation of this element of the marketing mix is elasticity of demand. *Elasticity of demand* refers to the degree of sensitivity or responsiveness of users of a program or service to changes in the price of the program (Howard and Crompton, 1980, p. 437).

Activity: Family swim membership
Organization: Private swim club
Pricing Approach: Average cost

$$\frac{\text{Total fixed cost}}{\text{No. of families}} \quad \frac{\$150,000}{300} \qquad \text{Average cost is } \$500$$

Activity: Senior citizens crafts classes
Organization: Community recreation center
Pricing Approach: Variable cost

$$\frac{\text{Total variable cost}}{\text{No. of participants}} \quad \frac{\$75}{15} \qquad \text{Variable cost is } \$5$$

Activity: Latchkey program
Organization: YMCA
Pricing Approach: Partial overhead

Average fixed + Variable   - United Way subsidy
$9   + $2   - $4 = $7 Partial overhead cost

Activity: Individual membership
Organization: Commercial sports and racquet club
Pricing Approach: Cost plus

$$\frac{\text{Total costs}}{\text{No. of members}} + \text{Markup of 20\%}$$

$$\frac{\$250,000}{500} + \$100. \text{ Cost plus price is } \$600$$

Figure 5.2.
Implementation Examples of Cost-Oriented Pricing

This concept attempts to address the question: how will a change in price impact upon the total amount of revenue generated from this program or service?

The reaction to a change in price of a program or service is not easily predicted prior to the actual implementation of the change. Prices for programs or services are considered to be either *elastic* or *inelastic:*

If demand is *elastic,* a change in price causes an opposite change in total revenue; an increase in price will decrease total revenue, and a decrease in price will increase total revenue. An *inelastic* demand results in a parallel change in total revenue; an increase in price will increase total revenue, and a decrease in price will decrease total revenue (Pride and Ferrell, 1983, p. 422).

If a recreation delivery system is considering a price change, it is important to clarify several things: the exact purpose of the price change (change in revenue or change in participation rates) and the price elasticity of demand related to this program or service. A public agency may want to lower prices to enhance participation by more residents. A commercial establishment may decide to raise prices to increase revenue or to restrict participation and contribute to its perception of exclusivity.

While it is difficult to ascertain the exact nature of the price elasticity of demand until the price change has been implemented, there are a number of factors that affect this elasticity, such as: the discretionary income of the target market, the stage in the life cycle of the program or service, the presence of competition or replacements, and the nonmonetary costs of participation.

An initial assessment point would be the ability of the target market group to pay for the program or service. If the target market does not have the additional funds to pay for the price increase, then one can be most certain that the demand will be elastic. It is important to note here that there is a meaningful difference between *ability* and *willingness to pay,* the latter being more difficult to discern. The social status and prestige associated with the program or service is also a confounding variable in this situation.

Another consideration is the stage in the life cycle of the program or service for which a price modification is being proposed. The introductory stage might indicate a low price to entice participation, while the take-off stage could probably adjust to a price increase. A program or service that is in maturity generally means the presence of competitors, so the price might well be elastic at this time, this elasticity would certainly be true of the saturation stage as well.

A critical consideration related to the price elasticity of demand is the availability of program or service substitutes. If a health club is the only one in a 15-mile radius as opposed to being one of three, this impacts upon price elasticity. This factor is composed of more than just examining the competition. The recreator must ask: how unique or irreplaceable is this program or service? There is only one Grand Canyon or one Yellowstone

National Park. Due to the unique nature of these two natural areas, it can be assumed that the price demand would be inelastic. People will pay most any reasonable price to visit either of these areas. However, if tourists are journeying through an area with multiple hotels and resorts all featuring swimming pools and tennis courts, then in this instance the price would most likely be elastic.

Additional implications to be examined are the indirect as well as the nonmonetary or social costs of the program or service. What price are users really paying for participating in this program or service? If the indirect costs of clothing and equipment or the nonmonetary costs of travel time and effort are already high in the minds of the users, then the additional increase in the direct price of the program must be modified with the additional costs considered. Social costs can work towards causing both elasticity and inelasticity in the price of a recreation program or service. If learning to swim as adults is too embarrassing for individuals, then any increase in price may be enough to cause elasticity. However, if membership in a particular fitness club is perceived as being socially prestigious, this factor contributes significantly to the inelasticity of the membership fee.

The elasticity of demand is an important ingredient for successfully establishing or changing the price of a program or service. However, it is one of those elements that is often difficult to measure specifically or accurately.

Nonrevenue-Generating Properties

It is commonly assumed that the sole reason to establish and charge a price for a program or service is for the purpose of generating revenue. There are additional reasons why recreation and leisure delivery systems might decide to charge a price for the use of their facility or participation in their program. This is especially true for programs and services offered in the public and nonprofit sectors, but many of these nonrevenue-generating properties apply to private and commercial recreation delivery systems as well.

By charging a price, recreation and park delivery systems are able to maintain control over the people using the facility. Public health codes and fire codes often dictate the number of people who can occupy a swimming pool or public building, and charging a fee would assist the recreation delivery system in complying with these standards. A small fee to reserve a picnic table in an urban park can improve control by mitigating against misunderstandings as to who claimed the picnic table first.

The charging of a fee also enables the organization to more accurately account for usage rates and patterns for their facilities, programs, and services. This is especially true for large facilities or parks where recreation usage is often through more passive or indirect services, making it more difficult to estimate number of participants, types of participation, and usage patterns. The price can also be varied to modify usage patterns in an attempt to adjust attendance over peak and slow periods.

When a fee, however small, is placed upon a program or service, it often has implications for influencing the perceptions of the users. By paying a fee to enter a park or use a facility or take part in a program, the user perceives the service as having a greater value than if it was free, and the payment of this fee often strengthens the commitment of the user to the facility or program. This commitment often results in reduced levels of vandalism and increased levels of attendance.

The price of a product, program, or service can also change the expectations of the users. People have come to expect that "you get what you pay for," and charging a price for admittance to a park or enrollment in a program often raises peoples' expectations of that park or program. Likewise, the prices charged by a recreation delivery system reflect upon the image of that organization. Prices relate to an organization's position. Is the organization perceived as being very expensive and therefore, quite exclusive, or is it perceived as being moderately priced with good quality? The prices charged by an organization can serve to maintain or even improve the image of the organization.

Psychological Aspects of Pricing

The pricing of a product or service also has a psychological side to it in addition to an economic one. One of the most common aspects of psychological pricing is *odd pricing*. Odd pricing is the tendency of organizations to offer admission for $1.99 as opposed to $2 and for program enrollment in an exercise class to be established at $24.99 so it is perceived as being under $25 per person.

Customary pricing is another issue related to the psychology of pricing. For instance, people may feel it is customary to pay a relatively higher amount for the greens fee on an outstanding private golf course that is open to the public, but would strongly object to paying more than a modest fee to use an outstanding public golf course. It is only natural to expect prices that are in line with the missions of various delivery systems and often have difficulty accepting fees that are not consistent with those missions.

Simply charging a price for a program changes the way users perceive themselves, the organization, and the program or service.   American consumers tend to be quite materialistic and believe strongly that "you get what you pay for." Often the economically disadvantaged members of our society prefer to pay a fee of some kind for recreational services provided by the public and nonprofit sectors because it affects how they view themselves and the provision of the service.

Psychologically, many people believe that the more costly the program or service, the better its quality. There are a number of examples of how a program offered at a modest price had to be cancelled due to lack of interest while the same exact program offered by another agency at five times the price was oversubscribed. A higher price also raises the users' expectations for quality. If one charges a higher price or even raises an existing price, participants will come expecting to see improvements or a higher quality program. Pricing impacts substantially upon users and their perceptions of themselves and the program or service (see Figure 5.3).

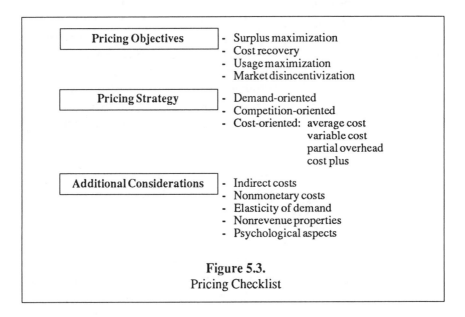

Figure 5.3.
Pricing Checklist

Price and Promotion

Price is often integrated into the promotional package of a product, program, or service. This is due to users' receptivity as it relates to the psychological implications of pricing.

There are a number of price-promotional strategies that are commonly used by recreation delivery systems when attempting to influence user behavior in relationship to its program or service. One of those strategies is the *early bird discount*. Public and nonprofit recreation organizations use this approach in an attempt to encourage people to sign up in advance for a program rather than at the last minute. Resorts and charter tours often use this same approach. The purpose of this strategy is to ensure enrollment in the tour or program as early as possible. This helps the agency to better plan and to improve cash flow as well.

Another such mechanism is *"2 for the price of 1."* In this instance, the organization offers this price incentive to increase levels of participation. Some organizations allow those users who sign up for one program to enroll in an additional program for half price. Some health clubs offer membership specials that invite an individual to join and to bring along a friend for the same price.

Package pricing is another promotion that attempts to use price as an incentive to influence user patterns. A community theatre group might be performing six plays in its upcoming season and offer a package plan of six plays for the price of four, thus encouraging would-be theatregoers to subscribe for the entire series rather than to just select individual plays.

Substantial price reductions are often used in the commercial sectors particularly in the travel industry whereby if a tour or cruise hasn't been sold out by a certain date, these accommodations are offered at a substantial savings to those individuals willing to make their travel plans with short notice.

Couponing is another price promotion often used. Many public park and recreation departments offer coupons good for one free session of one of their classes or workshops. Commercial establishments often offer coupons that may be redeemed for one free visit to their health or sports club. Coupons can also be used with a percentage of discount against purchase or membership enrollment.

While price pays only one part in the promotion process, it can often be a significant one in terms of motivation for users. Additional techniques of motivation will be covered in the following chapter, which deals specifically with the marketing mix element of promotion.

Summary

The third marketing mix variable is price. This particular variable is vital to the success of recreation delivery systems in reaching their target markets and meeting their revenue goals.

The pricing variable is quite complex in nature, having two dimensions—monetary and nonmonetary. These dimensions, direct and indirect price, must also be analyzed in view of the direct and indirect costs associated with participation in a recreation program or service. An understanding of these dimensions of price enables recreation delivery systems to more effectively manipulate the marketing mix to reach their goals.

The process of establishing a price for a recreation program or service must incorporate the establishment of pricing objectives as well as the development of pricing strategies. The delivery system must examine the specific objectives it hopes to accomplish by establishing a price. Such objectives can range from increased participation to increased revenues. The pricing strategies for programs and services must also be considered. Pricing strategies can incorporate the relationship of the cost of offering the program or service, to the demand for such a program, as well as the impact of competition.

Other factors that must be taken into consideration when establishing a price for a program or service as well as a pricing strategy are: elasticity of demand, nonrevenue-generating properties, and the psychological aspects of price.

The pricing variable is critical to the acceptance of a program or service by a target market as well as to the financial success of delivery systems. It is a complex variable that must be fully analyzed and addressed in conjunction with the other marketing mix variables.

Suggested Activities

1. Make a list of current programs and services offered by a delivery system and identify both the indirect and nonmonetary costs associated with these programs or services. Suggest ways in which these seemingly "invisible" costs could be reduced for users.

2. Select two current programs or services being offered by a recreation department. Assess your perception of the elasticity or inelasticity of demand for each of these programs. Provide a rationale for each of your designations. Suggest how these designations may impact upon pricing strategies.

3. Select one popular program being offered by a delivery system. Develop prices for this program utilizing each of the three pricing approaches. Which approach is currently being used in this situation? How would implementation of the other two approaches impact upon target market and the revenue picture of the delivery system?

4. Select one program or service that is in the maturation or saturation stage of the life cycle. Specify how price promotions might be utilized with this program or service.

5. Select one popular program or service being offered by more than one delivery system in your area. Examine the differences in pricing and explain these pricing differences on the basis of other marketing mix variables.

References

Crompton, J. L. and Lamb, C. W. Jr. (1986). *Marketing Government and Social Services.* (p. 316) New York, NY: John Wiley & Sons. 1986.

Howard, D. R. and Crompton, J. L. (1980). *Financing, Managing and Marketing Recreation & Park Resources.* (p. 437) Dubuque, IA: Wm. C. Brown.

Kotler, P. (1982). *Marketing for Nonprofit Organizations (2nd ed.)* Englewood Cliffs, NJ: Prentice-Hall.

National Park Service. *Marketing Parks and Recreation.* (pp. 29-30) State College, PA: Venture Publishing.

Pride, W. M. and Ferrell, O. C. (1983). *Marketing: Basic Concepts and Decisions.* (p. 422) Boston, MA: Houghton Mifflin.

Chapter Six

Promotion–The Final P of the Marketing Mix

Common Concerns for Parks, Recreation, and Leisure Delivery Systems

- A medium-size public recreation department utilizes press releases to communicate with its participants and debates the merits of replacing this method with paid advertisements.

- An island resort that specializes in providing a relaxing and unwinding vacation getaway considers the advantages of using the print media as opposed to radio or television.

- A suburban YMCA explores the possibilities of using existing members to recruit new members and participants.

- A corporate recreation coordinator regularly provides substantial in formation about programs and services to users and wonders if there are more effective ways to persuade people to participate.

Promotion

The final "P" in the marketing mix is *promotion*. A common misconception of marketing is that promotion and marketing are one and the same thing. Promotion is just one element of the marketing mix. The highly visible role of promotional techniques often contributes to this misconception.

Promotion is actually *communication*. It can be defined as communication designed "to facilitate exchanges with members of potential client groups by communicating the benefits offered by a program or service" (Howard and Crompton, 1980, pp. 448-449). The most essential purpose of this communication is to *inform,* to let people know what programs and services are being offered by a leisure delivery system. A second function of promotion is to *persuade.* While delivery systems utilize promotion to inform target markets about existing programs, they are simultaneously hoping to persuade these people to exchange discretionary time and money for benefits offered by the organization.

Promotional efforts can be influenced by target marketing strategies, stages in program life cycle, or other marketing issues. Although informing and persuading are the two most essential functions of promotion, there are also additional aims. Additional functions of promotion include: reminding, familiarizing, overcoming inertia, and adding perceived value to one's programs, services, or facility (National Park Service).

For instance, if a new program or service is being introduced the purpose of the promotion would be to *inform* people of the existence of this program or service. However, if the promotion reviewed existing programs or benefits of a well-established recreation facility, then the purpose would be more to *remind* the target market of the benefits related to such a facility. If a recreational delivery system is expanding its target marketing strategy to include a new user group, then the appropriate purpose of that promotion would be to *familiarize* target markets with the existence of the program or facility appropriate for them. Sometimes, it is necessary to use promotion as a tool to convince people who realize the benefits offered by the program but need some assistance in actually starting to participate. In this instance, the function of the promotion is to *overcome inertia* on the part of the target market. Often promotion is utilized to *add perceived value* to one's program or facility. If a program or service is similar to that offered by competitors, promotion can be used to associate the program with a particular image, enhancing its value to target market groups.

Framework for Understanding Communication and Promotion

In order to establish the proper framework to understand this fourth "P" of the marketing mix and to develop techniques for incorporating promotion into a marketing plan and strategy for your delivery system, it is vital to view promotion as part of the communication process. Years ago, Lasswell (1948, pp. 375-381) suggested that the communication process involved five areas to be addressed: *who . . . says what . . . in what channel . . . to whom . . . with what effect.*

This communication process involved in promotion is quite complex, requiring a host of insights, decisions, and progressions (see Figure 6.1). This chapter is designed to facilitate the understanding of this process for the recreator to enhance effectiveness when manipulating this "P" of the

Who	The park, recreation, or leisure delivery system initiating the communication
Says What	The actual message to be communicated; emphasis upon content and style
What Channel	The selection of specific media to be used: print, radio, TV, etc.
To Whom	Specific identification and description of target market groups to whom message is directed
What Effect	Identification of specific response from target market being sought by delivery system

Figure 6.1.
Decision Areas Within Promotion/Communication Process

Based upon information in Lasswell, H. D. (1948) *Power and Personality* (pp. 375-381). New York, NY: W. W. Norton & Co.

marketing mix. To do so, an overview of the conditions for successful communication, buyer behavior, hierarchy of response models, and impact of services advertising will be presented.

Some common examples of marketing and advertising mistakes actually refer to miscommunication. Just because promotion exists does not mean communication has occurred. Communication is a complex process, and Crompton and Lamb (1986) suggest that the following three conditions need to be met to ensure successful communication: a message designed and delivered to gain attention of the target market; a message addressed to the needs/wants of the target market along with suggested means for satisfaction; and correct positioning of the message for the target market (pp. 386-390).

How does an organization gain the attention of its target market? Its message has to literally *reach out* and *grab* the attention of the target market. It should be as if this message is for nobody else but them. The recent use of popular music from the 1960s advertising all kinds of products is an example of how advertisers targeting baby boomers as their market have utilized the music to speak directly to them and get their attention.

In addition, this message must address the wants and needs of the target market. Informing a target market of the existence of a fitness club will do little to address their needs and wants. The message needs to be customized to address the specific needs of the target markets, such as special weekend events for singles or low-impact programs for out-of-shape users. The message should also address the communication needs of the market. Do they need to be informed, persuaded, or reminded?

The third criterion relates to positioning, which was discussed at length in an earlier chapter. The promotion tool or message selected must be positioned correctly for the target market. It must have a look and feel that are consistent with the critical descriptors of the target market.

To incorporate the three conditions for successful communication as outlined by Crompton and Lamb, it is necessary for the recreator to have a better understanding of buyer behavior. How do people go about making decisions related to the purchase of a service? McCarthy and Brogowicz (1982) indicate that consumers go through a series of steps en route to this adoption of a service, as follows: awareness, interest, evaluation, trial, decision, and confirmation (pp. 139-140).

During the awareness stage, the consumer recognizes that such a service exists. This awareness is followed by the interest stage, in which the consumer begins to gather information about the program or service. During the evaluation stage, the consumer applies knowledge gained about the service to the consumer's own particular situation. The trial stage follows, in which the consumer actually purchases the service. During this trial stage, it is important to note that price plays a role. If the service under consideration is expensive, then it may not be as readily adopted. The trial stage is followed by the decision stage, in which the consumer decides whether or not to purchase. The decision stage is followed by the confirmation stage. It is interesting to note that even after the decision to purchase has been made, the consumer continues to think over this decision.

This series of steps involved in the consumer purchase process relates directly to the stages that recreation consumers go through en route to actual participation in a program or service (Figure 6.2). These stages in the participation process influence the type of communication response the recreation marketer may be seeking through promotion. The delivery system may be seeking cognitive, affective, or behavioral responses from the target market groups when designing promotional strategies (Kotler, 1980, p.475).

For instance, the recreation marketer may desire to gain the attention of a target market group to inform them of a program or service. In this case, a cognitive response is being sought. If the delivery system is interested in creating an interest on the part of potential users to become members of its facility, then it is seeking an affective response. When trying to convince recreation consumers to actually run out and participate in a program or join a facility, then recreators would be seeking a behavioral response.

The AIDA model of the response hierarchy relates to the potential response patterns being sought. This model indicates that buyers or potential consumers pass through the successive stages of awareness, interest, desire, and action en route to actual participation or purchase (Strong, 1925, p. 9). By utilizing this concept, the recreator is aware of buyer readiness or response stages. The readiness of target market group members to purchase a program or service in conjunction with the response hierarchy assists the recreator in selecting the appropriate response being sought through promotion. This relates to two of the suggestions made by Lasswell (1948, pp. 375-381). The delivery system needs to know *what to say* to target market groups and *with what effect*.

For instance, a potential member of a health club unaware that the club offers exercise programs and classes for people over the age of 50 would need to be informed or made aware of the existence of such a program or service. Individuals aware of the existence of such programs would be approached differently. Promotion to these people would be for the purpose of creating a desire, interest, or motivation for becoming involved. Other potential clients who already know of the existence of the club's programs

Purchase Process	Stages	ADIA	Focus of Promotion
Awareness	Cognitive	Attention	Inform target market of the existence of program or service
Interest	Affective	Interest	Remind target market of benefits or program
Evaluation		Desire	Persuade target market to become motivated to participate
Trial Decision	Behavioral	Action	Convince target market to actually register or participate in program
Confirmation			Continued contact with target market to assure continued participation

Figure 6.2.
Process and Stages Related to Promotion and Participation

Based upon information secured from the following sources: McCarthy and Brogowicz (1982). Essentials of Marketing (pp. 139-140). Homewood, IL: Richard D. Irwin; Kotler, P. (1980). Marketing Management 4th ed. (p. 475). Englewood Cliffs, NJ: Prentice-Hall; and Strong, E. K. (1925). The Psychology of Selling (p. 9). New York: McGraw-Hill.

and are motivated to begin exercising need to be faced with a promotional message spurring them into action so they will actually become a member of the health club.

Understanding the stages people go through enroute to actual participation enables the delivery system to more effectively plan the communication with them. A familiarity with this response model will also be helpful when designing actual promotional campaigns.

Another concept essential to effective promotion for parks, recreation, and leisure is services marketing. Joining a fitness club or registering for a softball league is quite different from purchasing a product. Since the provision of services consists of contact with the organization, in contrast to the purchase of a product where little or no contact with the producer is required, promotion for recreation and leisure should be developed according to the level of contact between the user and the organization (Edmonton Parks and Recreation, 1988, p. 27).

Since purchasing a service is different than purchasing a product, George and Berry (1984, pp. 407-411) provide six guidelines for improving the effectiveness of services advertising as follows:

1. Advertising must have a positive effect on contact personnel.
2. Advertising needs to capitalize on word-of-mouth.
3. Advertising should provide tangible clues.
4. Advertising needs to make service easily understood.
5. Advertising should contribute to continuity.
6. Advertising should promise what is possible.

These guidelines serve as strategies for enhancing the effectiveness of promotional techniques for parks, recreation, and leisure delivery systems.

When selecting promotional tools, designing promotional messages, or choosing media to be utilized, these guidelines should be considered. Recreation delivery systems should examine all elements within the marketing mix variables to strive to address these guidelines. How can the program or service be made more concrete to potential users? How can satisfied participants become part of the process? These are areas that can substantially enhance the effectiveness of the promotion of recreation and leisure programs and services.

The communication process between the delivery system and potential target market groups known as promotion is not a simple one. When undertaking the implementation of this fourth "P" of the marketing mix, recrea-

tors need to address the conditions for successful communication, buyer behavior, hierarchy of response models, and the implications of services
marketing.

Elements of the Promotion Mix

The promotional mix includes tools and techniques used by a leisure
delivery system to communicate with its public while attempting to inform,
persuade, remind, or familiarize its target markets with the programs,
services, or facilities offered by the organization. The types of activities
encompassed under this broad spectrum are both numerous and diverse and
can include (but are not limited to) the techniques listed in Figure 6.3.
Although the kinds and types of promotional tools and techniques that can
be utilized by a recreation delivery system to inform and persuade its target
market regarding its products, programs, and services vary, essentially each
of these activities can be grouped under one of the following four major
types of the promotional mix: *advertising, personal contact* or *selling, sales
promotion* or *incentives,* and *publicity.*

Advertisements	Demonstrations
Logo/emblem	Public speaking
Stationery	Decals
Press releases	Button/pins
News features	Bulletin boards
Brochures	Posters/signs
Flyers	Billboards
Annual reports	PSAs
Awards/citations	Radio/TV talk shows
Exhibits/displays	Contests
Video/slide presentations	Direct mailings
Free samples	Coupons
Catalogs	Trade shows
Open houses	Special events
Endorsements	Sponsorships
Word-of-mouth	Cable TV shows
Testimonials	Telemarketing
Celebrities	Sales presentations
Point of sales displays	Premiums
Newsletters	Pricing specials
Photographs	The Yellow Pages
Press kits	Reception procedures
Novelty items	

Figure 6.3.
Promotional Tools and Techniques

Howard and Crompton (1980, p. 456) define these four primary activities comprising the promotion mix as follows:

1. *Advertising*–Any paid form of nonpersonal presentation about an agency or its programs, which is paid for by an identified sponsor or developed by an identified sponsor and communicated through media as a public service.

2. *Personal Contact*–Direct oral presentation to one or more present or potential clients for the purpose of facilitating exchange.

3. *Incentives*–Something of financial value offered to encourage participation in a program or use of a service.

4. *Publicity*–Nonpersonal favorable communications in either print or broadcast media in which the sponsor is not identified and for which there is no payment.

While these four primary activities associated with promotion have an underlying common function for a delivery system, the tools and techniques associated with each, as well as implementation considerations, vary. An overview of these techniques and approaches will now be addressed. Please note that this chapter provides an overview of these categories of promotion only. Recreators interested in specific techniques for designing and implementing these categories are advised to consult the myriad of books written expressly for those purposes.

Advertising

Advertising is an impersonal form of communication with a target market presented through the media. This form of promotion must be paid for by an identified sponsor. Commercial recreation delivery systems have traditionally relied more heavily upon advertisement as a form of promotion. However, in recent years, as a result of increased competition for discretionary time and money, the role of advertising has become important to public and nonprofit delivery systems as well.

There are innumerable different promotional pieces that fall under the category of advertising. Any paid announcement on radio or television or in the print media, newspapers, or magazines, are considered advertising as well as posters, flyers, and brochures which are mailed directly to the target market or distributed in key locations.

One exception to the use of paid advertisements is the public service announcement (PSA). PSAs are advertisements that feature the aims, programs, or services of public or nonprofit organizations, and which appear at no charge to the organization because the space or time is donated by the media itself. The purpose of PSAs is to promote organizations or programs that are of value to the general public. The print media are not required to provide such services, but broadcast media such as radio and television stations are required by law to provide specific amounts of air time for the playing of public service announcements. PSAs are of interest to public and nonprofit organizations because they can provide free or low-cost avenues for promotion; it is therefore imperative that PSAs be considered when developing the promotional mix of these types of organizations. A drawback to use of PSAs, however, is that the timing and frequency of such advertisements are dictated by the media source providing the space or time, which limits the organization's control over the promotional message.

Although print ads differ from billboards and direct mail differs from radio commercials, there are some commonalities that can be addressed when coordinating the essential ingredients of advertising. Two salient points to consider in the development of advertising for one's recreation delivery system are the *message* and the *media*.

The Message

A number of relevant areas regarding the message itself are critical to the success and the efficacy of the promotional technique. There are three principal decision areas related to the message: *response, content,* and *style*.

The first consideration is the *type of response* the recreator seeks to get from the target market. Is the recreator hoping to inform them of the existence of a program or service, or is the recreator attempting to convince them to switch their participation patterns from their current recreation provider over to the recreator's organization?

A second consideration which is closely tied to response is *message content.* How does the response pattern, coupled with characteristics of the program or service, shape the actual message to be conveyed? If the program is in the maturation stage of the life cycle, it is necessary to highlight differences between one's program and the one offered by a competitor. If this is an expensive program involving a long-term commitment, the message needs to focus upon persuasion as well as information.

A useful framework incorporating aspects of both response and program characteristics influencing the actual content of the promotional message has been developed by Simon. Simon (1971, pp. 174-206) suggested a number of focuses for advertisement messages as follows:

> *Information*–presentation of straight facts
>
> *Argument*–utilization of a logical argument to substantiate a reason for purchase or participation
>
> *Motivation with psychological appeals*–incorporation of an emotional appeal to attempt to enhance the appeal of the program or service
>
> *Repeat-assertion*–utilization of a hard-sell approach that consists of restatement of one essential fact or factor
>
> *Command*–presentation of a direct order with the intent to influence behavior of the target market
>
> *Symbolic association*–utilization of a symbol to subtly promote one piece of information about a program
>
> *Imitation*–association of program or service with people or situations that are desirable to target market [11]

Each of these various approaches to message content of advertisements can be related to the three types of responses inherent within the hierarchy effects, cognitive, affective, and behavioral. Simon's framework is also useful for persuasion based upon characteristics of the program or service itself as outlined in Figure 6.4.

Type	Example	Useful With
Information	Ballet lessons for girls ages 10-14 on Mondays and Wednesday at 3:30 p. m.	Program that is routine or new program or service that is different or needs time or money committment
Argument	The time you spend sitting in traffic could have been better spent working out	New or high price program with hidden benefit or requiring action
Motivation with psychological appeal	Do you know how your child will spend his summer?	Stylistic, new; similiar to others; high price or hidden benefit
Repeat	Summer's coming—it's time for bathing suits	Established program: short-term or low price
Command	Don't spend your time watching—join now	Established program: short-term or low price
Symbolic association	Picture of people meeting others and enjoying life	Established program: low price; stylistic; short-term
Imitation	Use of a celebrity involved in program or service	Established program: stylistic; short-term; luxury

Figure 6.4.
Types of Advertising Messages

Based upon information secured from Engle, Warshaw, and Kinnear., *Promotional Strategy*, 5th. ed. Homewood, IL: Richard D. Irwin, Inc., 1983, pp. 320-333.

While the Simon framework incorporates a focus upon a specific, desired response and the characteristics of the program, it does not address lifestyle considerations, which more clearly delineate target market groups.

The final consideration for developing a message for an advertisement relates to *style*. Style can refer to a variety of different characteristics including the words selected, the tone of voice, and the overall feel of the commercial message. Any message can adopt different styles designed to better attract the interest and attention of specific target market groups. Kotler (1982, p. 365) provides marketers with some major advertising styles as follows: slice-of-life, lifestyle, fantasy, mood, musical, personality symbol, technical expertise, scientific evidence, or testimonial evidence. These styles expand the effectiveness of the advertising strategy by making the message attractive to different target market groups, as illustrated in Figure 6.5.

Style	Example
Fantasy	As parents complete registration forms for gymnastics and diving lessons for their children, they begin to daydream about their future participation in the olympic games.
Musical	A group of children are pictured singing on a merry-go-round extrolling the benefits of a day spent at the amusement park.
Mood	Young family strolling through nature trails of local park appear to be experiencing quality time with one another and nature.
Scientific Research	Interview with a physician who reviews research findings indicating that people who exercise regularly have fewer heart attacks.
Lifestyle	Busy, attractive career woman rushes to take her two young children to day camp and returns at the end of the day to find two happy, healthy children.
Testimonial	Group of three or four people deplaning share with one another the reasons why they plan on returning to Hideaway Resort on their next vacation.

Figure 6.5.
Examples of Advertising Styles

Based upon information secured from Kotler, *Marketing for Nonprofit Organizations,* *2nd ed.* Englewood Cliffs, NJ: Prentice Hall, 1982. p. 365

The message itself is obviously a very important component of the advertisement. It needs to grab the attention of the target market and create an interest on their part in the program or service being promoted. It should also foster a desire to take part in the program or service and culminate with members of the target market acting upon the information provided to them.

Integrating the AIDA (attention, interest, desire, and action) approach within the advertising message can be accomplished by making use of all parts of the advertising message, including the headline, subheadline, body copy, and the closing (Crompton and Lamb, 1986, pp. 419-420).

The attention of the target market needs to be attracted by the headline used in the advertisement while the subheading elaborates upon the benefits and creates an interest on the part of the target market. The actual message of the ad, usually called the body copy, would attempt to create a desire on the part of the target market to use this service or participate in this program. This is often accomplished by personalizing the copy and appearing to speak to the person directly. The closing portion of the ad needs to ask the target market member to do something. It should ask for their phone call or request that they complete the registration form.

The Media

Media is the second component of advertisement. There are a number of different methods available within media selection, including such options as radio, television, newspaper, magazines, direct mail, flyers and brochures, or billboards.

It is necessary for a recreation delivery system to select which media options are appropriate for its promotional purposes. Choices are often made on the basis of target market, product, message, and cost (Engel, Warshaw and Kinnear, 1983, p. 283). The recreator may want to review the media viewing patterns of the target market. Different target markets read certain magazines or certain sections of the newspapers, as well as having preferences and patterns for radio listening and television viewing. Flyers, posters, or billboards would need to address the traffic patterns of target markets (see Exhibit 6.1, p. 126).

Additional considerations in media selection relate to the product or program itself as well as the message to be utilized. Media choices vary according to each medium's effectiveness in promoting programs with different characteristics and messages with different purposes or styles. Newspapers are suited for well-known programs or services with an information message. However, television may be better geared for promoting a high-style service that requires a persuasive or motivational message.

The final consideration is, of course, cost. Television tends to be more expensive than the print media. The time of day selected for radio or television as well as the popularity of the program being broadcast all enter into the cost of the advertisement. The recreator needs to balance the effectiveness of reaching the target market with various media choices. Cost can often be a deciding factor in the media selection process.

Other factors related to media selection that need to be considered and which also affect the cost of the advertising are *reach* and *frequency*. Reach refers to the number of actual different people who are exposed to the advertisement, and frequency refers to the number of times those people are exposed to the advertisement (Simon, 1971, pp. 174-205). Direct mail provides a good example of this concept. What is an organization's reach or how many people receive a copy of the facility's brochure? What is the organization's frequency or how many of these mailings are sent to these people? The same concept applies to the other media options. There is a cost relationship between reach and frequency and the trade-offs between these need to be explored when developing the budget for a promotional package.

Exhibit 6.1.
Magazine Format for Program Brochure

Source: Prince William County Park Authority, Manassas, VA. Spring 1991

If the recreation delivery system attempts to make media choices on the basis of target market, program characteristics, message focus, and cost, then it is important to have an awareness that media differ substantially on many of these important criteria. Advantages and disadvantages involved in utilizing media choices are outlined in Figure 6.6. The advantages and disadvantages of each media type should be weighed carefully by the recreator in relationship to the specific objectives developed initially for the promotional package about to be undertaken.

Media	Characteristics
Newspapers	Broad reach for a variety of target markets Allows for in-depth examination Coverage is timely and flexible
Radio	Low cost with high frequency Reaches distinct, well-defined markets Can create exciting messages Timely and flexible
Television	Maximum reach but expensive Lacks selectivity of markets Tradeoffs between cost and effectiveness Good for physical demonstration Creates trust and believability
Billboards	Relatively inexpensive but effective Simple messages only Requires strategic location
Posters	Inexpensive means of promotion Success based upon location Message must be eyecatching
Magazines	Highly selective Can be expensive though efficient Able to access specialized groups
Direct Mail	Third largest method after TV and papers Opportunity for personalization Allows for selectivity, flexibility, and control Can be expensive "Junk mail" response

Figure 6.6.
Media Characteristics

Source: Adapted from National Park Service. *Marketing Parks and Recreation.* State College, PA: Venture Publishing, 1983, pp. 137-143

The final step in the utilization of advertisement is *evaluation*. Due to the extent of the resources used with advertisements, the agency needs to assess the effectiveness of specific ads. This can be accomplished in a number of ways.

Resorts who advertise in many different newspapers and magazines often request people interested in receiving additional information write to a specific post office box number, which varies based upon media used; in that way, these organizations are able to gauge the depth of response to various media sources. Advertisements on radio stations often inform listeners to ask for a certain person or product in an attempt to track the responsiveness of the radio ad. Likewise, public park and recreation departments often include a section on registration forms requesting participants to indicate where they heard about this program or service. In addition to these relatively simple forms of evaluation, marketing firms also use pre- and post-tests as well as recall and recognition tests to ascertain the effectiveness of television or magazine commercials or promotional campaigns.

Advertising may be an impersonal form of communication with one's target market, but it holds the potential for being highly effective as well as an expensive portion of the promotional mix. It is important that the recreator make careful decisions related to both the message developed and the media selected for such an undertaking. These decisions need to be made on the basis of objectives, target market characteristics, and program or service attributes, as well as cost.

Sales Promotion and Incentives

Sales promotion or incentives are an additional activity within the promotional mix with ramifications for parks, recreation, and leisure. Sales promotions or incentives have been previously defined as things with some financial or symbolic value offered to members of the target market for the purpose of encouraging them to participate in a particular program or to try a specific recreational service of some kind.

A wide variety of items are included in this classification. Crompton and Lamb (1986, p. 476) indicate that there are four general categories of such sales promotions: promotional pricing, free offers, prizes, and celebrities. Promotional pricing includes such incentives as discounts for limited time periods or off-peak hours, 2-for-1 offers, season passes, or discounts for groups. Free offer incentives can feature free passes for one member of the group or for children, with adults paying full price. This type of incentive can also consist of free open houses to sample a facility or its programs as well as opportunities to attend the first session of a program at no charge.

Prizes are also useful as sales incentives. The use of door prizes, contests, T-shirts, or premium giveaways are all examples of this use of sales promotion. Fitness clubs may offer free workout suits to new members enrolling by a specific date. Public and nonprofit organizations may use contests as a mechanism for encouraging people to register early for programs. Celebrities can be used as an incentive for attracting new people into an organization or for encouraging people to continue their participation.

The types and varieties of these sales incentives can be customized to reflect the programs and services offered by the leisure delivery system as well as the objectives which the agency wishes to attain. Ziethaml (1984, pp. 191-199) indicates that sales promotions such as guest discounts and privileges may be more effective promotional tools in the services industry than advertisements.

There are three different categories of sales promotions or incentives that can be utilized: consumer, dealer, and sales force (Kotler, 1982, p. 371). The aforementioned sales incentives offered to consumers are often referred to as external incentives. Such external incentives can be used to modify or regulate the behavior of users and nonusers.

However, there are other uses for such sales incentives. Dealer promotions such as free goods or discounts are incentives, as are cooperative advertising or sales contests. The purpose of these incentives is to encourage dealers to use or promote one's products or services for their own benefit. Sales force promotions are essentially the internal use of such incentives. Internal sales promotions could include bonuses, contests, free prizes, or trips directed toward personnel within the delivery system for accomplishing specific objectives such as increasing membership renewals or improving attendance. These prizes, awards, or contests are useful as a means for one's employees to encourage users to take specific action of benefit to the organization (see Exhibits 6.2 and 6.3).

Crompton and Lamb (1986, p. 475) offer the following steps as criteria for planning and coordinating incentive programs: specifying objectives, determining the inclusiveness, specifying recipients, determining direction, selecting type, establishing amount, and selecting time of payment. It

Exhibit 6.2.
Incentive Contest for Early Registration

Register during April and Win!

Register for any program or activity in this Guide Between April 3 and 28, and your name will be entered in a drawing for the following Parks and Recreation prizes:

- 4 sets of 2 tickets each for Tazz-Ma-Jazz performances
- 4 sets of tickets each for Livestock Musical Theatre's Summer shows
- 5 free pedal boat rides
- 2 Gold Musicards for Opus 89-90
- 1 Christmas wreath
- 2 free rounds of golf at Bryan Park
- 1 greens free package card at Gillespie Golf Course
- 1 free sailboat rental
- 1 free rowboat rental
- 1 free sailing class
- 1 free sweatshirt painting class
- 1 free session of tennis lesson

Winners will be drawn on **May 4** and notified by mail

Source: Greensboro, NC Parks and Recreation Department. 1989 Summer Brochure.

Exhibit 6.3.
Example of Sales Promotion and Co-Sponsorship

Source: Super Bowl Weekend Special Event Promotion: Mug with discount coupons, co-sponsored by Coca-Cola.™ MWR Department, Naval Air Station, Brunswick, ME.

is important to decide exactly which behavior the recreator wishes to change or modify, as well as specifying the exact group or groups of people to be targeted (e.g., users versus nonusers). The amount of money to be offered as an incentive or the cost of the promotion itself must be taken into consideration as well as the amount of time for the incentive offer. Due to the current and future financial impact of such promotions, all of these factors need to be addressed when developing and implementing this type of promotion.

Sales promotion and sales incentives can be an effective portion of the promotional mix for parks, recreation, and leisure organizations. They are useful for modifying the behavior of specific target market groups while simultaneously accomplishing objectives for the organization. It is imperative that adequate time and attention be provided for these incentives, as they are often responsible for raising the visibility of the organization as well as incurring expenses for the organization.

Publicity

An additional option within the promotional mix available to recreation delivery system is publicity. *Publicity* differs from advertising and sales promotion because it is not directly sponsored by the organization, and its purpose is usually to inform rather than to persuade people to participate in a particular program or service.

Publicity doesn't specifically promote a program or service but, rather, it serves as a mechanism to increase the visibility of an organization by drawing positive attention to it. The extent and variety of such public relations tools is substantial. Kotler (1982, p. 389) identified the following as major tools: written materials, audio-visual materials, corporate identity, news, events, and speeches. An additional category to be added to this list is technology. The use of telephone answering machines, cable televisions, and computers are additional techniques to be considered.

An overriding consideration when employing any of these public relations tools relates to credibility. The professional quality and presentation of written or audio-visual materials as well as speakers provided by an organization must be high quality. The other half of that credibility relates to the honesty and integrity of the organization and its uses of publicity.

Publicity can be of untold value to a delivery system for a number of reasons. It does not directly cost the organization the kinds of fees that would ordinarily be associated with such media coverage. It is not directly attributable to the organization, so it appears as if another organization such as a newspaper or TV station feels that the delivery system has value. In addition, it enables the delivery system to be associated with positive recognition.

However, publicity can work both ways. The free coverage afforded organizations in the media is not always favorable. For instance, Reebok® Shoes, well-known for its expensive sneakers, recently introduced a high-cost line of basketball shoes for playground play which appeared to be targeted for innercity youth. To counteract any potential negative publicity regarding these sneakers, the company has introduced a playground rehabilitation program whereby the company goes into urban centers and renovates playground basketball courts for use by youngsters.

There are a substantial number of events or activities that can enable a recreation delivery system to utilize publicity. Such things as sponsoring a road race to benefit the homeless or conducting a giant balloon launch to open a new facility can prove to be newsworthy enough to attract the attention of the local media.

It is recommended that organizations wishing to take advantage of opportunities for publicity do so by developing working relationships with members of the media and learning the media policies and procedures guiding such coverage, because due to the powerful and positive nature of publicity, a good deal of competition for such coverage exists.

Personal Selling or Personal Contact

The final option within the promotional mix is personal selling. *Personal selling* or *personal contact* includes direct, oral presentations made to current or potential users for the purpose of initiating or continuing participation in the service relationship. It is often associated with commercial recreation organizations, who sometimes maintain sales staff for the sole purpose of generating increased revenues through presentations to new or existing users.

However, it should not be misconstrued as solely a promotion option for commercial recreation organizations since public, nonprofit, and private recreation delivery systems often find the need to recruit or retain participants or members as well as being involved in other related activities such as fund-raising projects, capital campaigns, or campaigns for specific issues that might be related to passing bond issues or lobbying for tax considerations.

Every recreation delivery system, whether public or commercial, with or without a designated sales force, practices this form of promotion. Kotler (1982, p. 389) refers to employees who deal with people outside of the organization as *boundary* personnel and maintains there are two different categories of boundary personnel, which he refers to as *sales* personnel and *service* personnel.

Establishing a program of personal selling or contact requires the same kind of attention as the other categories of promotional techniques. Objectives need to be established and target markets need to be identified and selected. It is recommended that the AIDA method be applied to personal sales; this approach has been integrated into the seven steps of the personal selling process: prospecting, pre-approach, approach, presentation, objections, close, and follow-up (Crompton and Lamb, 1986, p. 459).

The prospecting and pre-approach steps of the selling process are related to identifying and selecting appropriate target markets and preparing the approach and presentation in such a manner as to gain the attention and the interest of the potential user, member, or customer. The close is the portion of the process that compels the potential customer to take some kind of action in relationship to enrolling in a program or becoming a contributor. The follow-up is not related directly to the AIDA process but is utilized to contribute to a continued relationship with the member, participant, voter, or contributor, depending upon the situation. These seven steps in the personal selling process attempt to move the potential buyer through the stages of readiness as addressed in other forms of promotion.

While the task of sales employees is quite apparent, it is important to note that the second category of employees designated as service employees also comes into extensive contact with the public. In addition to their obvious function within the organization, which may include such things as maintenance or answering the phone, these employees may deal extensively with users and potential users, and the outcome of these interactions can translate into renewed memberships or motivation to participate in activities. The role of service employees is so critical to recreation delivery systems that their role and performance will be profiled more extensively in the next chapter.

Personal contact or personal selling is not limited to employees of the delivery system. Recalling that one of the unique factors related to services advertising was word-of-mouth, park, recreation, and leisure delivery systems need to take into account the promotion power of their current and former users.

Ziethaml (1984) developed some hypotheses related to consumers' search for information and types of evaluation used in this process. Two of these hypotheses with substantial implications for leisure delivery systems include his belief that consumers seek and rely upon personal sources of information when purchasing a service and that consumers engage in substantial post-purchase evaluation when consuming a service (pp. 191-199).

These beliefs have widespread implications for recreation and leisure delivery systems. They need to recognize the importance of current users or participants as part of the promotional process. Involving them in sales efforts through testimonials or use of guest passes is critical to the effectiveness of such promotions. Such delivery systems need to take great care in meeting the needs of users and resolving any problems or complaints immediately. The need for this approach is two-fold. Such people can be powerful positive or detrimental sources of promotion for the organization. In addition, while participating in the program or service, they are continually evaluating the experience in an effort to assess their initial decision to participate.

The role and scope of personal selling or personal contact varies within recreation delivery systems and also varies based upon situational factors or current objectives of the organization. Generally, commercial systems have a greater focus and dependency upon sales personnel. However, various situations or needs of other delivery systems such as a referendum on a bond issue or major fund-raising efforts can dictate the inclusion of personal selling and contact as an appropriate form of promotion. Park, recreation, and leisure delivery systems also are afforded the unique opportunity to take advantage of word-of-mouth messages from users as part of personal contact or personal selling.

Coordinating the Promotion Mix

These four methods encompass the techniques and tools utilized by park and recreation delivery systems for the purposes of promotion. Although there are some basic variations between each of the four methods cited, essentially they are united in their fundamental purpose to assist the organization by informing target markets of its existence and by persuading them to take part in its programs or services.

These four different methods of promotion need to be considered and utilized in concert with one another. Publicity needs to be developed with an awareness of current advertising campaigns. Sales promotions and personal selling efforts need to be coordinated. When attempting to put together the promotional campaign for a program or service, a full-scale coordination effort is required. Four general areas of consideration need to be addressed as follows: organizational considerations, the target market, program or service attributes, and the impact of services advertising. An integration of these four areas of consideration with the process of communication and promotional decisions constitute the promotional mix.

Organizational considerations such as current position, objectives of the delivery system, and resources available, all need to be addressed. What is the current position of this delivery system? Is it perceived as being associated with one type of service or population group? Is it a market leader, or is there substantial competition for similar programs or services?

The mission of the organization as well as current objectives need to be considered. Whether the delivery system is public or commercial shapes the promotional mix. What are the current objectives? Does the agency hope to reposition itself or is it interested in increasing immediate revenues? Both of these areas shape the tone and eventual outcomes of promotional techniques.

The resources of the delivery system itself relate to the promotional mix. One obvious resource is funding. How much money is available for such undertakings? There are other resource considerations as well, such as ability and attitudes of service personnel; availability and aptitude of employees for speaking engagements; and the presence of nontangible promotional resources such as atmospherics.

Having reviewed the organizational considerations, the recreation marketer needs to focus upon the people or target market groups to whom the promotion is to be directed. What are the dimensions of the target markets on the basis of the common descriptors? What stage in the purchasing process is the target market and what response should be sought? Is there more than one target market for this program and if so, should responses sought be modified on this basis? Should users and nonusers be addressed differently? Can the promotional message be altered on the basis of differences in descriptors? Is geographic location as important as lifestyle preferences or is synchronographics a major focus?

The organization needs to clarify, for promotional purposes, the exact dimensions of its target market. The dimensions of the target market can then be related to promotional objectives, which may vary from one group to another. Refinement of target market groups enhances the delivery system's ability to make effective decisions related to methods and approaches undertaken.

The recreator also needs to examine more closely the program, facility, or service that will be featured in the promotion. This examination will hold considerable value towards the development of the promotion. What is the stage in the life cycle of the program or service? How will stage in the life cycle influence the objectives of the promotional message or approach? A re-examination of marketing strategies suggested for various stages of the life cycle will provide insight into directions of the promotions that will be most effective.

Other factors related to the product or program can also be examined for the purposes of providing additional information influencing participants' purchase and usage of one's program or service. Marketers generally classify programs and services on a number of different dimensions such as program characteristics, necessity or luxury, price range, similarity to competition, repeatability of purchase, and method of actual purchase; each of these areas affects the development and implementation of the promotional mix (Engel, Warshaw and Kinnear, 1983, p. 333).

Whether or not a recreation program is considered a necessity, a convenience, or a luxury in the minds of the target market makes a difference as to promotional focus selected. The cost of the program or service, ranging from minimal to fairly expensive, also influences the approach undertaken, as do factors like whether the selection of the program or activity is made on the spur of the moment or with extensive forethought. These are all factors related to the program or service that ought to be relevant to the coordination of the promotional mix.

The fourth area of consideration in the coordination of the promotional mix is the impact of services marketing upon the process. People view service organizations differently. People respond differently to promotion of a program as opposed to a product. Promotional efforts should try to make the program or service as tangible and as easily understood as possible. The appearance and attitude of service providers cannot be overlooked. The role of the satisfied, current user needs to be incorporated into the promotional message and approach.

There are a host of decisions that need to be made in this process of communication referred to as promotion. The process questions outlined by Lasswell related to the organization, the objectives, the target market, and the media utilized need to be addressed in light of the four areas of concern: the organization, the target market, the program or service, and services marketing. The integration of these two areas can then result in the selection of promotional techniques and the emphasis to be placed upon each form, as well as message and media decisions (see Figure 6.7).

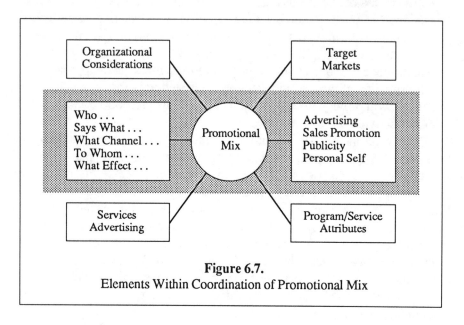

Figure 6.7.
Elements Within Coordination of Promotional Mix

Summary

The fourth and highly visible "P" of the marketing mix variable for parks, recreation, and leisure delivery systems is promotion. Promotion is actually a form of communication whose purpose is to inform and persuade potential customers to exchange discretionary time and money for one's programs and services.

Since it is a form of communication, promotion must incorporate areas of the communication process into its design and implementation. Essentially, promotion should address the following issues: who . . . says what . . . in what channel . . . to whom . . . and with what effect? These issues can effectively be addressed by an understanding of conditions for successful communication: stages in the purchasing process; stages in the response hierarchy; and implications of services advertising.

While there are countless different promotional tools and techniques utilized as part of promotion for park and recreation programs, there are essentially four distinct categories: advertising, personal contact or selling, sales promotion or incentives, and publicity. While these four categories possess an underlying common function, the design and implementation considerations for each vary.

Four common areas of consideration for all four categories of promotion are organizational considerations, target market descriptors, program/service attributes, and the impact of services marketing. A promotional campaign for a program or service may incorporate a mix of one or more of these basic categories, and the coordination between and among them is essential.

The importance and value of this fourth "P" of the marketing mix cannot be overlooked or taken lightly. The two basic purposes of promotion are to inform target markets of the existence of programs and to persuade them to become involved. Without adequate attention to promotion, the best designed programs and services would be incomplete without people participating due to lack of information or motivation to do so.

Suggested Activities

1. Select a specific promotional technique and assess its effectiveness in relationship to the three conditions for successful communication.

2. For that same promotional technique, attempt to determine the identity of the target market as well as the type of response being sought.

3. Collect all the promotional tools and techniques utilized by a specific leisure delivery system. Analyze these tools on the basis of the four categories of promotion. Suggest categories and techniques that could be included in the future.

4. Identify a recent ad released by a recreation delivery system. Critique the ad on the basis of the AIDA approach. Make suggestions for improving the effectiveness of this ad.

5. Select three advertisements developed by a leisure delivery system. Compare and contrast these ads on the basis of types of advertising messages and style considerations.

6. Identify a program or service that could benefit from a sales promotion. Brainstorm possible incentives to be used and develop a strategy for its implementation.

7. Review the publicity guidelines of an existing leisure delivery system. Identify techniques to enhance this cost-effective form of promotion.

8. Explore personal selling and personal contact opportunities for a leisure delivery system. Identify methods to be utilized to enhance the role this promotional tool plays within that organization.

9. Review the implications of services advertising and develop three specific suggestions or modifications that could be made to address these implications for a leisure delivery system.

References

Crompton, J. L. and Lamb, C. W., Jr. (1986). *Marketing Government and Social Services.* New York, NY: John Wiley & Sons.

Edmonton Parks and Recreation Department. (1988, June). *Marketing Plan 1988-1990* (p. 27).

Engle, Warshaw, and Kinnear. (1983). *Promotional Strategy 5th ed.* Homewood, IL: Richard D. Irwin, Inc.

George, W. R. and Berry L. L. (1984). Guidelines for the Advertising of Services, In Lovelock, C. H. *Services Marketing: Texts, Cases, and Readings* (pp. 407-411). Englewood Cliffs, NJ: Prentice-Hall.

Howard, D. R. and Crompton, J. L. (1980). *Financing, Managing and Marketing Recreation & Park Resources.* Dubuque, IA: Wm. C. Brown Company.

Kotler, P. (1980). *Marketing Management 4th ed.* (p. 475). Englewood Cliffs, NJ: Prentice-Hall.

Kotler, P. (1982). *Marketing for Nonprofit Organizations 2nd ed.* Englewood Cliffs, NJ: Prentice-Hall.

Lasswell, H. D. (1948). *Power and Personality* (pp. 375-381). New York, NY: W. W. Norton and Company.

McCarthy E. J. and Brogowicz, A. A. (1982). *Essentials of Marketing* (pp. 139-140). Homewood, IL: Richard D. Irwin.

National Park Service. (1983). *Marketing for Parks and Recreation* (p. 118). State College, PA: Venture Publishing.

Simon, J. L. (1971). *The Management of Advertising* (pp. 174-206). Englewood Cliffs, NJ: Prentice-Hall.

Strong, E. K. (1925). *The Psychology of Selling* (p. 9). New York, NY: McGraw-Hill.

Ziethaml, V. A. (1984). How Consumers Evaluation Processes Differ Between Goods and Services. In Lovelock, C. H. *Services Marketing* (pp. 191-199). Englewood Cliffs, NJ: Prentice-Hall.

Chapter Seven

Service Marketing

Common Concerns for Parks, Recreation, and Leisure Delivery Systems

- A public park and recreation department fears that long lines during registration periods may be discouraging participation.

- A MWR club director wonders if renovation of the interior of the club will positively impact upon its usage.

- A fitness club considers implementing a customer service training program for its employees.

- A resort installs a 24-hour guest "hotline" for addressing complaints and problems and hopes it will enhance customer service.

The Extra "Ps" For Leisure Delivery Systems

Exploration of the four "Ps" of marketing is not complete when addressing parks, recreation, and leisure organizations unless one gives thought and attention to the additional "Ps" of marketing that impact upon such a unique service field as parks, recreation, and leisure. Lovelock (1984, pp. 49-51) maintains that if users need to be physically present and must spend time while a service is performed, then their satisfaction will be influenced by interaction with service personnel, the nature of the service, facilities, and the character of other customers.

Since park, recreation, and leisure services are consumed and not just purchased, these peripheral factors augment the core benefits and need to be explored. Peripheral factors or other "Ps" that impact upon leisure delivery systems include: *physical evidence, participants, process and procedures, public image, and political impact.*

Physical evidence refers to those aspects of a service such as the facility itself and its environment. Lovelock believes that the more intangible the service the greater is the importance placed upon related tangible evidence (p. 43). What does the appearance of one's reception area say about one's organization and the services it offers? Is the exercise equipment in one's fitness center modern and in good repair? Is the park well-maintained and free of trash and litter?

Some of the benefits sought from leisure experiences such as escape, relaxation, socialization, or enjoyment are all intangible concepts. People seeking these benefits know instinctively when these occur and will assess the physical environment of the proposed activity in light of the probability that this need can be met.

Does one's area or facility have the "look" of a place where these kinds of things could happen? Ambience may be an overused expression of the 1980s, but it is an influential feature of the recreational experience. There is a growing preference on the part of participants for the right setting or ambience within which to experience various activities.

Many recreational pursuits do not enable the user to bring home tangible proof of the participation, such as a piece of pottery from enrollment in a pottery workshop. It is imperative that recreation delivery systems attempt to add a tangible element to the experience, such as T-shirts that boldly proclaim participation in a 10-mile road race, before and after exercise photos, bumper stickers that announce that this car climbed Pikes Peak, or daily notes overviewing campers' activities and experiences provided for parents at the end of the day or week.

The physical evidence surrounding an activity or inherent within an experience is a critical consideration for recreation delivery systems. Whether it includes such things as lighting, plants, or tablecloths related to socialization or relaxation or provides tangible evidence of sense of accomplishment or recognition, these peripheral images can substantially impact upon the success of a program or activity with specific target markets.

An additional "P" of recreation marketing is *people.* The people referred to within this factor are both other participants as well as service personnel. Lovelock (1984, p. 4) maintains that when users are involved in the production of the service, people and personnel often play an integral part in the experience.

Such is certainly the case with recreation services. Whether it be children going to summer day camp or adults selecting a tennis club, the people factor can come into play. A child may not want to go to camp due to the way the other kids at camp treat him or may eagerly await going to camp each day due to his relationship with a favorite counselor. Recreation activities certainly experience the double impact of the people factor.

When developing programs and services, the selection of personnel needs to be carefully integrated into the entire program package. Parents of young children may be influenced by the credentials of the camp staff and their look of maturity and responsibility; parents of older children may be looking for camp staff who they perceive as being able to amuse and entertain their children. The same is true of other recreational pursuits. Disney consistently employs people with a "wholesome, well-scrubbed look" to reinforce the image of family entertainment, and health clubs rarely hire people who are overweight or obviously out-of-shape as part of their staff.

While the personnel involved with a specific activity are relevant to the marketing process, the recreator must also be aware of the considerable influence of the other participants involved in the program or service. Who are these people? What do the participants have in common? How do they differ from one another? Will any of these similarities or differences impact upon participation patterns or attractions of specific target markets? Does age, skill level, or socioeconomic background make a difference in this particular instance?

Interpersonal behavior can and does play a role in the recreation experience. How much interaction is required with participation in this particular activity? This factor can be related to proximity of participation, the nature of the activity itself, and the nature of the participation. For instance, at a bowling center, participants would be in close proximity to people using the adjacent alley. Imagine placing a group of serious bowlers next to a young family interested in passing the time on a rainy day. Certainly the presence of both of these groups modify the experience of the others. However, when compared to membership in a health club where participants share locker and shower facilities with the same other people over an extended period of time, then the importance of intrapersonal behavior and attitude becomes quite significant. Service personnel in recreation facilities often find themselves managing user participation patterns so their behavior doesn't interfere with usage by others.

People make a difference in the recreation experience. Whether it be the service personnel who are physically present and involved when the participation takes place, or the presence and involvement of other users who may contribute or detract from the experience, this "P" called people is an outstanding feature of any recreational pursuit.

An additional "P" of marketing that is included as part of the peripherals of recreation marketing is termed *process* and *procedures*. This "P" most often relates to social and nonmonetary costs of participating in a program or service that are incurred due to the policies, procedures, rules, and regulations of a particular recreation delivery system. How do an organization's policies and procedures impact upon marketing?

Are people provided with information about the program or service over the phone, or must they come in person to receive that information? Can one register through the mail or pay by credit card? How far in advance are people allowed to make tee times or reserve court space? Can participants bring guests or nonresidents along with them? Must users provide identification each time they register or participate?

This "P" is one of those areas where the list of possibilities could be quite endless. In an effort to improve the efficiency and effectiveness of organizations, recreators often establish an extensive list of policies, procedures, rules, and regulations.   These well-intended factors can often substantially alter the experience of the recreation participant and in some instances create a social or nonmonetary price that may be too high to expend. Recreation delivery systems need to examine their policies and procedures with an eye for facilitating the participation by their target markets. Lovelock (1984) states that in the service sector, "the right way becomes as important as the right time or right place" (p. 31).

An additional category within the extra "Ps" of recreation marketing is *public image*. Like the ambience referred to in the "P" entitled physical environment, this factor is quite intangible. It relates generally to the perception both users and nonusers hold of a delivery system. In this way it is closely related to positioning but in this case the public image can be enhanced or changed through the *packaging* of one's program or service.

Due to the intangible and often abstract nature of recreation benefits and services, organizations need to strive to create a public image that reflects the nature and quality of the organization. Insurance companies that are plagued with a similar situation respond by making their service tangible through "giving people a piece of the rock" or "placing them under the umbrella." In a like manner, recreation delivery systems need to make their services as concrete as possible.

There are a number of techniques that could be utilized to address this situation (see Exhibits 7.1 and 7.2). The use of a logo or slogan or some combination of either could enhance an organization's tangibility. Club Med has been able to add meaning to its services by becoming "the antidote

Exhibit 7.1.
Sample Use of Logo

Logo utilized by the Edmonton, Alberta Parks and Recreation Department. Used by permission.

Exhibit 7.2.
Sample Use of a Mascot

"REX" short for Recreation, the mascot of the Wallingford, CT Recreation and Park Department making a guest appearance at the Annual Toddler Olympics.

for civilization." Sometimes organizations opt to use a mascot to make their service seem real. Certainly Mickey Mouse has come to stand for magic, family entertainment, and Disney.

Public image can consist of so many intangibles and unspoken ideas that can significantly impact upon the public's perception of an organization. A comprehensive tour package with an inexpensive price tag may send a message to potential users who may be concerned that the low cost of the trip translates into shoddy or unsafe transportation coupled with substandard accommodations. Likewise, promotional materials send additional image messages along with the primary message; the quality of programs or services offered by one's organization is suggested through the type of printing and the quality of the paper.

Public image is a substantive issue and concern for recreation delivery systems. They need to be concerned with their image among both users and nonusers. It is a factor that is often easily overlooked because it generally consists of intangibles or unspoken messages. However, effective utilization of this concept can translate into added marketing power for most organizations.

The final peripheral "P" to be addressed in this section is that of *political power.* Once thought to be solely the concern of public recreation agencies, this factor impacts upon all service delivery systems as they come under attack or receive accolades for how they conduct business. Organizations attempting to stem the tide of development and purchase additional open space areas for the purpose of preservation are the recipients of positive political clout as society turns its attention in the 1990s to environmental concerns. This same political shift may cause difficulty for ski areas and other recreational providers who come under close public and political scrutiny when applying to expand development and usage of national forest preserves in light of the current political climate.

Politics has an impact on all sectors of our society today and is not just limited to environmental issues. Public recreation organizations were changed following the passage of Proposition 13 and the accompanying anti-tax sentiment in the nation. Military recreation will face changes in light of the federal deficit and political changes in Eastern Europe. Non-profit organizations, especially YMCAs, are subject to political pressures as their nonprofit tax status is challenged by commercial organizations who maintain they represent unfair competition. Likewise, recreation delivery systems are able to use their political clout by amassing the support and action of groups of users or members who are able to collectively influence the political process on behalf of the agency or organization.

These five additional "Ps" of recreation marketing are not often found in marketing books or in the marketing handbooks of recreation delivery systems. However, their presence is real and their impact is extensive. With the increasing competition for the public's discretionary time and money, the battle over participants will grow and the ammunition will be found in the peripherals, those additional, often intangible "Ps" of recreation marketing, that subtly but surely influence participation patterns (see Figure 7.1).

Peripheral "Ps"	
Physical Evidence:	• Environment • Ambience • Tangible clues • The extras
Participants:	• Frontline staff • Other personnel • Other participants • Interrelatedness of contact
Process and Procedures:	• Registration procedures • Payment and refund policies • Guest usage • Advanced reservation procedures
Public Image:	• Users and nonusers • Slogan/mascot/logo • Type and quality of promotional materials
Political Impact:	• Current issues • Special interest groups

Figure 7.1.
Peripheral "Ps" of the Marketing Mix Variables for Leisure Delivery Systems

Role, Scope, and Importance of Customer Service

Peters and Waterman in their book *In Search of Excellence* focused America's attention upon the impact of service and rated service in this country as substandard. Since that time, customer service has become the buzzword of the day and the focal point of the future as recreation delivery systems, along with most other organizations in America, scramble to attempt to deal with this critical factor.

Parks, recreation, and leisure organizations are particularly reliant upon customer service. After all, participation in leisure activities is a voluntary activity, so consumers are not compelled to find the time and the money to participate in this activity. The advent of increased competition among types of activities and pursuits as well as with other delivery systems, all contribute to participants' emphasis upon customer service or the lack of it. An additional and most compelling factor is the realization that people intending to participate in a recreation activity often come to a facility or program badly in need of the "recreative" experience, and the last thing they need are additional problems as they attempt to fulfill this need.

Definition and Importance

Customer service can be simply defined as *meeting the needs of the user* or participant. Adequate customer service consists of conducting business in a timely and competent manner. Actual customers define high-quality service as meeting the following four criteria: *personal attention, dependability, promptness,* and *employee competence* (Zemke and Schaaf, 1989, p. 8).

Why is customer service so important? Good customer service relates to customer retention which translates into profit or loss for an organization. The Technical Assistance Research Programs Institute of Washington, DC found that one out of every four American customers is upset enough to stop doing business with a company and that 95 percent of these unhappy customers will switch companies rather than complain or fight for their rights (Zemke and Schaaf, 1989, p. 4). A study conducted by the Office of Consumer Affairs (Albrecht and Zemke, 1985, p. 6) revealed the following:

- The average business never hears from 96 percent of its unhappy customers, yet for every complaint received there are 26 other customers with problems, six of them serious.

- Fifty-four to seventy percent of complaining customers will do business with an organization again if a complaint is resolved, with the percentage rising to 95 percent if it is handled promptly.

- The average customer with a problem will tell 9 or 10 other people about the problem with the organization, and 13 percent of them will tell more than 20 people.

It is fairly clear that users, members, guests, or participants who are not having their needs met are taking their recreation and leisure participation elsewhere, which impacts upon an organization's viability. In addition, their unhappiness further contributes to loss of participation for the organization by their desire to tell other potential users of the poor treatment they received while doing business there.

Desatnick reports that it is five times more expensive for an organization to secure a new customer as it is to keep an old one (1987, p. 3). This reinforces the value of providing good customer service as part of regular practice, since the cost of advertising coupled with the difficulties in communicating with potential target markets make Desnatnick's findings important to park, recreation, and leisure delivery systems.

Organizational Components of Customer Service

In their book, *Service America: Doing Business in the New Economy,* Albrecht and Zemke cite the following three basic elements as cornerstones of customer service management, which they refer to as the service triangle: *a service strategy, customer-oriented frontline people,* and *a customer friendly system* (1985, p. 39).

Constructing this service triangle is not an easy task. If one looks at these three components, it appear as if customer service includes everything. SuperAmerica, a food service company cited by Zemke and Schaaf (1989), defines customer service from the customer's point of view as follows: "If you can see it, walk on it, hold it, hear it, step in it, smell it, carry it, step over it, touch it, use it, even taste it, if they can feel it or sense it, then It's Customer Service" (p. 333). Notice how similar this quote from SuperAmerica is to the peripherals cited in the additional "Ps" of recreation marketing.

The initial imperative is a well-conceived *strategy for service* that defines the recreation delivery system and serves as a unifying theme, slogan, or belief that guides all additional actions within the organization. It needs to be a simple, concise statement that is easily translated into policy, procedures, and practices.

For instance, Disney is most likely one of the undisputed leaders in the recreation and entertainment business. This organizations knows quite clearly that it stands for service to the customer in the way of providing wholesome enjoyment for all ages. Walt Disney's philosophy was very simple. Employees were there for the customer and every employee was in the entertainment business. This helps to explain why at Disney there are no customers, only guests. There are no employees, only cast members who wear costumes and who, when at work, are "on stage." Employees clearly know that they are part of the show and there to help the guests in any way possible.

Before embarking upon a customer service strategy, an organization needs to turn its mission statement into a clear-cut motto or slogan that accurately reflects what it is trying to accomplish for its customers. While the strategy planners get started, they might want to consider what they call these customers. Are the customers of public departments referred to as residents or taxpayers? Are employees enrolled in the corporate recreation club referred to as employees or members?

The strategy must underline the basic premise that the customer is number one and is the reason for the organization's existence. It is surprising just how many recreation delivery systems may forget that they exist for the user and that they would not be in business today if it was not for the customers.

Albrecht (1988, p. 134) suggests that in order for a service strategy to become a reality, an internal service triangle needs to be developed that encompasses elements of culture, leadership, and the organization.

The culture of the organization must be permeated with commitment to the customer. The culture must literally eat and breathe a customer-first orientation. In addition, the leadership of the organization must be designed in such a way as to empower the employees so that every employee can make instantaneous decisions and take immediate action when in the best interest of the customer. The final part of Albrecht's internal service triangle addresses the organization itself; he maintains that the organization needs to treat both customers and employees well, incorporating the premise that employees will treat customers as they are themselves treated.

The second component of the service triangle as developed by Albrecht and Zemke is the existence of *customer-oriented frontline people.* Naturally, the employee needs to be competent. However, customer-oriented employees are those who can "tune into the customer, assess the need, situation, and outlook and be response, attentive, and willing to help" (Albrecht, 1988, p. 33). In this day and age of shortages of labor in some parts of the country and shortages of motivated, well-trained employees in many parts of the country, this is not simple task.

Even though it is not a simple undertaking, it is nevertheless a significant one for any leisure delivery system. A Cambridge Report Survey reveals that peoples' perception of service includes personal attention, responsiveness, and politeness, and the customers think they know the service staff's attitude towards them (Zemke and Schaaf, 1989, pp. 17-18). Therefore, when a frontline service employee is chewing gum, looking bored, or taking personal phone calls while attending to a customer, the message is quite clear. The customer is not important and has perceived that without the employee or the organization telling them that.

The attitude of frontline personnel can be critical to a delivery system. A SuperAmerica manager mentioned in *The Service 101* was reported to have posted the following under the heading, "Why Customers Quit Shopping at a Place of Business":

1 percent—Die
3 percent—Move away
5 percent—Start buying from someone they know
9 percent—Find a more competitive price
14 percent—Are dissatisfied with the product
68 percent—Are dissatisfied with the ATTITUDE of a company
          employee
_____
100 percent
(Zemke and Schaaf, 1989, p. 333)

If the attitude and performance of frontline personnel are so important to a leisure delivery system, how then does one ensure quality in this area? Desatnick (1987, p. 72) believes that organizations desiring to build customer-oriented work forces must emphasize that priority from the very beginning and must take steps to ensure that employees realize that their job security is dependent upon the organization's ability to satisfy its customers. He maintains that creating a customer-oriented workforce is a full-time process and suggests that "the process starts with establishing clear corporate values of service superiority, then proceeds to recruit and hire people who share those values and, finally, continually reinforces those values from the first day of orientation all the way to the retirement party" (p. 74).

The recreator needs to examine the personnel practices of the organization from start to finish. What is the wording and tone of its job announcements? Disney is quite clear that it is looking for friendly and enthusiastic cast members to become a part of the show.

How are prospective employees selected? Many organizations have found that interviews conducted by people currently in frontline positions are better mechanisms for selecting people who will share the organization's culture and value system. Desatnick (1987, p. 36) recommends a patterned interview focused upon behavioral characteristics. This patterned interview, which allows the candidate to talk more than 70 percent of the time, is structured to reveal behavioral characteristics such as communication skills, decision making, problem solving, and other characteristics that constitute a good service orientation.

A logical progression in this process would be substantial time and attention devoted to an employee's orientation program as a vehicle for welcoming the employee into the organization, instilling the culture and values of the organization, as well as providing the employee with the training necessary to carry out the job responsibilities. It is important to note that training should not end with the completion of orientation, and that the outstanding organization places a great deal of emphasis on continual training of its employees throughout their employment with the organization.

Placing enthusiastic, well-trained personnel into frontline positions is a natural start to this process of having customer-oriented frontline employees, but there are additional steps that should be taken to ensure this component of service management. Employees require feedback. They need to know exactly what it is they should be doing, what the standards of performance are, and how they are measuring up against these standards.

This involves ongoing research and evaluation. Effective guidelines for such measurement include utilization of both qualitative and quantitative data that are collected frequently, with the results shared in a useful, employee-friendly, visible manner (Zemke and Schaaf, 1989, p. 55). Employees need to know exactly what is expected of them, and these expectations can be translated into service procedures that can then be measured. The results of these measurements must be shared with employees to enable them to utilize the results and make improvements within their areas.

A final component to this part of the process which is recommended by most authors writing about customer service management relates to employee motivation. When feelings are involved in job performance as they are in frontline customer-service positions, employees often suffer contact overload, which is characterized by apathy, fatigue, tension, and irritability (Albrecht, 1988, p. 111). Dealing with people on a regular basis and doing one's best to meet their needs is a highly charged, emotional challenge that can result in some of the aforementioned syndromes. Organizations need to recognize contact overload and develop techniques to address it.

Maintaining the motivation and morale for service management employees should be an ongoing process. How can one keep employees interested and committed to the customer? There are a variety of contests, awards, and methods of recognition and achievement that can be utilized, such as employee of the month, job rotation, employee social events and parties, which are used effectively in a number of organizations.

However, Albrecht suggests that quality of worklife is crucial to maintaining high quality, motivated, frontline employees. He cites such factors as a worthwhile job, safe and secure working conditions, adequate pay and benefits, job security, competent supervision, feedback on performance, opportunity for growth, advancement on merit, positive social climate, and fair play (p. 169).

An important concept that needs to be integrated within this section on creating customer-oriented frontline personnel is the role of management in this process. Albrecht (1988, p. 20) maintains that there is no longer a need for a customer services department within an organization because it is everyone's job. Every employee within a recreation delivery system, even if the employee is not primarily responsible for serving the member or the participant as would be the case with management personnel, is in the business of customer service.

Albrecht and Zemke (1985, p. 105) point out that if "your job is not serving the customer, then you'd better be serving someone who is." In a service organization such as a parks, recreation, and leisure organization, the role of management is to support, encourage, and facilitate the performance of the frontline personnel in their quest to serve the customer.

The last component of the service management triangle refers to the creation of a *customer-friendly system*. This refers to a recreation delivery system that thinks people-first and attempts to devise a system that is convenient, accessible, and pleasant for the recreation user as opposed to what might be easiest for the organization itself.

Although there are any number of techniques that could be utilized in the modification of an organization to ensure that it is customer-friendly, the following represent broad parameters to be considered: fulfilling user *needs*, adapting *cycle of service,* and *empowering employees* to ensure customer satisfaction.

Fulfilling the needs of the user or participant relates to marketing decisions regarding the service package. A recreation delivery system needs to carefully decide which *core benefits* the user is seeking and at the same time determine which *peripherals* (or those smaller, often intangible extra "Ps" of marketing) that the participant may be seeking. Albrecht and Zemke (1985, p. 80) maintain that these benefits should not be a hodge-podge of extras, but a carefully developed package of peripherals which they believe become key factors to customers once the core benefits have been met. In order to develop a customer-friendly system, it must meet both the core and peripheral benefits being sought by the target market.

A second element of a customer-friendly system is the identification and modification of the *cycle of service.* Cycle of service refers to that continuous chain of events that a customer goes through as he or she consumes the service (Albrecht, 1988, p. 33). It is of value to recognize that recreation participants, club members, or guests at a resort do not visualize a chain of command or a departmentalization of an organization. Rather, they envision a rather natural pattern of recreational participation or usage.

A recreation organization needs to visualize this cycle of service as a repeatable sequence of events in which various people try to meet the needs and expectations of the guest or participant. Albrecht and Zemke (1985, pp. 33-38) recommend attempting to discover each critical moment of the service cycle by identifying all small episodes and drawing a diagram of the repeatable cycle (see Figure 7.2).

It is vital to this identification that every small episode be included in the diagram, because each time a participant comes into contact with any aspect of the organization it impacts upon the user's perception of the quality of the program and service and the organization as well. Jan Carlson, the president of Scandinavian Airlines, calls these small episodes of contact with an organization "moments of truth" (Albrecht and Zemke, 1985, p. 27). The system of a recreation organization can best be analyzed in light of service and convenience for the user or participant by examining each of the moments of truth associated with the facility or organization. An analysis of these moments of truth could include the initial phone contact with the organization up until the time a participant completes a 10-week program with the agency.

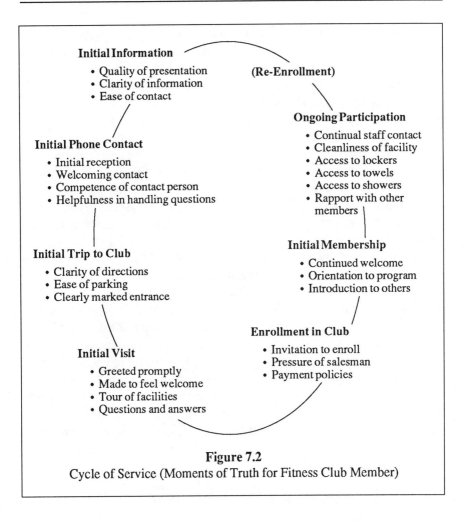

Figure 7.2
Cycle of Service (Moments of Truth for Fitness Club Member)

In the course of examining the cycle of service that has been developed through the compilation of moments of truth, the role and importance of the employee again comes into play. It is clear that the service cycle and moments of truth are heavily dependent upon the attitude, performance, and action of frontline personnel. *Employees* must be *empowered* to solve problems, make decisions, and take action to *make things rights for the customer,* which can be referred to as *directed autonomy* (Zemke and Schaaf, 1989, pp. 57-58).

Since most delivery systems are organized by departments or according to function, there is virtually no one person assigned to ensuring that the service cycle is effective and satisfying for the participant. Therefore, the recreator needs to allow employees the flexibility to ensure this satisfaction. An additional factor related to ensuring customer satisfaction is the fact that it is virtually impossible to entirely systematize a service because a service is not actually created until it is consumed by different people in varying circumstances. Frontline employees need to be allowed and furthermore encouraged to make modifications that result in meeting the needs and expectations of the recreation consumer.

A leisure delivery system does not exist or would be unable to continue its existence without its members, users, guests, or clients. The recreation customer, regardless of what he or she is referred to, is the central core of every recreation organization and it is imperative for the delivery system to integrate this fact into practice. The recreation customer is the reason for an organization's existence and is of great value to the delivery system.

Stew Leonard, the now-famous owner of the "Disney" of dairy stores in Norwalk, CT, suggests that organizations look at customers as an *asset* whose value grows over time. For instance, Leonard estimates that each of his grocery customers is worth $100,000 to him, or $100 worth of expenditures per week at 50 weeks a year over a 10-year period (Zemke and Schaaf, 1989, p. 317). This philosophy and perception of the customer has enabled Stew Leonard's Dairy to become ten times more successful than other grocery operations. The same transition is required for recreation delivery systems. A user should not be viewed as just one person who happened not to get the court-time reservation he or she wanted, but rather as an asset of the organization that spells participation and revenues over a substantial time period.

Customer Care–The Cutting, Competitive Edge

Regardless of what one calls it, customer service is important. Albrecht and Zemke referred to it as service management, while Peters and Waterman started it all with their reference to "the smell of the customer" in *In Search of Excellence: To smell your customer* is to know them thoroughly, and to be so close to them that you are able to meet their needs and expectations as a matter of course.

However, customer service cannot be considered just an extra that an organization chooses to provide, nor can it be considered a satisfactory way to conduct business. Tom Peters, in the foreword of *The Service Edge—101 Companies that Profit from Customer Care,* states that "superb service is becoming a requirement for survival in our fragmenting, fast-changing, quality-conscious, and ever more competitive markets" (Zemke and Schaaf, 1989, p. xi).

If customer service was the buzzword of the 1980s, then *customer care* will be the cutting, competitive edge for the 1990s and beyond as we shift to a service-based economy. Customer care differs from customer service because customer care refers to organizations who practice superb, high-quality service that is customized to enhance the expectations of those they serve.

Why customer care? Can it possibly be worth the resources required to implement such a practice? The Strategic Planning Institute of Cambridge, Massachusetts, through its computerized PIMS (Profit Impact of Marketing Strategy), found that businesses practicing *high quality customer service* differed from companies with below-average service in that they:

(a) charge 9 to 10 percent more for their service;
(b) grow twice as fast;
(c) increase market share by 6 percent per year as opposed to a loss of 2 percent per year; and
(d) have an average return on sales of 12 percent versus 1 percent (Zemke and Schaaf, 1989, p. 8)

Customer care, a high quality approach to customer service, enables these successful organizations to increase market share, growth rate, and profitability. It will certainly be the competitive watchword of the future.

Albrecht and Zemke describe service management as a transformational concept that is "so conceptually simple but given the monolithic resistance to change displayed by most organizations, it is almost always a tall order" (1985, p. 30). It has been demonstrated to be a difficult and challenging concept to introduce, implement, and integrate into an organization. Yet there are a number of organizations from a wide variety of service ventures, such as travel, health care, food services, entertainment, and hotels, which have succeeded by profiting from customer care and superb customer service.

Albrecht, in his book, *At America's Service,* reviewed the process and procedures of a number of outstanding customer service organizations, which he refers to as the *champions,* and devised a list of suggestions that reflect how those champion businesses go about creating and continuing outstanding customer service as follows:

- Have basics down pat
- Believe quality drives profit
- Know the customers
- Focus on MOTs (moments of truth)
- Have a "whatever it takes" attitude
- Recover skillfully
- Support service people
- Have management viewed as help
- Care about employees

(Albrecht, 1988, p. 38)

A recreation delivery system could review this list developed by Albrecht in light of its current or proposed service management process. Areas could be identified as contributing to the success of the customer care program with concerted effort made to continue in this direction. Suggestions that are not currently being implemented or utilized could be developed by the organization.

One of the most complete overviews of service organizations that operate on the cutting edge with customer care is *The Service Edge-101 Companies that Profit from Customer Care,* by Zemke and Schaaf (1989). The authors provide the reader with an overview of guiding principles for customer care, but also detail specific practices utilized by outstanding businesses in travel, hotels, health care, entertainment, food service, and public service, that have applications for the variety of delivery systems in parks, recreation, and leisure.

The first guiding principle offered by these authors is to *listen, understand, and respond to the customer* (Zemke and Schaaf, 1989, p. 29). What does this mean for parks, recreation and leisure? How can these organizations structure themselves in such a manner that they are so close to the customer that they can truly have a feel for the customer's needs and expectations and respond to them?

Some of these approaches simply involve regular review and implementation of elements of the marketing process. How is the target market changing? Are some of these changes reflected in differences in needs and wants of one's users? An organization cannot expect to remain stagnant in the provision of its services in light of ongoing changes in interests and expectations of recreation participants.

One of the techniques recommended by customer service experts is *recovery.* A focus upon recovery assumes that something will go wrong and provides a mechanism for frontline personnel to make things right for the customer. Working to normalize relations with a dissatisfied or unhappy user is one of the most important activities to be undertaken by a service provider and includes the following five ingredients: apology, urgent reinstatement, empathy, symbolic atonement, and follow-up (Zemke and Schaaf, 1989, pp. 22-25).

The process of recovery is an organized approach to enable frontline personnel to deal with those problems that are certain to arise. The first step is to apologize to the user in a sincere manner, and to follow this with the urgent reinstatement. It is important that employees relay to the unhappy user that they also share the user's sense of urgency regarding the resolution of this problem and that they are genuinely interested and intent upon doing so.

The emphasis is upon treating the person first, then the problem. The fourth step in the recovery process is symbolic atonement, which involves offering some type of goodwill gesture that indicates that the organization would like to make this problem or inconvenience up to the user. This cycle of recovery is completed with the follow-up, whereby the employee or the organization checks back with the user following the incident to ensure their satisfaction with the outcome.

How can a delivery system truly come to understand the moments of truth as experienced by its participants or members? Organizations need to listen closely to their customers, and this can be accomplished through such market research techniques as focus groups, surveys, service audits, and utilization of the mystery guest technique.

The organization should not overlook information gathered by its frontline personnel. While an official complaint and comment mechanism can be introduced, frontline personnel should be monitored for information they have secured related to users needs, wants, and problem areas.

The second operating principle identified by Zemke and Schaaf (1989) is the *definition of superior service and development of service strategy* (p. 37). Does the delivery system have a statement of service intent that differentiates the organization from its competition and has value from the perspective of its users? Are all members of the organization–management, frontline personnel, and users alike–aware of exactly what it is the organization intends to accomplish for its participants? Zemke and Schaaf (1989, p. 43) suggest that there are different approaches to this communication: cascading and cloning.

A *cascading communication* is a simple, highly detailed message that flows from one unit to another. Five years ago, the Foothills Metropolitan Recreation and Park District in Colorado repositioned itself as a park and recreation provider that facilitates wellness for its participants. The organization accomplished this by developing a six-point definition of wellness and specifying how different departments would integrate this concept into their ongoing services. On the other hand, Club Med practices a cloning form of communication, in which a simple service message, such as its "antidote to civilization," can be interpreted by the individual clubs, with their diversity in target markets, programs, and natural resources, as they see fit.

Zemke and Schaaf (1989, p. 47) introduce a third operating principle for customer care that includes *setting standards and measuring performance.* Does the recreation delivery system decide service expectations for the organization and establish standards related to those standards? Has the recreator determined exactly what service components are to be measured and implemented a plan to measure them accurately and frequently using a variety of different methods? These procedures will be examined more completely in the chapter on market research. This principle reflects the belief cited earlier that employees in service organizations perform more effectively when they know very specifically what is expected of them and are then informed on a regular basis in a nonthreatening manner of their performance on these standards.

The next principle established by Zemke and Schaaf (1989, p. 58) is to *select, train, and empower employees to work for the customer.* It is maintained that the ultimate success or failure of a service organization depends upon what happens between the customers and the frontline people. Selection and training are naturally key components related to this principle, as well as the recreator's recognition of the stress related to continual frontline, customer-oriented employment. Disney employs a practice of allowing frontline employees to take a time-out and go backstage when they feel the need to do so. This seemingly small technique would be a boon for recreational delivery systems where an overtired or distracted employee could contribute to a problem or a less-than-satisfactory exchange with a user or participant.

The final operating principle for superb service management or customer care is to *recognize and reward accomplishment* (Zemke and Schaaf, 1989, p. 70). This principle recognizes that customer care is an ongoing process that must be practiced seven days a week for 52 weeks a year, every year. Recognition involves a means of acknowledging employees for their continued practice of customer care or for a specific incident of outstanding customer care. This can involve anything from seemingly casual time and interest on the part of management to full-blown celebrations of people and

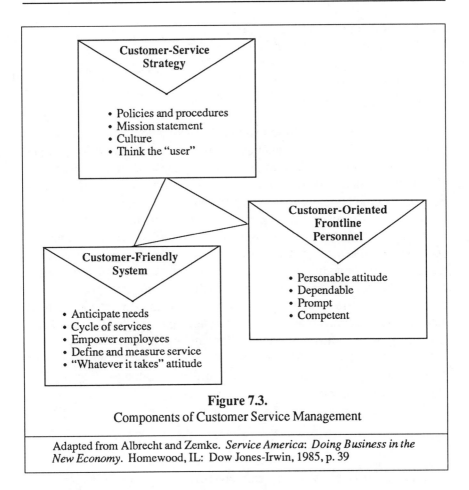

Figure 7.3.
Components of Customer Service Management

Adapted from Albrecht and Zemke. *Service America: Doing Business in the New Economy.* Homewood, IL: Dow Jones-Irwin, 1985, p. 39

positive incidents. The recognition/rewards can be both symbolic as well as tangible, such as pay for performance incentives, which are more easily utilized in the private sectors than in public organizations (Figure 7.3).

Customer Service to Customer Care: The Choice of the Organization

It is important to recognize that every recreation delivery system is practicing some level of service to its users or participants, whether it is making a concerted effort to do so or not. Albrecht (1988, p. 11) suggests that there are five different levels of service:

1. Going out of business
2. Dogged pursuit of mediocrity
3. Present and accounted for
4. Making a serious effort
5. Service as an art form

The choice is entirely up to the recreation organization. The effort or lack of effort expended by an organization will relate to the organization's success and viability. It will impact upon the agency's market share and ability to maintain or increase this factor, as well as the financial performance and ultimately the success or failure of the organization.

Each participant or member is an asset for the organization. They represent not only continued participation and revenue over an extended period of time, but also serve as spokespersons for the organization by either recommending or warning friends and acquaintances about their treatment and experiences with the organization. In the long run, it is more efficient as well as more effective to implement a service management approach. A general rule of thumb regarding customer service is that "it takes 12 pluses to make up for 1 minus in service" (Albrecht and Zemke, 1985, p. 79). A proactive approach to customer service by recreation delivery systems appears to be the most cost effective and the most competitively sound approach to undertake.

Summary

Recreation and leisure programs and services are activities and experiences that are consumed as opposed to purchased. Since participants partake directly in the process, the elements of the marketing mix need to be expanded to include additional "Ps" of service marketing: physical evidence, participants, process and procedures, public image, and political impact. The role and scope of these peripheral Ps need to be addressed by park, recreation, and leisure delivery systems.

An overriding concern of service marketing is customer service. Customer service may be simply defined as meeting the needs of the user. Recreation and leisure delivery systems can address this concern by focusing upon factors inherent within the cornerstones of customer service management, which include a service strategy, customer-oriented frontline people, and a customer-friendly system.

Attention to the peripheral "Ps" of service marketing and implementation of customer service management will enable recreation and leisure delivery systems to confront this new and very real area of competition for the 1990s.

Suggested Activities

1. Select a park, recreation, or leisure delivery system and conduct an audit of the peripheral "Ps" of service marketing.

2. Assume the role of a recreation participant in a delivery system and construct a cycle of service by enumerating the moments of truth for the user.

3. Visit a delivery system with which you are not currently familiar and assume the role of a user. Attempt to ascertain the customer service strategy and suggest recommendations for improvement.

4. Develop standards of service and measurement for one phase of a recreation or leisure delivery system.

5. Examine the personnel policies and practices of a park, recreation, or leisure delivery system. Suggest modifications related to improving customer service in the areas of recruitment, selection, and training.

6. Identify three common customer problem areas within a delivery system. Construct role play exercises that frontline employees could utilize to handle recovery situations.

References

Albrecht and Zemke (1985). *Service America: Doing Business in the New Economy.* Homewood, IL: Dow Jones-Irwin.

Desatnick, R. L. (1987). *Managing to Keep the Customer.* San Francisco, CA: Jossey-Bass.

Desatnick, R. L. (1987, March). Building the Customer-Oriented Work Force. *Training and Development Journal,* p. 72.

Lovelock, C. H. (1984). *Service Marketing.* Englewood Cliffs, NJ: Prentice-Hall.

Zemke, R. and Schaaf, D. (1989). *The Service Edge: 101 Companies That Profit From Customer Care.* New York, NY: New American Library.

Chapter Eight

Strategic Marketing Planning

Common Concerns for Parks, Recreation, and Leisure Delivery Systems

- A community center requires extensive renovations and the department considers various space utilization plans to address the future needs of the community.

- A MWR department explores future management directions based upon changing enlistment patterns and government policies.

- An urban YMCA questions its viability over the next 20 years due to changing demographic projections.

- A resort considers repositioning itself as a "family" place and wonders about the long-range implications of such a move.

While there are a multitude of uses for marketing within leisure delivery systems, one application that is especially critical to the future and ongoing viability of such organizations is strategic marketing planning. *Strategic marketing planning* enables organizations to identify their *unique strengths* and to *build strategies* for the future on that basis. It provides a mechanism for *understanding* and *cooperation* among members of an organization to shape a *vision* for a *preferred future* by fostering an *action plan for today that addresses the needs of tomorrow.*

What can strategic market planning do for park, recreation, or leisure delivery systems? This type of planning differs from other, more traditional approaches to planning in a number of ways. Its unique focus upon the customer, along with its identification and inclusion of factors within the environment, make it a more comprehensive and useful method for ongoing management of a delivery system.

Strengths and weaknesses of the organization can be isolated while identifying *opportunities and threats* facing the agency currently and in the future. With this SWOT approach to planning (strengths, weaknesses, opportunities, and threats), an organization can make the most of its resources today while simultaneously preparing for the future.

Strategic market planning through the SWOT approach focuses upon "doing the right thing" as opposed to "doing things right." Tom Peters in his book, *Thriving on Chaos-A Handbook for a Management Revolution,* states that "Managers do things right. Leaders do the right thing."

There is a significant difference between these two phrases as they relate to the continued viability and success of a park, recreation, or leisure delivery system. A community park and recreation department serving dual-career and single-parent households may be running its summer playgrounds correctly in terms of hiring quality staff and scheduling appropriate activities and may be puzzled as to why the playground programs are not well attended. While the department may be running the playgrounds correctly, it may not be doing the right thing in view of the family composition of the community. Strategic planning would enable the department to examine the changing family structure and modify its services to offer more structured summer programs or day camps for these children, who require more structure and supervision than is inherent within traditional playgrounds.

An additional benefit of the strategic planning process is its involvement of all members of the organization. Due to the nature of the process, it lends itself to input and feedback from people employed in all phases and levels of the operation. This involvement contributes to the completeness of the process and enhances the acceptance of changes required as an outcome of the process.

Steps in the Strategic Market Planning Process

The corporate sector embarks upon the strategic market planning process by undertaking the following:

(a) analyzing current performance and identifying future opportunities and threats,

(b) determining organization's mission and objectives,

(c) setting objectives and developing strategies for each organizational unit, and

(d) modifying/managing mission and strategies to achieve organization's overall and unit objectives

(Cravens, 1982, p. 15)

This same process can be adapted for utilization by parks, recreation, and leisure delivery systems.

The first phase of this process consists of a situational analysis whereby the organization examines both internal and external factors impacting upon the organization overall and for each of its subunits. These designations of subunits would vary for each organization, but may be similar to existing program or cost centers such as community centers, golf courses, stadiums, youth programs, and so on.

This situational analysis process consists of three components: *environmental scanning, market assessment,* and *organizational inventory,* which together lead to the desired outcome of identifying *strategic advantages and goals* for the delivery system (Anthony, 1984, pp. 12-16). These three phases enable the leisure delivery system to address factors both within and outside of its control and to focus upon the people it serves or wishes to attract to its organization. It accomplishes this while utilizing and building upon the unique resources of the organization (see Figure 8.1).

The first phase in the process is termed environmental scanning. *Environmental scanning* requires that the organization look at factors and forces in the environment, those outside influences which are beyond the control of the agency. The organization would identify factors and forces

Figure 8.1.
Steps in the Strategic Marketing Process

in the environment under the following categories: economic, legal/ political, sociodemographic, technological, and competitive (Anthony, 1984, pp. 12-16). Each of these subcategories would be further broken down and labelled as being an *opportunity* or a *threat* for the agency. Current factors within each of these categories are identified, with an attempt made to project trends or directions for each of these within the next 5 to 10 years (see Figure 8.2 and Exhibit 8.1).

Economic factors involved in the environmental scanning portion of this process would include such things as rate of employment, prime rate, inflation, and any factors that could reflect upon the costs of operation for the organization as well as the discretionary income and spending patterns of user groups. For instance, a high unemployment rate could be perceived as an opportunity, with a sizeable number of people having time for recreation and leisure. However, this same factor could translate into lack of money to participate in recreation pursuits.

Legal/political factors present an interesting category. In this instance, legal refers to actual laws with potential impact, while political refers to those less formal influences within the environment. For instance, Proposition 13 and Proposition 2 1/2 were laws passed in California and Massachusetts. However, the political impact of taxpayers'unrest spread to other states across the country informally without the actual passage of legislation that impacted significantly upon public park and recreation agencies.

OPPORTUNITIES		THREATS

Economic
(income, inflation, interest rates)

Legal/Political
(laws, special interests)

Technological
(computers, medical advances)

Sociodemographics
(age, gender, marital status)

Competition
(other agencies/products)

Figure 8.2.
Factors Within Environmental Scanning

Adapted from Anthony, "Effective Strategic Planning." *The Nonprofit World Report*, July-August, 1984.

Exhibit 8.1.
Environmental Scanning for Calgary, Canada
Parks and Recreation Department

Marketing Strategy for 1988-1989

ENVIRONMENTAL FACTORS

Economic
- Calgary has been in a general recession for the last three to four years.
- There is an increasingly competitive marketplace for all companies in the recreation and sport field.
- Private sector recreation and sport facilities and businesses are going out of business.
- If dollars were spent wisely on surveys, needs assessments, and advertising, many would still be in business today.

Political
- The annual Department budget is decreasing each year.
- An increasing demand for greater accountability and better recovery rates on programs and facilities.
- Public demand for lower yearly tax increases.

Social and Cultural
- Lifestyles are constantly changing with less reliance on the public sector.
- The family unit is changing with more single parent households and working mothers.
- General demographics indicate that Calgary is becoming an aging population.
- "Participation" has increased the awareness of sport and recreation in the minds of the general public; this in turn, has increased the need for the delivery of a variety of related activities.

Technology
- Computerization is making many of Calgary Parks and Recreation procedures more efficient. Need still exists, however, for computerized procedures that *directly* impact the public (i.e., registration for Summer In The City).
- Technology, through the development of time-saving devices, has given the average Canadian more time to spend on leisure-time activities.

Source: Calgary Parks and Recreation Department's Strategic Marketing Plan, Fall 1987, pp. 10-11.

A third category within environmental scanning is *technological* influences or changes. Technology is an area that can be critical to the identification of changes in today's world. These changes can present both opportunities and threats to leisure delivery systems, which can be organizationally specific or more global in nature with implications for changes in work and lifestyle.

For instance, the advent of computerization within organizations can spell opportunities for improving services through more efficient systemization of registration procedures or maintenance schedules. However, this same technology changes the way Americans live, work, and play. The advent of cable television and VCRs has given rise to people who stay within their homes and the creation of "couch potatoes," a term unheard of 10 years ago.

Employment shifts from the industrial to the service sector may influence the types of benefits participants are seeking from recreation and leisure experiences. Will people working with computers all day long feel an increased interest in socialization? After a full day of dealing with people, will service workers need to relax in more isolated ways? These changes brought about by technology can pose either a threat or an opportunity for delivery systems, based upon the timely manner in which organizations identify and address these changes.

While technology will provide an array of opportunities and threats for leisure delivery systems, the same is true of changes inherent within the category of *sociodemographics*. Sociodemographics can include a host of different factors and influences (see Exhibit 8.2). Within this area, such things as the aging of the population, the rise of two-career couples, changing marital patterns, and the increase in minority populations will all influence the role and direction of leisure delivery systems in the future. A resort electing to attract adults and senior citizens to its facilities could perceive these changes as being opportunities for the organization, rather than threats to it. Morale, Welfare, and Recreation units of the military recognizing the changing employment and marital roles among their enlisted personnel could capitalize on this change by providing on-base daycare and recreation opportunities to accommodate the needs of working families.

An examination of the aforementioned factors would not be complete unless the delivery system addressed the potential impact of *competition* to their organization. The organization needs to identify specific competitors and the nature of that competition. Key questions that need to be addressed

Exhibit 8.2.
Demographic Changes
Edmonton, Alberta Parks and Recreation Department

Demographic Changes

Likely the most important change in the environment since 1985 is the aging of the baby boom population. As is the trend across Canada, Edmonton's population is getting older. Between 1976 and 1986 the 65 and older age groups increased from 32,940 to 44,972 and an 8 percent share of the total population. By 1989 it is projected this figure will increase by another percentage point for an additional 8,708 persons and will continue to increase. By 2001 seniors will comprise 11.7 percent of Edmonton's population (79,550 persons).[6] Note that the elderly of the future will differ financially from the elderly of 1987.

Other age distribution changes of note are declining numbers in the 10-29 age group and increasing numbers in the 30+ age categories (except 50-54). There has been a slight increase in the 0-4 age group over the last three years.

For example, day hiking, canoeing and cross-country skiing peaks between the ages of 35 and 44 and then declines with increasing age. Other sports activities likely to decline because of an increasing age barrier include baseball, hockey, aerobics and fitness, racquetball, jogging or running and downhill skiing. Conversely, participation rates for curling, fishing, golfing, hunting, picnicking and walking for pleasure increases in the older age categories.

Changing birth rates impact the department initially with altered market size for child activities. Edmonton's marriage rate has dropped from a high of 11.7/1,000 persons in 1971 to 9.4/1,000 in 1984. This social phenomenon has been accompanied with declining fertility and birth rates. The 1966 fertility rate was 97.0/1,000; by 1984 it had dropped to 68.2/1,000.

The live birth rate in 1966 was 22.0/1,000, dropping to 16-17/1,000 between 1972 and 1980, and then increasing slightly again in 1982 and 1983 to 19.5 The result was a decline in the 0-4 year old population and an increase in 1986 compared to 1983.

In the ten-year period between 1971 and 1982 the number of single parent families increased from 11,345 to 17,305. Single parent families comprised 14.6 percent of the total number of Edmonton families (134,540) in 1982

The average number of persons per family, as well as the average number of children per family has been dropping during the past two decades. In 1971 there was an average of 1.7 children/family and an average of 3.6 persons/family. These figures dropped to 1.2 and 3.1, respectively, by 1981. Municipal recreation agencies are often perceived to be only providers of children's activities.[7]

In addition to the trend of today's families comprising fewer children is the disappearance of the traditional female "homemaker." In 1971 one in three Canadian households consisted of the wife staying at home with the children. By 1981 only one in five fit this traditional image; analysis predict that even fewer women will remain in the home in the future. This will have impacts upon the scheduling of activities and availability of customers for 'family' markets.

Source: Edmonton Parks and Recreation Department's Marketing Plan for 1988-1990, pp. 7-8.

during this part of the process include such considerations as the strengths and weaknesses of these competitors, and an identification of how they compete on such things as costs and fees, access to clients, image, and type of client base (Anthony, 1984, pp. 12-16).

For instance, a community recreation department might identify a local YMCA as a competitor, while the YMCA might include commercial fitness clubs as its competition. It is important to recognize that competition need not always be specific organizations, but could also be products provided by technology, such as cable television, pay-for-view, or home fitness equipment.

The outcome of this first phase of strategic market planning would result in a comprehensive list of opportunities and threats to the leisure delivery system. It is important to note that some factors may indeed pose an opportunity and a threat concurrently. An overriding premise of this phase of the process is that most factors and influences are no longer threats once they are identified. The actual identification of a threat before it becomes operational can actually be utilized as an opportunity for the organization by adapting to the situation and incorporating those adaptations into the ongoing direction and operation of the agency.

Market Assessment–The Second Phase

The second phase of strategic market planning is the market assessment. The *market assessment* is actually a *participant profile,* which is another reason for the importance and value of strategic market planning to recreation delivery systems. Park, recreation, and leisure organizations deal with people. As such, recreators need to give substantial attention and focus to these people and this phase of the process facilitates that attention.

Market assessment requires that the organization look at its participants in a variety of ways. It is of value to identify and address changes and projected changes of the people one serves in the following areas: demographics, lifestyles, motivation, and program/service expectations (Anthony, 1984, pp. 12-16).

This process is significantly enhanced when the organization examines these factors over a period of time. It is recommended that leisure delivery systems identify these key factors for past, current, and future participants or users to view changes in perspective and to better hypothesize future changes and directions.

A natural starting point for the market assessment is to identify clearly and concisely the specific dimensions of one's current markets or participants. These participant dimensions could then be examined in light of demographics. This information, coupled with current U. S. Census Bureau projections and other sources of trend analysis, would facilitate the projections related to this category for the next 5 to 10 years. How will the demographics of the people served change? Will they be older? Will recreators see more women and minorities? Will there be more singles? Will they have more or less discretionary income to expend? These are all areas for discussion and projection.

The identification of demographic changes, then, provides a basis for pinpointing current lifestyle profiles and suggesting future directions in this area, which is crucial to the provision of leisure services. How much time do current participants have for recreation? How much effort are they willing to expend? How does their current family or lifestyle situation impact upon their usage of the organization's programs and services?

These are all areas that need to be explored by the organization with an objective of identifying ways in which lifestyle patterns may change in the immediate and distant future and how these patterns will impact upon the programs and services offered by the organization. For instance, will the pattern of women's involvement in the work force continue or abate? Will the trend for inner-directedness change recreational patterns? Will commuting patterns, which have impacted upon the programs and services of many park and recreation organizations, change? Will technology and the movement to working at home cause a change in these patterns within the next five years?

If demographics and lifestyles are areas that make an impact upon a recreation delivery system, then motivation is certainly a consideration. Will people be making trips to resorts for total escape and relaxation, or will they be looking for socialization or the status associated with certain kinds of trips? Will parents be looking for quality leisure experiences for their children during the summer months, or actually seeking dependable avenues for daycare?

The suggestions compiled through examination of motivation for programs and services will naturally impact upon service expectations, the final heading under this category. Program and service expectations reflect the changes identified for demographics, lifestyle, and motivational influences previously noted. Does the recreator need to change the hours at the fitness club? Do organizations need to address the amusement of teenagers being taken on vacations with their families?

The market assessment of the customer/member/user/participant profile enables the organization to identify and visualize changes and influences that may substantially impact upon the recreational needs and patterns of the organization's current target markets. It also affords the organization the opportunity to conceptualize these changes prior to the demand for them, which can enhance the continued viability of a delivery system or present it with new market opportunities (see Figure 8.3).

Factors	Yesterday	Today	Tomorrow
Demographics (age, gender, income, etc.)			
Lifestyles (psychographics, patterns)			
Motivation (belonging, socialization, etc.)			
Program/Service Expectations (price, amenities, etc.)			

Figure 8.3.
Market Assessment/Participant Profile

Adapted from Anthony, "Effective Strategic Planning." *The Nonprofit World Report*, July-August, 1984.

Organizational Inventory–The Third Phase

The third phase in the strategic market planning process is the *organizational inventory.* At this juncture, the delivery system has examined two important areas: the environment or impact of outside factors, and participants' profiles. The next logical step is the analysis of strengths and weaknesses of the organization itself, which is exactly the purpose of the organizational inventory.

The organizational inventory focuses upon developing a balance sheet for the organization by taking an inventory of both the strengths or assets of the organization as well as any weaknesses or problem areas. Areas examined in this step include such factors as personnel, physical facilities, equipment, location, cash, and other assets such as reputation, special products/services, markets served, or market position (Anthony, 1984, pp. 12-16).

The organization would develop a list of its resources and then designate each of those resources as a strength or a weakness. The organization needs to objectively identify *what it does well* as well as honestly assessing *problem areas*. It is imperative when developing this list of resources to bear in mind that an organizational inventory needs to address all of its resources, both tangible and intangible. The location of a facility is a tangible resource, while the reputation or market position of the organization is an intangible factor. Each of these factors may be deemed as being positive or negative for the delivery system.

It is also important to note that an identified current strength may require modification based upon future changes and influences in order to remain a strength. Each weakness identified does not necessarily mean that the organization must improve upon it, once identified. For instance, just because a commercial fitness club does not particularly appeal to families with small children as well as the local YMCA, does not necessarily mean that the fitness center should take steps to attract children or families.

The organizational inventory is the final step in this three-prong approach to strategic market planning. It is critical to the success of the process because it requires a thorough and honest assessment of the strengths and weakness of the organization, which can then be integrated with the initial steps, environmental scanning and market assessment.

Strategic Advantage and Goal Setting

The findings and suggestions collected from the environmental scanning, the market assessment, and the organizational inventory are now brought together to be utilized to explore the strategic advantages of the delivery system. *Strategic advantages* consist of those *major advantages* currently held by the organization, as well as those *viable directions* for a preferred future for the agency.

This phase of the process involves the implementation of the SWOT approach. The agency identifies its strengths and weaknesses as well as opportunities and threats. This process allows the organization to create its preferred future by utilizing this information to address the strategies to be undertaken.

During this stage of the process, the organization needs to address a variety of questions. Where are we now? Where should we be going? How does our organization need to change in the next five years and beyond?

How will our programs and services change in view of changes in the environment and the people we serve? What is it that our organization can do better than our competitors? The culmination of this process results in the creation of a vision of what the organization will look like, whom it will be serving, and how these programs and services will be delivered to customers, users, members, or participants (see Exhibits 8.3 and 8.4).

Strategic market planning recognizes that an organization is obligated to both plan and carry out those plans through the final step of strategic goal setting. If the strategic advantages provide the long-term direction and vision of the delivery system, then the development of *strategic goals* provides for the short-term guidelines for action.

Exhibit 8.3.
General Opportunities for Edmonton Parks and Recreation Department

Opportunities

Opportunities are identified and incorporated into strategies in each service area marketing plan. General opportunities are identified here.

1. Individuals indicated that they like to participate in groups instead of individually for recreation activities. Group opportunities should be created.

2. The seniors market will double by the year 2000. Plans should be considered now for serving that market.

3. Neighborhoods are becoming heterogeneous and there are more special interest groups. Therefore, geographic segmentation may become inappropriate.

4. Promotions should not be pursued where less than 50,000 coupons are distributed.

5. Advertising should be structured so as to stimulate word-of-mouth advertising.

6. Programming must match the target market's expectations and wants.

7. Opportunities exist for serving society's current interest in health/wellness.

Source: Edmonton Parks and Recreation Department's Market Plan for 1988-1990. p. 3

The strategic goals developed and utilized in this process are actually an application of management by objectives (MBO). The strategic goals complying to the criteria established by the MBO process should be clear and concise statements developed for realistic action that specify criteria for monitoring progress and measuring achievement (Raia, 1974). In order to actuate strategic goals in the MBO manner, it is necessary that for each major step or action to be undertaken, the strategic objectives specify *who* will do *what, when,* and *how* the progress will be measured.

Exhibit 8.4.
Strategic Marketing Objectives for Calgary Parks
and Recreation Department

Objective: 4.   To continue to improve public relations efforts with an emphasis on customer services.

Strategies/ Description	Time Frame	Needs	Responsibility	Evaluation
a. Set-up an ongoing "Mystery Shopper" type program to assess the level of Customer Service available at the arenas.	Set-up system Summer 1987 Winter 1987	Free passes	- Marketing section - Facility manager - Student research - Marketing person	One completed assessment each spring.
b. Conduct a monthly, on-site survey of arena users.	Ongoing	Minimal	- Marketing section - Arena management - Arena foreman	Monthly survey summaries.
c. Increase Customer Relations training for field staff.	Fall 1988 Ongoing	Minimal	- Arena management - Staff training and development for staff	Training seminar offered.
d. Provide an improved experience for arena users and spectators through: 1. Improved catering 2. Better seating 3. Better temperature control	Ongoing	Operational	- Arena management - Arena foreman	Monthly surveys will indicate improvement.
e. Develop an on-call lottery list for last minute ice rentals.	Fall 1987	Minimal	- Arena management	On-call list completed and utilized by arena managers.

Source: Calgary Parks and Recreation Department's Strategic Marketing Plan, Fall 1987, p. 83.

The outcomes of the strategic market planning process may have a variety of impacts upon the delivery system. Its impact may be somewhat substantial, as would be the case if the delivery system perceived that based upon this process it needed to reanalyze the mission of its organization; or, the impact might be more of a redirection or reapproach, as the organization focuses upon the selection of target markets for the future and marketing strategies related to these groups.

Strategic market planning is by design proactive, and its purpose is to enable organizations to gain insight into the future so they are able to select and plan for the organization's future viability and market position. A well-known example of marketing myopia as identified by Levitt (1975) is that of the railroad, which perceived itself as being in the "train" business as opposed to the "transportation" business, and how such an approach nearly led to the extinction of passenger rail service in the United States.

The YMCAs, whose original mission was the spiritual, physical, and mental development of young, Christian men relocating to urban areas, is an example of this. Recognizing changes in the environment and participants' profiles, the YMCAs redefined their mission.

Not all recreation delivery systems will find themselves in the position of needing to substantially change the basic purpose or mission of their organizations. Most organizations will find it necessary to change or refocus target markets and to revise or modify marketing strategies in light of the information secured and the directions uncovered.

Revisions or modifications of marketing strategies would closely reflect the types of alternatives discussed previously in the section on program life cycle, which explored various strategies related to changes required over time. Options such as market penetration, market development, market extension, or market reformulation strategies, as well as retrenchment and selected demarketing strategies for programs or services that no longer reflect the best utilization of the organization's resources, would be explored (Crompton, 1983, pp. 56-61).

Approaches to Strategic Analysis

While there are a number of alternative approaches to strategic analysis utilized in the corporate sector, two such approaches are particularly applicable to park, recreation, and leisure delivery systems. These two approaches are a growth-share analysis, often referred to as the Boston Consulting Group (BCG) method, and the multiple factor screening method, often referred to as the GE Nine Cell Approach.

Boston Consulting Group Method

The *Boston Consulting Group (BCG) method* implements this critical decision-making process by *identifying individual business units* and analyzing these units on the basis of two factors, *market share* and *market growth rate* (Cravens, 1982, pp. 64-66).

To adapt and utilize this approach for leisure delivery systems, the organization would begin by identifying all major programs, facilities, or services provided by the organization. A large public department may identify such units as parks, golf courses, sports facilities, and recreation programs, while a smaller department might utilize such cost centers as parks, community centers, youth programs, adult programs, and special events as the units they seek to analyze.

The selection of units will vary for each organization. However, Kotler (1980, p. 76) identifies several characteristics that could assist the delivery system in making decisions about program or service units to be utilized, based on whether the unit:

(a) is a single business or collection of related businesses;
(b) has a distinct mission;
(c) has its own competitors;
(d) consists of more than one program or functional units;
(e) has its own manager;
(f) can benefit from strategic planning; and
(g) can be planned independently of other units.

These guidelines should be considered and modified by the delivery system as related to its specific situation.

The identified units are then analyzed on the basis of market share and market growth rate. Market share refers to the delivery system's sales or participation figures in relationship to that of its leading competitors; market growth rate is the projected rate of growth of the particular program, product, or service for that market (Kotler, 1982, pp. 94-95).

The success of this approach to strategic analysis and planning is based on the assumption that the higher the market share of the delivery system for a particular program or service, the greater profitability this program or service has for the organization. For instance, if a YMCA currently has a large percentage of adults working or living within its catchment area as members, this sizeable percentage of market share would bode well for the organization's continued success in the area of fitness as well as with this age group.

The same is true for the second factor, market growth rate. If the delivery system is currently providing programs and services that appear to be destined for continued or increasing popularity among the target market or potential target markets, then this factor would positively impact upon the attendance, participation, and revenue generation of this activity, facility, or service.

After analyzing each of the major programs, services or, units offered by the organization on the basis of these two factors, each unit is placed on a grid. The unit's placement on the grid reflects its market share and market growth rate. Each program or service is represented as a circle and the size of the circle is made proportional to the revenue it generates. Public or non-profit organizations may want to determine size of designation for each unit on the basis of participation levels, or some combination of revenue and participation, rather than solely on the basis of revenue generation.

The BCG method's grid consists of a vertical and a horizontal axis. The vertical axis represents market growth rate and the horizontal axis represents market share (Cravens, 1982, p. 66). On the basis of "high" and "low" designations on each of these two factors, the grid is divided into four separate quadrants and each of the major programs, facilities, services, or units utilized in this analysis will be placed into one of these quadrants based on the interrelationship between market share and market growth rate.

Since the category of market share is divided into high share and low share and the designation of market growth rate is segmented into high growth and low growth, the four quadrants each reflect different types of designations and subsequent strategies. The popular names associated with these four quadrants are *stars, cash cows, question marks,* and *dogs* (Kotler, 1980, p. 77). Each of these designations is indicative of a particular situation that the organization can now easily identify, which will facilitate the identification and implementation of appropriate marketing strategies.

Stars are those programs or services which are characterized by both *high market share* and *high market growth rate.* Due to the program/ service's current success coupled with the projected increases in demand, the agency needs to *increase resources* for these programs and services. Stars will become the cash cows of the future.

Cash cows are those programs/services which are currently very popular and well attended, thus generating revenues–which is how the term originated. While this designation is characterized by *high market share,* it has been found to have a *low market growth rate.* The delivery system's strategy, therefore, is to continue to offer these programs/services to *maintain* their viability and revenue. However, the revenues from these programs will be used to *subsidize* or *contribute* to the development of those programs/services designated as stars.

Question marks are those programs/services which are characterized by *low market share* in an area which is perceived as having a *high market growth rate*. These may be programs/services recently introduced by the agency or those impacted upon by situational changes such as shifts in the environment or increased competition. This creates difficulty in the decision-making process. Does the delivery system continue to support these programs and services hoping to create additional stars, or does it withdraw resources from them? Generally, additional study is required for program/services located in this portion of the grid.

Dogs are those programs or services with *low market share* coupled with *low market growth rate*. These are often programs/services that have been offered for a long period of time with ever-diminishing popularity, or recently introduced programs or services with little evidence of potential for increased success. The delivery system needs to employ *demarketing* or *termination* strategies with these programs/service to better utilize their existing resources in other areas.

An example of the Boston Consulting Group method is found in Figure 8.4. A resort hotel seeking to attract new target markets and ensure year-round occupancy recently added a spa operation to the resort. A wide variety of activities and services are offered at the spa. After one year of operation, the resort employed the BCG method to ascertain appropriate strategies for each of the activities and services.

A review of the quadrants reveals that the traditional services such as massages, individual assessments, and skin treatments are serving as the cash cows for this operation by generating the largest portion of revenue. It has been determined that services such as nutrition counseling, spa cuisines, and adventure-oriented out-trips are increasing in popularity. These services have been designated as stars and the spa will make a concerted effort to utilize its resources to expand in these growth areas.

Swimming and hair care are found in the lower right-hand quadrant, indicating their designation as dogs. It was determined that guests wishing to swim generally use one of the two existing pools at the main hotel and that most spa clients are more interested in fitness and wellness than in hair and nail care. Resources allocated to these two phases of the operation will be reduced, and space and staff will be reconfigured to accommodate programs and services designated as stars. The fitness classes and the special events

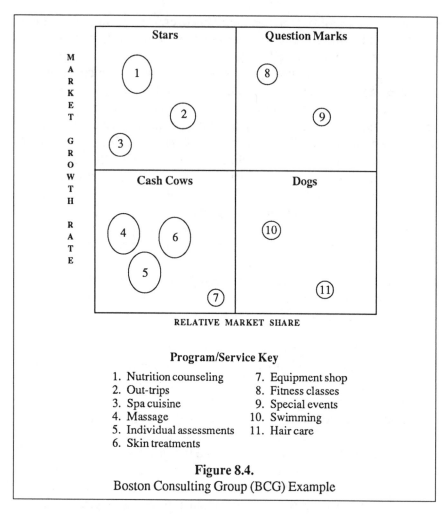

Figure 8.4.
Boston Consulting Group (BCG) Example

offered at the spa have been designated as question marks. Although both of these activities appear to have a high rate of market growth, participation by clients of the spa has been minimal. Resources to these two program areas will most likely be reduced or modifications will be made.

Use of the Boston Consulting Group method for strategic marketing planning enables park, recreation, and leisure delivery systems to objectively rate the potential of their programs and services. It allows for resource allocation decisions to be made on the basis of market share and market growth rate in an attempt to prepare for the future.

GE Nine Cell Approach to Strategic Planning

The GE Nine Cell Approach holds potential for usage by park, recreation, and leisure delivery systems. This approach enables an organization to examine different programs and services being offered. It can readily be adapted for either large or small delivery systems.

The first step in implementing the GE Nine Cell system is for an organization to list all major programs, facilities, or services to be examined. Those major headings are then examined on the basis of two key factors, *program/service potential* and *organizational capability,* to determine *overall attractiveness.*

Program/service potential refers to the potential a specific program or service has for the future in terms of growth and continued viability. Factors included for examination under this heading are market size, market growth rate, profit margin, competition, cyclicality, seasonality, and scale economies (Kotler, 1980, p. 79).

The first factors included in program potential refer to markets. Market size refers to the total number of people likely to be interested in the particular program or service being examined. Naturally, the larger the size of this group, the higher the rating it would receive. For example, if an organization was located in a community where a "mini" baby boom was occurring, then the size of the market for infant and toddler programs would be quite large, in contrast to the same market in a community where the largest percentage of the population was 50 or over.

Market growth rate relates to the projected or future growth patterns of a specific target market. For instance, the mature market, individuals 50 years of age or older, are being projected as a rapidly growing market for the 1990s, and therefore would bode well for programs and services that attract this age group.

Another factor included under the examination of program potential is profit margin. Profit margin pertains to the amount of revenue generated by a program or service after expenses. An examination of various programs or services will reveal that the costs incurred by different activities may vary substantially. Obviously, those programs and services which generate a higher profit margin for the organization will receive a higher ranking in this category.

When analyzing the profit margin of a program or service, competition can play a role. The nature and extent of the competition for a particular program or service impacts upon pricing thresholds and subsequent profits. If one has the only large, moderately priced facility in the area available for rental, then this lack of serious competition may enhance its profitability. The reverse would be true for an amusement park surrounded by similar attractions competing for the same discretionary dollars.

Scale economies also relate to profitability. Scale economics refer to additional profits an organization could generate through increased participation. For example, a corporate fitness center has a sizeable number of fixed costs. If membership were to increase, the organization would benefit by being able to generate additional membership revenues without substantially increasing fixed costs.

Two additional factors included in the analysis of program potential that particularly impact park, recreation, and leisure delivery systems are cyclicality and seasonality. Activities such as gymnastics and ice hockey follow cycles of popularity based upon outside factors such as the Olympic Games. There are a number of recreation and leisure pursuits, such as skate boarding and video games, whose participation levels vary over time.

Seasonality is yet another factor to be considered. Some programs or services such as snow skiing and outdoor swimming naturally lend themselves to varying participation levels based upon seasonal changes. Most ski areas today attempt to add amenities such as spas or golf courses to address this factor, and resorts have long been adjusting to seasonality by attempting to attract convention groups during nonpeak seasons. Both of these factors can impact upon the potential a program or service may have for the delivery system.

The GE Nine Cell Analysis requires the examination of a second major factor, *organizational capability*. This refers to the ability of the delivery system to successfully offer particular programs and services. Factors examined under this category include: market share, price competitiveness, program or service quality, knowledge of target markets, and sales effectiveness (Kotler, 1980, p. 79).

A critical factor in this analysis is market share. Market share refers to the percentage of a particular target market participating in an organization's programs or services. A high market share contributes to the delivery system's strength. A YMCA whose latchkey program consists of 35 percent of the target market possesses a sizeable portion of that market.

Another area to be examined is price competitiveness. A delivery system needs to ask how competitive it is on this issue, and whether or not it could continue to offer the same program or service at the same or lower rate in the future and still remain profitable. Other areas addressed within this factor include price competitiveness related to peripherals offered by the organization, as opposed to those of the competition.

Sales effectiveness and knowledge of the customer are the final two components within the organizational capability factor. These two elements are closely related. If the recreator were interested in introducing a service for older adults and the current clientele are young, single adults, then the recreator's knowledge of the customer is diminished. Sales effectiveness relates to the delivery system's ability to communicate with target markets and attract them to its programs and services. An organization's current market share with the designated market impacts upon both of these factors.

Implementation of the GE Nine Cell Approach

The implementation of the GE Nine Cell Approach to strategic marketing planning involves the identification of major programs and services to be included in the process. These programs and services are rated by members of one's organization on the basis of the two overall factors, program/service potential and organizational capability.

A rating scale similar to the one presented in Figure 8.5 could be utilized. Points are assigned for each indicator and then averaged to assign each program or service a rating for *overall attractiveness* for the delivery system. It is possible to weight these factors by assigning a numerical indicator of importance to each of the factors being examined. For instance, if market size or program quality are deemed to be more important than other factors, the level of importance can be addressed through such a weighting procedure.

When the assessment for each program or service has been completed, they can be placed into the nine cells. Each program or service will have two scores: program/service potential, which is designated as high, medium, or low; and organizational capability, which is designated as strong, average, or weak (Cravens, 1982, p. 78).

The GE Nine Cell is a matrix divided into nine cells with three different zones. The three cells in the upper left are designated as the green zone. The red zone consists of the three cells in the bottom right and the yellow zone is the three diagonal cells from the lower left to the upper right.

Programs or services designated high or medium on program/service potential and strong or average on organizational capacity are placed in the green zone. Programs or services ranking low or medium on program/service potential and average or weak on organizational capability are

Program/Service Under Consideration_____

PROGRAM POTENTIAL (PP)

(rank in order of least importance)	(multiplied by weight)	(assign score of 1-5 with 5 as excellent)
_____	Market size	_____ = _____
_____	Market growth rate	_____ = _____
_____	Profit margin	_____ = _____
_____	Competition	_____ = _____
_____	Cyclicality	_____ = _____
_____	Seasonality	_____ = _____
_____	Scale economies	_____ = _____
	Total for PP:	_____

ORGANIZATIONAL CAPABILITY (OC)

_____	Market share	_____ = _____
_____	Price competition	_____ = _____
_____	Program quality	_____ = _____
_____	Knowledge of user	_____ = _____
_____	Sales effective	_____ = _____
	Total for OC:	_____

Overall Attractiveness Score = PP + OC
(for plotting on GE Nine-Cell Grid)

Figure 8.5.
Analysis Format for GE Nine Cell Approach

assigned places in the red zone. Those programs or services not being designated as red or green would be placed in the center yellow section for caution.

The overall attractiveness of the programs and services offered by the delivery system are then reviewed. Programs falling into the section designated green for "go" hold a high priority for being introduced or continued as services offered by the delivery system. The resources of the organization should be focused here. Those programs or services falling into the red "stop" zone are activities that should be eliminated or phased out over time. Those activities present within the yellow "caution" zone require additional research before decisions about their future can be made.

A community center example is illustrated to better describe the scope of this approach to strategic planning. This community center was charged with raising revenues by 40 percent within a two-year period and utilized the GE Nine Cell Approach to facilitate its planning (see Figures 8.6 and 8.7).

The activities of dance, fitness, and center rental were placed in the green zone due to their attractiveness on both factors. High levels of market share coupled with profit margin led to these placements. The after-school program and kiddie camp were placed in the red zone, meaning that these programs should be phased out. This determination was made on the basis of the ranking, which identified low market share, high levels of competition, and declining growth of this target market. Instructional programs and special events fell into the yellow caution zone because there was so much variation found between individual types of classes and special events, it was determined that these areas required further investigation before decisions were made.

The GE Nine Cell Analysis is a particularly valuable approach to strategic marketing planning for park, recreation, and delivery systems. The use of the two factors, program/service potential and organizational capability, are quite practical for utilization by such delivery systems. The use of the nine cell grid with the accompanying strategies for each zone enables a park, recreation, or leisure delivery system to make both short- and long-term decisions for an organization.

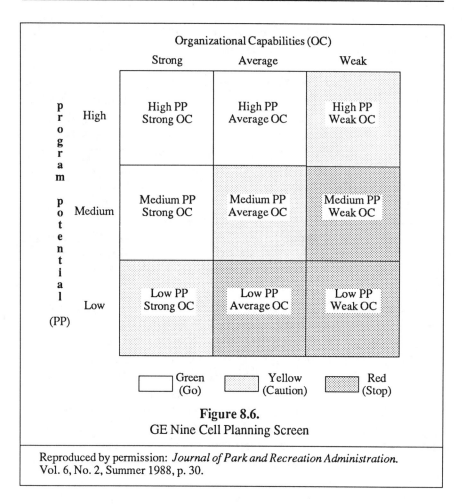

Figure 8.6.
GE Nine Cell Planning Screen

Reproduced by permission: *Journal of Park and Recreation Administration*. Vol. 6, No. 2, Summer 1988, p. 30.

Summary

Since change makes a continual and substantial impact upon today's world, park, recreation, and leisure delivery systems need to manage their systems to address these changes. Strategic marketing planning is a process enabling such organizations to create a vision for their preferred future rather than rely upon a reactive approach to management.

The strategic marketing process consists of three phases of analysis: environmental scanning, market assessment, and organizational inventory. The completion of these three steps results in the identification of strategic advantages for the delivery system, which can then be translated into strategic goals for implementation.

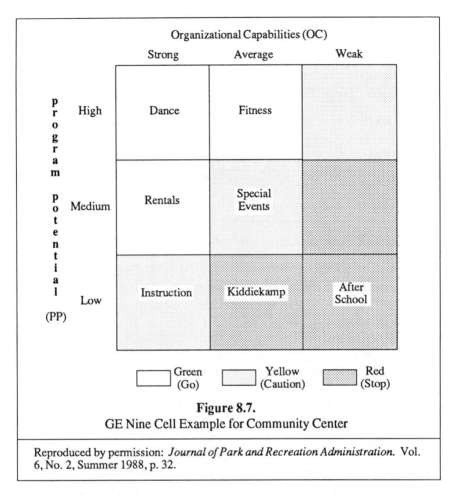

Figure 8.7.
GE Nine Cell Example for Community Center

Two approaches with potential for adoption by leisure delivery systems are the Boston Consulting Group method and the GE Nine Cell approach. The Boston Consulting Group (BCG) method relies upon analysis of market share and market growth rate to arrive at strategic decisions. The GE Nine Cell approach incorporates the analysis of two factors, program/ service potential and organizational capability, as a mechanism for making strategic marketing decisions regarding the organization's resources.

Suggested Activities

1. Examine the steps in the environmental scanning process and develop a list of potential sources of information and activities related to the implementation of this process.

2. Interview several leisure delivery systems managers and ask them how their target markets have changed over the past 10 years. Uncover specific examples as to how programs and services have been modified to address these changes.

3. Select a leisure delivery system and complete the first three steps of the situation analysis. Based upon this information, identify strategic advantages and develop strategic goals.

4. Conduct a strategic marketing analysis for a leisure delivery system using the Boston Consulting Group method. On the basis of this analysis, what recommendations would you make to this organization?

5. For the same organization examined in the previous activity, conduct a second strategic analysis using the GE Nine Cell approach to strategic marketing. Compare and contrast the recommendations of the two approaches.

References

Anthony, W. P. (1984 July-August). Effective Strategic Planning. *Nonprofit World*. pp. 12-16.

Cravens, D. W. (1982). *Strategic Marketing*. Homewood, IL: Richard D. Irwin.

Crompton, J. L. (1983, July). Formulating New Directions with Strategic Marketing Planning. *Parks and Recreation*. pp. 56-61.

Kotler, P. (1980). *Marketing Management: Analysis, Planning, and Control (4th ed.)* Englewood Cliffs, NJ: Prentice-Hall.

Kotler, P. (1982). *Marketing for Nonprofit Organizations (2nd ed.)* (pp. 94-95) Englewood Cliffs, NJ: Prentice-Hall.

Levitt, T. (1975, September-October). Marketing Myopia. (with retrospective commentary) *Harvard Business Review.*

Raia, A. (1974). *Managing by Objectives.* Glenview, IL: Scott, Foresman and Company.

Chapter Nine

Marketing Research

Common Concerns for Parks, Recreation, and Leisure Delivery Systems

- A county park and recreation department spending more and more money on brochures would like to assess the effectiveness of these expenditures.

- An executive director of a suburban YMCA conducts an annual survey of members and wonders if additional, ongoing methods of research should be undertaken.

- The marketing director of a large resort system considers developing a new "off-season" package program and questions its acceptance.

- The manager of a sports and racquet club uses a suggestion box system for members and is dissatisfied by its results.

Marketing Research and Marketing Information Systems

Marketing research can be defined as "the systematic and objective process of generating information for aid in making marketing decisions" (Zikmund, 1989, p. 5). All the steps in the marketing process whether it be selection of target markets, manipulation of marketing mix variables, or strategic planning, require decision making. The effectiveness of these decisions is based upon the availability and quality of pertinent data and information.

Park, recreation, and leisure delivery systems need to utilize marketing research as that link between their participant, member, or guest and the organization. Marketing research functions as a mechanism for "identifying problems and opportunities; generating, refining, and evaluating marketing actions; monitoring marketing performance; and improving marketing as a process" (Boyd, Westfall and Stasch, 1989, p. 9).

To a large extent, recreation and leisure delivery systems have relied upon a practice of "playing a hunch" or intuitively assuming what the user needs or wants and hypothesizing as to how marketing mix variables can be manipulated to meet these needs and wants. The purpose of marketing research is to better understand the consumer and improve marketing effectiveness on the basis of data and information rather than conjecture.

This process is greatly enhanced through the creation of a marketing information system, known as MIS. A marketing information system (MIS) is defined as "an organized set of procedures and methods to continually gather, sort, analyze, evaluate, store, and distribute pertinent, timely, and accurate information for decision making" (Zikmund, 1989, p. 18).

Such a system is critical to the effectiveness of park, recreation, and leisure delivery systems. Obviously the scope and extent of such an MIS would vary based upon the size of the organization and its mission. However, before recreators dismiss the practicality of establishing such a system, it is important to reexamine this definition of a marketing information system and focus upon the key words within this concept.

The key words in this definition are *organized procedures and methods*. Many of the activities inherent within such a system are currently conducted and utilized in most park, recreation, and leisure settings. An awareness of the importance and value of such activities, coupled with the implementation of a systemized approach, is generally all that is necessary for the use of MIS within a delivery system.

Components of the MIS

While there are a wide variety of methods and strategies for gathering the types of information needed in the MIS, the required data and information essentially falls into three broad categories: *internal information, standardized information,* and *special research projects* (Cravens, 1988, p. 430). Utilizing these three broad categories of data and information, park, recreation, and leisure delivery systems can undertake the creation of an MIS for their organization.

All information secured through marketing research can be labelled as either internal or external. *Internal* information refers to the data or information collected by an organization in the course of its regular operation (Kotler, 1982, p. 152). Additional pertinent information, termed *external,* is information originating from outside the daily operation of the agency and can consist of both primary and secondary sources. *Primary data* are specific types of information gathered specifically for the agency's use while *secondary data* refers to general information collected by outside organizations for general use (Boyd, Westfall and Stasch, 1989, pp. 21-22).

Internal Information

The first category of information is internal and obviously refers to the data and information collected by the park, recreation, or leisure delivery system as a matter of course. These are records and accounts that are a part of normal business operations. The type and scope of these internal record keeping procedures vary based upon the organization but may consist of such things as participant registration forms, usage pattern tallies, fees collected, rental or occupancy rates, phone calls and inquiries, sales receipts, program cancellations, and suggestions or complaint letters.

Since these are generally records and procedures that are part of the daily operations of the delivery system, the transition from standard business operations to the creation of an MIS involves a few modifications. The delivery system staff would need to focus upon systemizing their usage, ensuring accuracy, expanding the information base, and utilizing the information.

For instance, phone calls and inquiries coming into an organization can be revealing if the information is recorded and used. A simple tally sheet to record types of calls, general demographic or geographic information about the caller, and types of questions or recommendations communicated might provide useful information for the organization. Do people seem unclear about the program or service? Are they put off when the price is quoted? Would they like to see the service modified in some way? Are most of the callers female or male? Are similar complaints or suggestions received over a given time period?

Resorts, amusement attractions, and tourism bureaus can use written inquiries as part of an MIS operation. A simple tally of postmarks or return addresses can provide information about the geographic parameters of their target markets. If they use multiple sources of advertisement, a coding of these forms can enable them to assess the effectiveness of various types of advertisements.

Examination of program and attendance records can be valuable if systemized and used regularly. Which programs or services seem to be entering a new stage in the life cycle? Was there any impact upon participation levels when changes were made in personnel, or the time or location of the program? Was the impact positive or negative? Could pricing strategies be introduced to alleviate overcrowding at certain facilities during peak periods? Accuracy of information should be stressed in this instance. Personnel should be cautioned to represent accurately the number of users for a particular program or facility.

Analysis of existing participant/member/guest registration forms should be made (see Figure 9.1). What kinds of information are included on these forms and how can this information become part of the MIS? These forms might be further examined to identify additional questions that could be included without substantially impacting upon the time and effort required

---

Family Lifestyle: Please check the one description which best describes your household.

___ Single adult living alone   ___ Family with teenagers
___ Single adult living with others   ___ Family with no children living at home
___ Married couple without children   ___ Retired
___ Family with infants or preschoolers   ___ Single parent with children at home
___ Family with young children

Time Preference for Participation: Please indicate those days of the week and times which would be most convenient for you.

___ Weekdays (Mon.-Fri.)   ___ Early mornings (6:00 a.m.-7:30 a.m.)
___ Weekends (Sat./Sun.)   ___ Mornings
                             ___ Lunch time (11:30 a.m.-1:00 p.m.)
                             ___ Afternoons
                             ___ Early evenings (5:00 p.m.-7:30 p.m.)
                             ___ Evenings (7:30 p.m.-10:00 p.m.)

How did you hear about this program? Please indicate how you found out about this program, activity or service by checking appropriate category.

___ Newspaper article
___ Newpaper ad
___ Department brochure
___ Friend
___ Other: please specify: _____

Figure 9.1.
Suggested Questions for Use in Registration Procedures

for completion. Such things as address, general age categories of the registrant, or usage status would all be helpful in providing for a more complete marketing picture.

Collection of fees or check-in practices at parks, beaches, or tourist attractions can be revealing. How many people are in the car entering the area? What are the age and gender breakdowns of the occupants? Is the car licensed in-state or out-of-state? All of these pieces of information, when utilized in conjunction with a marketing plan, can assist the organization in better understanding its market.

These internal data can be very revealing by providing a myriad of information regarding the customer. In most instances, it is not a question of creating these systems, since they may already be in place. The focus for the recreator in this instance is to *organize* the collection of this information, to *expand* upon existing information collected, and to then *analyze* and *use* the findings. These data, when integrated, form the basis for the internal data portion of the MIS.

Standardized Information

The second category of information required for MIS is *standardized information*. This type of information refers to data and information collected externally to the organization by a variety of organizations and groups. Organizations such as the Census Bureau, chambers of commerce, public libraries, trade and professional organizations, government agencies, as well as research companies are sources of these types of information. This type of information can be accessed by a park, recreation, or leisure delivery system. The cost varies from no charge to a nominal fee, or is set on a contracted basis, depending upon the source.

Since this information is secondary data, it is important to note that this information will not specifically relate to the organization. It may provide the organization with trend analyses and statistics that can assist the recreator in identifying opportunities or challenges for the organization as well as changes in demographics or psychographics.

Much of this information, such as shifts in demographics or changing trends in participation patterns, is readily available from a variety of sources such as government reports, professional journals, trade newsletters, and related periodicals and publications. *USA Today* regularly features articles and statistics reflecting time usage patterns and lifestyle interests. The

Programmers Information Network (PIN), a quarterly newsletter published by the National Recreation and Park Association, usually includes pertinent facts and projections related to changing programmatic patterns. Periodicals such as *U.S. News and World Report, Newsweek, Journal of Marketing,* and *Entrepreneur* quite often feature articles of interest and use to leisure service providers.

Government publications, particularly those disseminated by the U.S. Census Bureau, provide a large collection of statistics for only a nominal cost (see Exhibit 9.1). Since this collection of information is so extensive, it is recommended that recreation marketers make use of the *Census Catalog and Guide,* published annually, which lists all current and previous census publications. Publications by the Census Bureau that may be of interest to recreators include:

Current Population Reports–monthly report which updates and expands upon the 10-year census, featuring data on personal and family characteristics as well as consumer patterns and living arrangements.

Census of Service Industries–data related to sales and employment patterns for service industries such as hotels, advertising, amusement and recreation services.

County and City Data Book–statistical information for each census region, published every five years.

State and Metropolitan Area Data Book–statistical items for states, metropolitan areas, and central cities.

Census of Outlying Areas–statistical items for smaller population regions of the country.

Statistical Abstract of the United States–large annual publication containing an extensive list of charts and tables overviewing a myriad of consumer patterns.
(Boyd, Westfall and Stasch, 1989, pp. 175-178)

All that is required by a delivery system to incorporate these findings into its MIS is the systematic collection of this information. This information should be shared with members of the organization along with suggestions for monitoring or modifying program and service patterns.

Exhibit 9.1.
Personal Consumption Expenditures for Recreation: 1970 to 1987 from Statistical Abstract

No. 377. PERSONAL CONSUMPTION EXPENDITURES FOR RECREATION: 1970 TO 1987

(In billions of dollars, except percent. Represents market value of purchases of goods and services by individuals and nonprofit institutions)

TYPE OF PRODUCT OR SERVICE	1970	1975	1980	1981	1982	1983	1984	1985	1986	1987
Total recreation expenditures	**42.7**	**70.2**	**115.0**	**128.6**	**138.3**	**152.1**	**168.3**	**185.7**	**201.7**	**223.3**
Percent of total personal consumption[1]	6.7	6.9	6.6	6.7	6.7	6.8	6.9	7.1	7.2	7.4
Books and maps	2.9	3.6	5.6	6.2	6.6	7.2	7.8	8.1	8.6	9.7
Magazines, newspapers and sheet music	4.1	6.4	10.4	11.0	11.4	12.0	12.7	13.2	13.9	15.8
Nondurable toys and sport supplies	5.5	9.0	14.6	16.0	16.8	18.0	19.7	21.1	23.1	26.8
Wheel goods, durable toys, sports equipment[2]	5.2	10.5	17.2	18.7	19.3	20.4	24.8	26.7	29.8	33.4
Radio and television receivers, records and musical instruments	8.5	13.5	19.9	22.0	24.5	28.2	31.5	37.0	38.9	41.2
Radio and television repair	1.4	2.2	2.6	2.7	2.8	2.8	2.8	3.2	3.3	3.7
Flowers, seeds and potted plants	1.8	2.7	4.0	4.4	4.5	4.8	5.2	5.5	6.1	6.7
Admissions to specified spectator amusements	3.3	4.3	6.5	6.9	7.8	8.6	9.5	9.5	10.2	11.1
Motion picture theaters	1.6	2.2	2.7	2.9	3.3	3.6	3.9	3.6	3.8	4.1
Legitimate theaters and opera, and entertainments of nonprofit institutions[3]	.5	.8	1.8	2.0	2.1	2.4	2.7	3.0	3.4	3.7
Spectator sports	1.1	1.3	2.0	2.0	2.3	2.6	2.9	2.9	3.1	3.3
Clubs and fraternal organizations[4]	1.5	1.9	3.0	3.4	3.8	4.2	4.5	4.8	5.0	5.4
Commercial participant amusements[5]	2.4	4.9	9.7	11.7	12.5	13.6	14.1	15.1	16.0	17.3
Pari-mutuel net receipts	1.1	1.7	2.1	2.2	2.2	2.3	2.6	2.6	2.6	2.7
Other[6]	5.1	9.7	19.4	23.4	26.0	30.0	33.1	38.9	44.1	49.3

[1]See table 693.   [2]Includes boats and pleasure aircraft.   [3]Except athletic.   [4]Consists of dues and fees excluding insurance premiums.   [5]Consists of billiard parlors, bowling alleys, dancing, riding, shooting, skating and swimming places; amusement devices and parks; golf courses, sightseeing buses and guides; private flying operations and other commercial participant amusements.   [6]Consists of net receipts of lotteries and expenditures for purchase of pets and pet care services, cable TV, film processing, photographic studios, sporting and recreation camps, and recreational services not elsewhere classified.

Source: U.S. Bureau of Economic Analysis. *The National Income and Product Accounts of the United States, 1929-1982*; and *Survey of Current Businesses,* July issues.

Small organizations may want to designate one employee as the individual who collects these pieces of information from other members of the organization and is responsible for disseminating these statistics and facts on a monthly or quarterly basis. Larger organizations may designate a specific department as being responsible for this function or contract with information or research firms.

Many commercial leisure delivery systems address this need of MIS to collect and utilize standardized information by choosing to purchase such information from private research firms. These syndicated service research firms, such as Nielsen, the American Research Bureau, Simmons Market Research, or Target Group Index, provide consumer and trade information on a fee basis to their subscribers (Kotler, 1982, p. 156).

Special Research Studies

The third category of information to be secured as part of the MIS is *special research studies*. These types of studies are usually undertaken in response to a specific problem, special situation, or lack of information. While the focus and purpose of such studies vary widely, there are some principles and practices that need to be addressed which are consistent for all such types of studies.

The major steps involved in planning and conducting a formal research study are as follows:

1. *Definition of the problem*–clear and specific identification of the exact type(s) of information to be secured through this study

2. *Research design*–identification and selection of the type of research methodology to be employed in this study (i.e., descriptive, experimental, exploratory)

3. *Data collection techniques*–selection of methods for securing needed information (i.e., mail, phone, interview, observation)

4. *Sampling design*–determination as to how respondents will be identified and selected

5. *Field data collection*–collection and processing of information obtained from sample

6. *Analysis and interpretation of data*–utilization of appropriate techniques to analyze data followed by determination of findings

7. *Research report*–communication of key methodology and findings of the study
(Cravens, 1982, pp. 434-435)

Park, recreation, or leisure delivery systems can choose to conduct these special research studies on their own or may elect to utilize outside experts to conduct such studies. For instance, many public and nonprofit recreation delivery systems regularly conduct needs assessment studies as part of their ongoing operation utilizing current employees. Some organizations elect to utilize outside consultants or marketing research firms to conduct such studies.

The National Recreation and Park Association recently utilized a marketing research firm to identify psychographic clusters of individuals who could be targeted by public park and recreation delivery systems. The eight leisure-based clusters, grouped by psychographics were identified as follows:

Cluster	Percent of U.S. Households
Young Optimists	3.48
Upscale Couples	3.86
Upscale Families	17.91
Golden Years	1.19
Young and Restless	6.02
Blue Collar Families	41.98
Social Security	7.02
Need-Driven	18.46

Park, recreation, or leisure delivery systems desiring to utilize outside consultants or marketing research firms can either contact area colleges or universities or consult *Bradford's Directory,* which lists both custom and speciality-line marketing firms throughout the country.

Types of Marketing Information Required

Although there are many different types of information that could be secured through marketing research, there are some types of information which are of particular value to park, recreation, and leisure delivery systems. This valuable information can be categorized under the following general headings: marketing opportunities, target markets, marketing mix, customer satisfaction, and marketing performance.

In this ever-changing society within which we live, peoples' needs and interests seldom remain constant over an extended period of time. Due to these changes, it is vital that leisure delivery systems utilize marketing research as a diagnostic tool to identify and evaluate market opportunities.

Programs and services that are currently well-received may or may not be as popular in the future. It is incumbent upon the MIS within a delivery system to identify potential opportunities and conduct research to help managers make better decisions regarding these future ventures.

The initial stage of identification of potential opportunities is often uncovered utilizing standardized information available through MIS. A review of census data, statistics compiled in journals and newsletters, and features in newspapers and periodicals often leads a delivery system to focus upon a trend or projection that may hold value for the delivery system.

For instance, recent findings indicating a growing preference for weekend travel prompted many tourist attractions and resorts to modify their marketing mix to offer special weekend getaway packages rather than focusing upon a one- or two-week vacation. Demographic reports revealing the maturing of American society along with a "mini" baby boom has prompted some recreation and leisure delivery systems to modify programs to attract the older American, while still other organizations have launched programs for babies and toddlers.

While secondary data are generally the source of identification of these potential opportunities, the MIS may then conduct additional research that evaluates the potential of this opportunity for the specific delivery system. Needs assessment surveys or focus groups are often used for just this purpose. Often a delivery system may test-market the new program or service by offering it in a limited area, such as one resort or one community center.

An additional area of information that is often required by park, recreation, and leisure delivery systems is target marketing. There are a number of questions that require answers related to this area of the process. Who are the current users? What are their characteristics on the basis of the five target market descriptors? How do users differ from nonusers? What differentiates heavy users from light users?

Delivery systems have a number of options for exploring the answers to these target marketing issues. They can make use of any or all of the three categories of information within their MIS. They may wish to add additional sets of questions to existing registration forms or introduce tally sheets for phone calls and inquiries as a way of incorporating this research into their internal information process. The delivery system may elect to draw conclusions from Census information to compare how current users differ from the general population, or they can conduct (or contract a marketing research firm to conduct) a study to identify the specific parameters and characteristics of their target markets.

A third part of the marketing process that can benefit from marketing research relates to the marketing mix variables. There is an extensive array of information that can be secured related to marketing mix variables. How important is time of day and location of activity or service to participation? Does pricing play a role in usage? What attributes or peripherals need to be present in order to attract target market groups? Should the program or service line be expanded or reduced? How effective is the facility's brochure?

A final area commonly associated with marketing research is the analysis of marketing performance. This is referred to as performance-monitoring research, which is designed to "regularly, perhaps routinely, provide feedback for evaluation and control of marketing activity" (Zikmund, 1989, p. 14).

Much of the information secured in this area would relate to the internal information which is collected routinely as part of normal operations, such as tracking of program attendance, analysis of sales receipts, or user feedback forms. Once these patterns have been established, they can be monitored by MIS on a regular basis. The information secured in this area can facilitate decision making regarding scheduling of employees during peak and nonpeak hours of participation, modification of programs reaching the later stages of the program life cycle, and the impact of changes in the marketing mix variables such as new personnel or price increases.

Often the purpose of this type of marketing research is to identify situations where things are not going as planned or as usual. Special research studies such as importance-performance studies or focus groups could then be instituted to identify the exact nature of the difficulty.

Commonly Used Research Techniques

The purpose of this chapter is not to provide the recreator with the specific tools and techniques contributing to the validity and reliability of research studies, which can be found in a variety of research books. However, it is important that types of research techniques that are commonly used in marketing research be overviewed. Therefore, the following techniques and approaches will be mentioned: focus groups, importance-performance analysis, test marketing, user satisfaction measures, recall and recognition tests, and need assessment applications.

Focus Groups

Focus groups are a qualitative form of research that is unique to marketing. They are not designed to provide the organization with scientific or hard data. They are useful for providing specific feedback from users or nonusers on a variety of topics when the recreator requires additional insights. They often uncover interesting and useful information that may not have been revealed through quantitative research methods. Objectives that can be accomplished through focus group interviews include:

    (a) develop hypotheses for further testing,
    (b) provide information for structuring questionnaires,
    (c) provide overall background information on programs,
    (d) solicit patron impressions about new program concepts,
    (e) stimulate new ideas about older programs,
    (f) generate ideas for new programs, and
    (g) interpret previously obtained quantitative results.
(Rossman, 1989, p. 140)

    Focus groups can be conducted by a trained member of the organization or by an outside marketing firm. Initially, the researcher needs to select a focus or decide exactly what types of information the organization is seeking. The specific focus of the group will relate to the informational or research needs of the delivery system.

    The second step when using this technique is identifying the people to participate in the focus group. The selection of the sample composing the focus group is important. There are two issues requiring attention in this area: number of groups to have, and makeup of each group (Boyd, Westfall and Stasch, 1989, p. 103). It is generally recommended that one never use just one focus group, but rather hold a number of them until one stops receiving new ideas or information.

    Selection of group members is important. The recreator should be sure to select people who possess the information the organization is seeking and are representative of the target market group under examination. Members of a fitness club who have dropped out or have not renewed their memberships may be randomly selected for participation in this process. Teenagers who might be potential participants in a proposed trips program might serve as members of the focus group.

It is recommended that the size of the focus group be limited. The exact number of participants may vary, with recommendations ranging from 6 to 15. One might consider offering some kind of incentive for their participation, such as free use of the facility for a day or a discount coupon or gift certificate for use within the organization.

In addition to selecting the participants for the focus group, the recreator needs to select the time and location scheduled for this process. It is important to select a time and location that is convenient for the focus group members. If the group will include current users of programs or services, it would be appropriate to schedule the focus group immediately before or after their regularly scheduled participation patterns. Participants for the focus group should be invited ahead of time so they can set aside time for this purpose. It is also recommended that the room where the focus group is conducted be relatively free from interruptions or distractions.

Additional suggestions that may be helpful and contribute to the success of focus group interviews are as follows:

- Be sure of the focus—what topics, ideas the recreator wants to cover.

- Invite the appropriate people and if possible try to select a representative group.

- Don't include more than 15 people in the group.

- Briefly explain the process and identify the focus/topics to be covered.

- Use a tape recorder—eventually the participants will become accustomed to its use.

- Encourage everyone to participate, but ask them to keep their responses brief.

- Allow everyone's input and don't allow one person to dominate.

- Occasionally, take a break and restate the focus or summarize ideas.

• Don't insist upon consensus from participants.

• Limit the interview to one hour or less.

• Close the interview by reiterating themes and ideas.
(National Recreation and Park Association, 1989, p. 8)

Following the focus group interview, it is advised that the interviewer organize notes and review the tapes as soon as possible. Additional recommendations include acting upon the information gathered in the focus group interview and sharing the information with other members of the organization as well.

Importance-Performance Analysis

Importance-Performance Analysis has been utilized by marketers as a mechanism for examining the desirability of product attributes. It is based upon research indicating that participant satisfaction is a function of both user expectations about attributes of the program/service they consider important, and their assessments of the delivery systems' performance related to these attributes (Mantilla and James, 1979, pp. 77-79). Use of this type of analysis is especially valuable for leisure delivery systems because it provides a dual mechanism for assessing users' preferences for certain components of a program/service as well as evaluating customer service standards by analyzing the performance of the delivery system.

The first step in undertaking this analysis is to generate a list of program/service attributes related to the program under examination. A review of various marketing mix variables facilitates this process. This list of pertinent attributes is then developed into a survey instrument for participants. The users are asked to rank the attribute list twice.

They first rank the attributes based upon *how important* they perceive these variables to be related to their participation. For instance, how important is the leader of a fitness class, or how important is the price of the program? They then rank the identical set of attributes based upon their perceptions as to *how well* the delivery system is *performing* in relation to these variables. Completion of these two identical sets of attributes provides vital information for the organization. They allow the organization to identify the marketing mix variables that are important to participants while simultaneously assessing how well the organization is performing on these factors.

The results of these two rankings are then plotted on an Importance-Performance grid (see Figure 9.2). The vertical axis is used to plot importance scores and the horizontal axis plots performance, resulting in the creation of four quadrants. The upper left-hand quadrant consists of those attributes users perceive as being important but not offered at the desired performance level. Hence, the label "concentrate here" is assigned to this quadrant. The quadrant in the lower-left shows minor services that are being performed in an average way but don't require attention, since they are not very important. This quadrant is designated as "low priority."

The two quadrants to the right include attributes that are designated as being important to the user with accompanying high levels of performance by the agency. The upper right-hand quadrant shows important services which the agency is performing well. They need to continue in this way. Hence, the designation "keep up the good work" is assigned to this quadrant. The lower right-hand quadrant shows minor services that are being performed very well by the agency. Therefore, this quadrant is designated as "overkill" and the organization need not concentrate its efforts here.

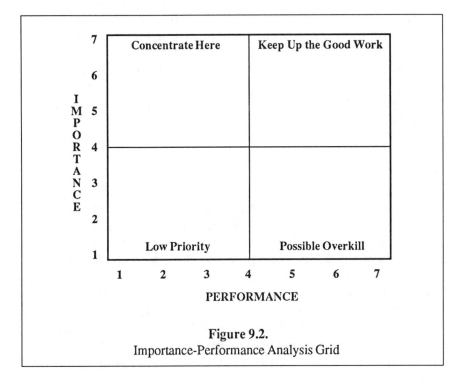

Figure 9.2.
Importance-Performance Analysis Grid

The Importance-Performance Analysis is a boon for recreation marketers. It enables them through a relatively simple research process to identify important marketing mix variables while simultaneously assessing the delivery system's performance on these attributes. The placement of this data on the grid allows the organization to readily make decisions regarding resource allocations, since each program/service attribute is placed in a quadrant revealing a specific strategy for the organization. The efficacy of this research approach is related to the proper selection of attributes or program/service factors, so recreators are cautioned to ensure the proper selection of these factors through an examination of the marketing mix variables and a review of pertinent literature.

An Importance-Performance Analysis of fitness classes held at at a recreation center is presented in Figure 9.3. A 15-item list of attributes was generated for this analysis, including a variety of marketing mix variables.

The results of this analysis indicate that the recreation center is doing an above-average job of both assessing the needs of its clientele as well as delivering the program, as indicated by the large number of attributes that are clustered in the upper right-hand quadrant labeled "keep up the good work." Attributes plotted in the two lower quadrants would most likely not be addressed by the recreation center, since these variables are deemed either "low priority" or "possible overkill." The upper left-hand quadrant reveals that three of the attributes–registration procedures, parking, and other participants in the class–are areas where the organization should consider making changes or improvements. A brief set of follow-up questions may be required to determine the exact nature of the problems within these three attributes.

Test Marketing

An additional marketing research technique utilized by park and recreation delivery systems is test marketing. *Test marketing* is a procedure whereby an organization tests on a small basis the viability of a marketing plan for a new or modified program or service (Boyd, Westfall and Stasch, 1989, p. 711). In this way the organization is able to try out ideas generated in focus groups or modify marketing mix variables for programs in later stages of the program life cycle without investing substantial resources.

Test marketing is useful for recreation delivery systems in two ways: it enables them to estimate outcomes of alternative courses of action, and it allows them to correct or modify programs/services before being fully

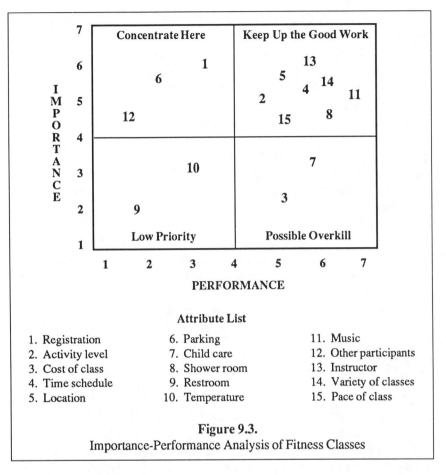

Figure 9.3.
Importance-Performance Analysis of Fitness Classes

introduced to their users (Zikmund, 1989, p. 307). Utilization of test marketing varies based upon the size of the organization but can be helpful for both small and large delivery systems.

A small community recreation department considering adding an after-school play program for its residents might test market the program in one neighborhood before introducing it community wide. A chain of resorts might implement test marketing by introducing new pricing for full-service packages in one or two of its operations before extending the concept throughout the entire organization. In both of these instances, the delivery systems are able to try out a new program or modify existing ones on a small basis without committing major resources to the change. The findings from these test markets enable them to anticipate user acceptance and profitability while making needed changes prior to full-scale adoption.

While test marketing can be a useful research tool, recreation delivery systems should be cautioned as to the importance of sampling with this technique. It is vital that the test market or markets be as representative as possible of the entire user population. The test market should be similar to the general user population in terms of target market characteristics and competition patterns.

If the community recreation department had test marketed the after-school play program in a neighborhood with substantially higher percentages of children and working parents, then they would be unable to accurately predict its profitability for all areas of the community. Likewise, if the resorts selected for test marketing the complete pricing package were located in areas where competition was unusually high or nonexistent, the same would be true.

Test marketing is a powerful tool for parks and recreation. It is an opportunity to introduce new programs and services and to test their acceptance and profitability without overcommitting resources. It also provides them with the advantage of improving upon new programs and services before offering them on a large scale.

User Satisfaction

Since recreation delivery systems are dependent upon the satisfaction of their users, participants, or members in order to remain viable, this is an important area of market research. There are a variety of satisfaction research techniques that could be utilized, ranging from very casual to highly structured approaches and revealing either qualitative or quantitative data.

The range of approaches varies based upon the "customer-service" orientation of the organization, and it is becoming increasingly common for parks and recreation agencies to utilize a variety of approaches for determining user satisfaction. Some of the methods utilized include: sales-related methods, complaint and suggestion systems, and user satisfaction surveys (Kotler, 1982, pp. 66-69).

Sales-related methods are commonly used by those recreation delivery systems where profitability or self-sustaining services are criteria for success. While revenue growth patterns and loss of market share are indicators of users' satisfaction and should be utilized by recreation delivery systems, revenue figures should not be used as the sole criterion.

One critical factor to be addressed is that of demand. If a day camp sponsored by a public park and recreation department is operating at 100 percent of enrollment capacity, it doesn't necessarily indicate users' satisfaction. This department needs to analyze its capacity in relation to the size of the target market as well as the availability of other moderately-priced options for a similar service. If there is little competition for a program or service accompanied by high levels of demand, then enrollment or revenue figures do not necessarily indicate high levels of participant satisfaction with the program or service.

The demand factor can also work in reverse. A ski area with reduced revenue figures or a resort in a remote tourist destination cannot assume that users are dissatisfied with their services. Such fluctuations in revenue can be attributed to economic conditions, airline schedules, or weather patterns. Sales and participation patterns are internal marketing research methods that are useful when other factors are taken into consideration as well.

It is becoming increasingly common to see recreation and leisure delivery systems using complaint and suggestion systems for assessing users' satisfaction. Suggestion boxes can be strategically placed in highly trafficked areas of a facility. Comment cards placed at the program or service area or distributed at the conclusion of the experience are becoming commonplace (see Exhibit 9.2). Some hotels and resorts are now providing a service where guests can contact by phone or in person an employee designated to resolve their complaints or problems on a 24-hour-a-day basis. Another form of user satisfaction assessment being used by resorts and other recreation delivery systems is the mystery guest. Using this research method, research firms or volunteer guests are used to visit a facility or participate in a program or service and report their treatment and experience back to the organization.

These qualitative forms of marketing research actually serve a dual purpose. They provide useful information for the organization while making users feel as if they are important and of value to the organization. An important reminder when using any of these techniques is to make use of the information received. People will refrain from using suggestion boxes if they never see changes implemented. Some organizations post the suggestions received on a daily or weekly basis along with the action taken. Complaints or comments should be shared with employees so they can assess their performance. This information should also be monitored so the delivery system can identify marketing mix variables requiring attention or modification or identify patterns of trouble.

Exhibit 9.2.
User Comment Card

Thanks for using our facility. Our best ideas come from you. Please help us serve you better by completing this reply card and sending it via Guard Mail or leaving it in any MWR suggestion box. Thank you.

What would you like to tell us about your experience with MWR today? _____

_____

_____

Would you like to thank a particular MWR employee? What is that employee's name and where does that employee work? _____

_____

_____

You would like us to provide what special services for you?_____

_____

_____

How can we improve our service? _____

_____

_____

_____

How would you rate the MWR facilities? (Check One)
☐ THE BEST
☐ BETTER THAN MOST OTHER BASES
☐ AVERAGE
☐ POOR

If you would like us to respond to your comments:

Name: _____   Phone Number: _____

Address: _____

Source: Morale Welfare Recreation Department, Naval Air Station, Brunswick, Maine

User satisfaction surveys are still another method to be used. This can include both formal and informal methods. Some organizations make it a policy for middle managers or even direct-service employees to randomly call five participants or members each week to find out what they liked and disliked about the facility, program, or service (see Figure 9.4).

Other organizations supplement this approach by conducting regular measures of satisfaction. Two approaches to this measurement are directly reported satisfaction and derived satisfaction (Kotler, 1982, pp. 69-70). To ascertain directly reported satisfaction, the organization would periodically sample users by mail or phone and ask them how satisfied they felt with a particular program or service. The scale could be constructed to use an odd number of intervals such as 3, 5, or 7 and would indicate to the organization the self-reported feelings of satisfaction of the users.

Measurement of derived satisfaction is conducted by asking users how well the program or service satisfied them as well as their expectations related to a program or service attribute (see Figure 9.5). This approach is based upon the assumption that an individual's perception of satisfaction is based on the person's expectations. A similar odd-number interval scale

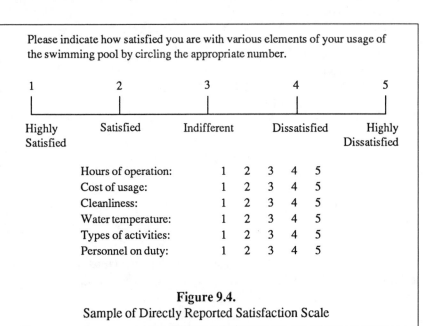

Figure 9.4.
Sample of Directly Reported Satisfaction Scale

Adapted from Kotler, Phillip. *Marketing for Nonprofit Organizations,* 2nd ed. Englewood Cliffs, NJ: Prentice-Hall, 1982, pp. 70-71.

would be developed for use in this method, but with this method the respondent would be asked two questions related to each attribute. A "need deficiency" score can then be determined by subtracting the answer to the first question from the answer to the second. It would then be determined that the higher the need deficiency score, the greater the degree of dissatisfaction or the smaller the level of satisfaction (Kotler, 1982, pp. 69-70).

Please indicate your opinion regarding the quality of various activities and services provided by this resort by circling the appropriate number.

The quality of our staff:
How much is there now:
(min.)   1   2   3   4   5   6   7   (max.)
How much should there be?
(min.)   1   2   3   4   5   6   7   (max.)

The variety of activities for children:
How much is there now:
(min.)   1   2   3   4   5   6   7   (max.)
How much should there be?
(min.)   1   2   3   4   5   6   7   (max.)

The variety of evening activities for adults:
How much is there now:
(min.)   1   2   3   4   5   6   7   (max.)
How much should there be?
(min.)   1   2   3   4   5   6   7   (max.)

Figure 9.5.
Sample of Derived Satisfaction Scale

Adapted from Kotler, Phillip. *Marketing for Nonprofit Organizations,* 2nd ed. Englewood Cliffs, NJ: Prentice-Hall, 1982, pp. 70-71.

Measures of users' satisfaction are becoming an increasingly important component of marketing research. With the growing emphasis upon providing excellent or outstanding service to customers, recreation and leisure delivery systems are making use of the variety of techniques available to them to assess their performance in this area and to enhance their viability by retaining users, participants, or members who are well-satisfied with the programs and services.

Promotion and Public Relations

An additional area of interest to recreation marketers relates to the level of success of promotional and public relations efforts. Since this phase of the marketing process involves substantial resource utilization, it is advisable to determine the effectiveness of various techniques employed. Marketing research methods can be employed to address this concern.

Since the purpose of promotion is to both inform and persuade target market groups to utilize an organization's programs or services, it is necessary to determine the efficacy of different methods employed. Recreation and leisure delivery systems usually make use of different methods and use various channels to serve as outlets for this information.

How is one to determine which types of promotions or which channels of communication are most effective? One recommended method is to track the results of one's promotional distribution. This can be undertaken in a variety of ways. The recreator can request that frontline employees who serve as the initial user contact with an organization inquire as to how the potential user heard about a particular program, service, or facility. This information can be recorded and used to assist in promotional strategies.

An additional method involves the coding of brochures, press releases, or advertisements. Registration forms or mailing labels can be coded with designated codes or symbols according to distribution method and the efficiency of that location or method can be analyzed when registration forms are returned to the agency (Tracking, 1989, p. 3). This same coding procedure can be adapted for tracking the effectiveness of advertisements placed in more than one newspaper or periodical. The inquiry portion of the ad can be varied to include different box numbers or different names to which inquiries are to be directed. The inquiries or registrations can then be traced to their origin, assisting marketers in determining the effectiveness of various promotional channels.

In addition to assessing promotional effectiveness, these methods can also be related to target marketing. A resort can analyze inquiries on the basis of geographical regions or zip codes to identify those areas of the country or neighborhoods within regions where target marketing efforts are either succeeding or failing. Target marketing strategies can then be adjusted accordingly.

The effectiveness of advertising messages can also be ascertained after the completion of the campaign. The two most commonly used methods are recognition and recall tests. With recognition tests, members of the target market are shown the ad and asked whether they have seen it or not; with recall tests, target market members are asked if they can recall seeing any particular advertisement without being shown the specific ad (Crompton and Lamb, 1986, p. 426). Use of either of these two techniques assists in assessing the effectiveness of a specific ad.

Public relations is another area of interest to recreation marketers. The recognition of an organization by the general public as well as the public's perceptions related to the organization's visibility or market position can prove revealing. To ascertain levels of public awareness and market position, the agency can conduct recall or recognition tests as well. Randomly sampled members of the target market can be contacted and asked to name various programs or services being offered by the delivery system or asked to mention the names of delivery systems in the area who offer particular kinds of services.

The results of this method enable the delivery system to identify programs or services requiring heightened promotional efforts. It is also useful in determining the public's perception of the organization and its relationship to that of its competitors. Such recall or recognition tests can also be used to measure the effectiveness of a logo or slogan change or the efficacy of a particular public relations effort when conducted on a pre- and post-test basis.

The use of research methods to track and assess promotional and public visibility techniques is critical to the success of a delivery system. An organization can be developing target-market oriented programs and services and yet, if this group is not aware of the existence of the agency or such programs and services, then the marketing process will be incomplete.

Target Markets

There are a plethora of research questions that can be generated around the topic of target markets. Who are they? Where do they live? What are their needs and interests? What are their lifestyle tendencies? What is our agency's market share? How can we project future target market demand for a program or service?

While many of the aforementioned research methods reveal information about target markets if analyzed correctly, the most commonly associated technique utilized in this endeavor is the needs assessment (see Exhibit 9.3). Needs assessment can consist of a variety of approaches that can be conducted on an daily or weekly basis as well as via a systematized, periodic approach.

Exhibit 9.3.
Recognition Rating Results

Name three facilities or services operated by the Parks and Recreation Department

Mention	First	Second	Third	Total	% of Total
Muttart	85%	53%	0%	138%	16%
Kinsmen	23%	65%	3%	91%	10%
JJNC	32%	8%	16%	56%	6%
Swimming	72%	41%	8%	121%	14%
Golf	71%	81%	4%	156%	18%
MWRC	11%	17%	19%	47%	5%
Stadium	19%	12%	20%	51%	6%
MW pool	15%	12%	5%	32%	4%
Rundle/Hawrelak	26%	41%	12%	62%	7%
Valley Zoo	23%	12%	10%	45%	5%
Total	398	369	111	878	100%

Facilities or services which own and manage tourist attractions

First Mention	City/P&R	Triple 5	Prov. Govt	Do Not Know	Private
Edm Space Sc Centre	60% (60/0)	5%	5%	30%	
Fort Edmonton	55% (53/2)		7%	39%	
Muttart Conservatory	50% (50/0)		7%	35%	10%
Valley Zoo	25% (25/0)			75%	
W.E.M.		86%		12%	
River Valley	75% (75/0)			25%	

Facilities or services which own and manage recreation facilities

First Mention	City/P&R	Prov. Govt	Kinsmen	Club	Do Not Know
Kinsmen	43% (41/2)	2%	7%	15%	26%
City pools	58% (50/8)				42%
MWRC	46% (46/0)				54%
Club Fit	10% (10/0)				90%

Source: June 1986 Tracking Survey, Edmonton Parks and Recreation Department

For instance, internal marketing methods such as including additional questions on registration forms or accounting for those participants who are heavy users as opposed to occasional users can become part of one's needs assessment approach. The use of secondary data information can also be incorporated into needs assessment. The market potential for golf in Amherst, MA was determined by integrating Census information with Simmons Market Research data, as illustrated in Exhibit 9.4.

Exhibit 9.4.
Market Projections for Golfers

Amherst Population 1980, 1988, 1993 Population by Age	1980 Census Number	1988 Estimate Number	1993 Projection Number
0-4	892	842	738
5-9	1,106	838	777
10-14	1,413	917	771
15-19	3,156	2,780	3,030
20-24	7,070	3,427	3,913
25-29	2,589	3,030	1,430
30-34	1,717	3,606	2,658
35-39	1,306	1,984	3,257
40-44	912	1,384	1,768
45-49	779	1,037	1,260
50-54	769	820	940
55-59	705	702	725
60-64	526	663	649
65-69	475	516	535
70-74	325	387	424
75-79	294	293	293
80-84	200	213	221
85+	180	216	249
Total	24,414	23,659	23,634

Golf Projections	Year 1980	1980	Simmons Participation Rate for '79	Projected Participants	Agency's Share
Total adults (18-65+)		21,003	8.5%	1,785	
18-24		10,226	7.9%	808	
25-34		4,306	9.4%	405	
35-44		2,218	9.8%	217	
45-54		1,548	10.0%	155	
55-64		1,231	9.3%	114	
65 or older		1,474	4.4%	65	

Golf Projections	Year 1988	1988	Simmons Participation Rate for '87	Projected Participants	Agency's Share
Total adults (18-65+)		21,058	10.9%	2,295	
18-24		6.207	11.3%	701	
25-34		6,636	13.7%	909	
35-44		3,368	12.3%	414	
45-54		1,857	10.6%	197	
55-64		1,365	9.2%	126	
65 or older		1,625	6.1%	99	

Golf Projections	Year 1993	1993	Simmons Participation Rate Projected	Projected Participants	Agency's Share
Total adults (18-65+)		21,352	12.1%	2,584	
18-24		6,943	12.5%	868	
25-34		4,088	14.9%	609	
35-44		5,025	13.5%	678	
45-54		2,200	11.8%	260	
55-64		1,374	10.4%	143	
65 or older		1,722	7.3%	126	

Source: Warnick, Rodney B. "Golf Players in Amherst, MA 1980, 1988 & 1993." Presented at National Marketing Forum of the National Recreation and Park Association, Cromwell, CT, May 1989 based upon Census data and Simmons Market Research Bureau. *Study of Media and Markets.* Volume P-10 Sports and Leisure.

Internal marketing research and use of secondary data are two options available to delivery systems related to target market research. Delivery systems can also utilize specialized research projects as well. Many factors related to target marketing can be explored with such methods. The delivery system may choose to identify market segments for its organization as is represented in Exhibit 9.5, with a market segmentation profile of primary and secondary markets as conducted by the Edmonton Parks and Recreation Department.

Exhibit 9.5.
Market Segmentation for Edmonton Parks and Recreation

Representations: x - primary market
o - secondary market
( ) - percentage of population

Demographics:	Athletic Flds.	Fitness Cts.	Golf Courses
Male (50%)	x	x	x
Female (50%)		x	o
15-24 yrs. (20%)	o	o	o
25-34 yrs. (32%)	o	x	
35-54 yrs. (18%)			
55+ (10%)			
Under $20,000 (16%)			
$20-$39,000 (50%)	o	o	o
$40,000 and over (34%)	o		
Psychographics:			
Belongers (38%)	x		x
Emulators (8%)		x	o
Achievers (21%)			
I Am Me's (3%)	x	x	
Experientials (5%)		o	o
Socially Conscious (12%)		o	
Integrateds (2%)			

Source: Adapted from Marketing Plan for Edmonton Parks and Recreation Department. June 1988, p. 11.

Delivery systems can also choose to develop more specific profiles of user groups for specific programs or services. An example of such an usage profile is contained in Exhibit 9.6, which overviews the user characteristics of golf participants with the Calgary Parks and Recreation Department.

Needs assessments related to target markets are a crucial part of marketing research for a delivery system. While there are a variety of methods that can be incorporated into this process, ranging from informal solicitations of qualitative information to highly structured research methods, it is important to the success of the interpretation of these research efforts that the marketer adhere to sampling procedures and safeguards for reliability and validity for research projects. Such accepted research practices and techniques are detailed in a variety of sources such as marketing research

Exhibit 9.6. Profile of Golfers		
General Profile of Golf Course Users: 96 Percent of Population Participating 34 Percent of Adults Use Municipal Golf Course at Least Once Per Year		
USER CHARACTERISITCS	PERCENTAGE	
Gender	**1984**	**1985**
• male	75	65
• female	24	35
Household Marital status of users:	**1984**	**1985**
• married	80	75
• single	13	19
Size of household of users	**1984**	**1985**
• 2	63	51
• 3	12	17
• 4	13	14
• 1	7	7
• 5 or more	5	10
Number of people in household that golf:	**1984**	**1985**
• 2	45	50
• 1	44	31
• 3 up	11	18
Source: Strategic Marketing Plan, Calgary Parks and Recreation Department, Fall 1987		

or research methodology books, and it is recommended that delivery systems utilize these sources when developing specialized research projects.

Another factor to take into consideration when conducting user or needs assessment surveys is the interpretation of the data. Decisions related to data analysis need to be addressed prior to constructing the survey and should focus upon "what is going on" as well as "why it is occurring." An important consideration related to this issue involves the coding of the data. It is recommended that data be collected in such a manner that important target market descriptors can be included and analyzed. For instance, asking whether or not people have children 18 years of age or under living at home is not as revealing as determining stage in the family life cycle (preschoolers, high-school-age children, etc.) (Hudson and Witt, 1984, p. 22). The ability to analyze more than one variable is also critical. Analyzing responses on the basis of age, gender, income, or other target market descriptors provides the delivery system with more extensive information than analyzing the data collectively.

There are a variety of options available to park, recreation, and leisure delivery systems to assist them in better understanding their target markets. The use of multiple mechanisms enhances the capability of the delivery system to design and modify programs and services for those target markets they seek to attract.

Summary

All steps in the marketing process require decision making and the effectiveness of this decision making rests upon the use of marketing research. Such marketing research procedures are enhanced by the establishment of a marketing information system (MIS).

The organized procedures and methods of the MIS consist of methods and strategies to gather three types of information: internal, standardized, and specialized research information. Utilization of all three of these categories of information is key to the success of the marketing process.

Although there are a myriad of types of information secured through marketing research, those areas of particular importance for parks, recreation, and leisure delivery systems include: marketing opportunities, target markets, marketing mix, customer satisfaction, and marketing performance. While there are a plethora of research methods to employ, those of particular value for parks and recreation include: focus groups, importance-performance analysis, test marketing, users' satisfaction, promotional and public relations effectiveness, and target markets.

The completeness of the MIS along with the accuracy of research methods utilized to collect information contribute to the effectiveness of a recreation delivery system in continuing to respond to the ever-changing needs of target markets and variations within the competitive environment.

Suggested Activities

1. Select a specific park, recreation, and leisure delivery system and examine activities currently being conducted which constitute MIS.

2. Examine the internal records and forms of a delivery system. Identify specific ways in which internal marketing research efforts could be enhanced through minor modifications to these materials.

3. Examine appropriate periodicals including newspapers, journals, and newsletters published in the past three months. Select articles or statistics that could be useful as standardized sources of information for parks, recreation, and leisure. Suggest specific modifications or decisions that need to be undertaken on the basis of the information uncovered for a particular delivery system.

4. Identify programs or services that might benefit from the use of focus groups. For one of these programs or services, select people to be included in this process and develop a list of appropriate questions to be used.

5. Select one specific facility, program, or service and develop a list of attributes that could be utilized in the construction of an importance-performance analysis.

6. Observe the day-to-day operations of a specific organization or facility. Based upon your observation, suggest both informal and formal techniques which might be implemented to measure users' satisfaction.

References

Boyd, Westfall, and Stasch. (1989). *Marketing Research—Texts and Cases (7th ed.)* Homewood, IL: Richard D. Irwin.

Cravens, D. W. (1982). *Strategic Marketing.* Homewood, IL: Richard D. Irwin.

Crompton, J. L. and Lamb, C. W., Jr. (1986). *Marketing Government and Social Services* (p. 426). New York, NY: John Wiley & Sons.

Hudson and Witt. (1984, April). Beyond Frequency Counts: How to Get More Out of Community Surveys. *Journal of Park and Recreation Administration,* p. 22.

Kotler, P. (1982). *Marketing for Nonprofit Organizations (2nd ed.)* Engle wood Cliffs, NJ: Prentice-Hall.

Mantilla and James. (1979). Importance-Performance Analysis. *Journal of Marketing 41* (1), pp. 77-79.

Programmers Information Network (PIN). National Recreation and Park Association. Vol. 1 No. 1, January 1989, p. 8.

Rossman, J. R. (1989). *Recreation Programming--Designing Leisure Experiences* (p. 140). Champaign, IL: Sagamore Publishing.

Tracking...How to Verify the Results of Your Brochure Distribution. (1989, July-August). *Marketing Recreation Classes* (p. 3).

Zikmund, W. G. (1989). *Exploring Marketing Research (3rd ed.)* Chicago, IL: The Dryden Press.

Chapter Ten

Future Trends and Target Markets

Common Concerns for Parks, Recreation, and Leisure Delivery Systems

- A YMCA with a strong market position with children and youth examines the potential impact the aging population may have upon the organization.

- A chain of resorts considers the influence changing family characteristics and household patterns may have upon vacation packages.

- An urban park and recreation department undergoing a major renovation program for parks and community centers considers the role of changing community demographics upon these plans.

- A municipal golf course considering expansion wonders if this recent, dramatic increase in participation is a trend or a fad.

Impact of Societal Change

Marketing is the creation and distribution of goods and services and as such does not exist in a vacuum. The process of marketing is not static and is continually impacted upon by changes within society.

When discussing rapid changes within society, Margaret Mead was said to remark that the world into which one is born is not the world in which one will live or die. In today's world, it is challenging to even begin to come to grips with the accelerated pace of change.

Societal and technological changes influence all phases of our society. Recent changes and advancements determine how we live, how and where we work, as well as modifying values and attitudes about our leisure time. Oftentimes seemingly small advances and shifts have a far-reaching impact upon all aspects of life.

The focus of this chapter is not to address the ramifications of each and every one of these changes and advances, but rather to identify current trends within our society which substantially influence recreation and leisure, leading to the creation of new target market groups that will be viable for organizations in the future.

Pertinent Trends and Directions

While a vast array of societal changes have created trends and directions for the future, a number of these changes require examination due to the many ways they will impact upon use of leisure time and the marketing of such programs and services. Such trends and directions to be examined include shifting demographics, technological advances, and changes in values and attitudes.

Changing Demographics

One of the major demographic shifts relates to the maturing of the population. This age wave consists of two demographic groups of particular interest to leisure delivery systems: baby boomers and senior-seniors.

The baby boomers born between 1946 and 1964 are 76 million strong, constitute nearly half of America's adult population, and are entering mid-life (Farrell, 1989, p. 112). This group, by its sheer numbers, has shaped society since their beginnings. First, they caused school overcrowding; more recently, they created a boom for the housing market. The baby boom generation was among the first to be reared in the "recreation mode," as evidenced by their participation in everything from little league to piano lessons, and as a group they believe strongly in recreation as a right rather than a privilege. The sheer size of their numbers and their predilection for recreation will make them a force for the future.

An almost accidental demographic offshoot of the baby boomers is the resurgence of parenthood. Many baby boomers are becoming parents and the baby boomlet created by this pattern is changing the demographic makeup of this country as well. Babies, toddlers, children, and teens are now growing target market groups.

The greying of America includes not only the baby boomers but also those individuals currently 55 and over who will create an entire spectrum of grey for the country with a range of different age groups. According to the Census Bureau, the two next fastest-growing age groups in this country are those 85 and over and those people 75 to 84. By the year 2000, it is predicted that there will be almost 35 million people age 65 or older (Godbey, p. 9). The increased longevity of these more mature age groups coupled with vast differences in levels of health and income will create a host of heterogeneous lifestyle groups to be targeted by park, recreation, and leisure delivery systems.

Another demographic pattern with potential for impact upon parks, recreation, and leisure is the increase in the number of singles, nonfamily households, and fragmented families. The rise of alternative lifestyle choices along with divorce and the creation of single-parent households contribute to the increase in this demographic trend. Nonfamily households account for one-fourth of all households and single-parent households constitute about 13 percent of the population (Godbey, p. 30). Family patterns as well as stage in the family life cycle have long been considered elements with far-reaching impact upon recreation and leisure patterns. The diversity created in this socio-demographic target market descriptor will continue to grow in importance.

A final demographic trend with implications for the field is the increase in minority populations. Minorities constitute a growing percentage of the U.S. population, with the number of blacks and Hispanics rising significantly. The Hispanic population, which increased 34 percent since 1980, will become the largest minority group in the United States by 2010 (Leisure Industry Digest, 1989, p. 1). More than half of the growth in the country will be due to immigration with people from Latin America and Asia accounting for much of the influx (Kelly, 1987, p. 15).

Recreation and leisure delivery systems provide programs and services for people and as people change, these delivery systems will find the need to change by modifying their programs and services to adapt to the changes in the needs and interests of their target markets. The demographic shifts reflect some of the major trends with potential impact upon this field.

Impact of Technology

Scientific advances and technological changes within recent years have had considerable impact upon lifestyles and recreation behavior. Video games, microwaves, cable television, automated teller machines, and VCRs have substantially changed the way we live, work, and play. Medical research and breakthroughs have impacted the quality and length of our lives as well as provided directions for how we should live our lives. Computers, FAX machines, and robotics have influenced employment and work patterns as well.

Americans born in recent decades can expect to live longer. The increased life expectancy coupled with extension of the life cycle will change both expectations of and participation patterns in leisure in the future. Computerization and robotics will create a different picture for the work world. Jobs requiring physical exertions will be phased out and replaced by service sector employment opportunities. Computerization and advances in communication will enable Americans to work at home and away from urban centers. The conveniences and alternatives provided by cable television and VCRs will alter both the opportunities and expectations Americans hold for recreation and leisure pursuits.

We are virtually in our infancy as it relates to scientific and technological changes and advances. The current impact of such changes coupled with advances we may have difficulty even conceiving of at this time will combine to alter lifestyles, recreation participation patterns, and the expectations of recreation users.

Changes in Values and Attitudes

Peoples' attitudes and values lead them to make choices in their lives about how they live, work, and play, so they hold profound importance for the recreation and leisure field. Daniel Yankelovich, a social researcher, in his book, *New Rules: Searching for Self-Fulfillment in a World Turned Upside Down,* points out that as a nation we are in search of new rules with which to face the future, since the old rules of post-World War II just don't work anymore. This search for new rules governing our day-to-day lives has led to changes in society.

Joseph Plummer (1989) maintains that we are in the midst of a paradigm shift–*"a fundamental reordering of the way we see the world around us"*– caused by satisfaction of basic needs and the impact of technology and its subsequent economic changes (pp. 10-11). These shifts from traditional values to new values, with particular impact upon recreation and leisure, are as follows:

Traditional Values	_to_	_New Values_

Traditional Values	New Values
Self-denial ethic	Self-fulfillment ethic
Higher standard of living	Better quality of life
Traditional sex roles	Blurring of sex roles
Accepted definition of success	Individualized definition
Traditional family life	Alternative families
Live to work	Work to live

(Plummer, 1989, pp. 10-11)

This gradual move from traditional values to new emerging values is being adopted by an ever-growing number of people. Stanford Research Institute (SRI), initiator of VALS (Values, Attitudes, and Lifestyles), predicted that there would be a shift from outer-directed to inner-directed people; this shift is documented through market research conducted by Young and Rubican Ventures, where Plummer serves as the managing director.

Social forecasters Naisbitt and Aburdene, in their book, *Megatrends 2000–Ten New Directions for The 1990s,* cite multiple examples and statistics indicating a move away from the more traditional, outer-directed approach to living and support the rise of a new social paradigm. Three of these megatrends particularly related to this shift are: a renaissance in the arts, the religious revival, and the triumph of the individual (1987, p. 84).

Of particular interest to this field is the shift from a sports culture to an arts focus. Naisbitt and Aburdene maintain that during the nineties we will "shift from baseball to ballet with the arts replacing sports as society's dominant leisure activity," and they indicate that this transition is already in progress (p. 84). A report by the National Endowment for the Arts calculated that Americans now spend $3.7 billion attending arts events as compared with $2.8 billion for sporting events (Naisbitt and Aburdene, 1987, p. 84). Additional statistics cited led them to suggest that "in less than a generation Americans have reversed their leisure spending habits" and relate these shifts to the coming of age of the baby boomers (p. 84).

The triumph of the individual relates to a number of factors, including technological advances in communication, which provide options for freedom in work patterns as well as an increasing focus on global issues and culture. This renewed interest in sense of community bodes well for a growing interest and acceptance of environmental concerns.

The religious revival that encompasses both fundamentalism and the New Age movement underscores this shift to a new social paradigm. It is estimated that evangelicals number nearly 40 million people and this, coupled with the 5 to 15 percent of the population who are New Agers seeking personal development and insight through the metaphysical, signifies such a shift (Naisbitt and Aburdene, 1987, pp. 278-280).

What these value and attitude changes mean for recreation and leisure is predictable and many of the manifestations of these changes are already present. The interest in wellness encompassing changes in lifestyles along with participation in individual physical activities such as walking, hiking, and cross-country skiing is already apparent. The increased interest in the arts through attendance at concerts and performances as well as enrollments in art-related classes are well noted. The growing popularity of travel and the heightened interest in leisure adventures and experiences all are indicators that the value and attitude shift is already happening as is the renewed and enthusiastic attention being generated by environmental concerns and outdoor recreation.

Plummer (1989) feels that the research on changing values indicates that organizations need to rethink the old rules and recognize the emerging new rules and changes. He suggests that marketers analyze and act upon these changes by recognizing the following:

(a) new focus on individuality favoring high levels of creativity, flexibility, and responsiveness;
(b) the greater value being given to experience prompting the growth of travel, the arts, sports, and lifelong education; and
(c) the shift in health behavior from curing sickness to promoting wellness. (p. 13)

The world is changing and these changes are not just related to politics, technology, and the economy. Such changes lead to shifts in values and attitudes. This new social paradigm consisting of renewed interest in the individual, creativity, quality of life, the arts, and wellness all have substantial implications for parks, recreation, and leisure.

There is a plethora of societal changes and technological advances with potential impact upon parks, recreation, and leisure delivery systems. While it is not feasible to identify and examine each of these changes or the specific impacts for every organization, it is important that recreators be cognizant of some of these trends and directions and identify those with greatest potential impact upon their delivery system.

Potential Target Market Groups

Our society continues to grow more diverse. This diversity leads to the creation of a plethora of subgroups whose needs and interests vary based upon their lifestyles. While target marketing has long been recognized as a substantial contributor to the success of a delivery system's marketing plan, the identification of specific target market groups now assumes an even more important role. There are a number of target market groups with potential for leisure delivery systems in the future such as baby boomers, older Americans, minorities, children, young adults, fragmented families, and some new clusters identified through Prizm and VALS.

Baby Boomers

One such target market group with potential for leisure delivery systems both now and in the coming decades is the baby boomers. This generation, consisting of 76 million people or one-third of the entire population, will be very important to recreators.

This entire generation "lurching into middle age" will question what they're doing and why they're doing it (How the Next Decade Will Differ, 1989, p. 143). *Adweek* reported that this group of Americans sees leisure as a birthright (Russell, 1987, p. 138). Market researcher Judith Langer has identified a new attitude among people in their thirties and forties that she terms "backing off workaholism" (Russell, 1987, p. 76). Life changes such as attitudes towards work and career coupled with attitudes towards leisure will make a difference to the park, recreation, and leisure industry. Previously ambitious employees no longer satisfied with work rewards will seek other vehicles such as recreation and leisure pursuits to fulfill their changing needs.

Some of the key issues for this "maturing" generation of baby boomers will be quality of life and the environment as they search for sense of self, well-being, community, and meaning (How the Next Decade Will Differ, 1989, p. 143). Baby boomers experiencing the physical changes of aging will seek out physical activities in their free time. Concerns for quality of life, sense of community, and meaning will push them towards environmental issues and outdoor recreation pursuits, as well as other alternatives related to recreation.

This search for quality of life coupled with their possession of nearly one-half of the nation's discretionary income will make them profitable target markets for parks, recreation, and leisure. A word of caution is in order regarding their selection as a target market. The baby boom generation is quite diverse and defies categorization when it comes to purchasing behavior (Sneak Preview, 1989, p. 47). Leisure delivery systems will need to examine this group carefully and subsegment the baby boomers accordingly for effective manipulation of marketing mix variables to attract these subgroups.

Are they worth the extra effort required of an organization? Not only are they an especially viable target market for today, but by the year 2030 there will be 77 million of them retired, and their combined discretionary income and time make them worth the pursuit (The Grey Boomers, 1990, p. 55).

The Age Wave

Another target market group worthy of a leisure delivery system's consideration is the new cohort group of Americans currently retired or rapidly approaching retirement. Coming soon to leisure delivery systems everywhere is the *age of the aged*. This bulging "silver market" (50 and over) accounts for approximately 64 million Americans and represent 75 percent of the nation's wealthiest people. Between 1990 and 2000, they will account for 18.5 percent of the population growth, while Americans under the age of 50 will grow by only 3.5 percent (Shades of Grey, 1989, p. 60).

Their impact as a target market is already being felt. Television shows, movies, commercials, and even magazines now all feature older adults. With money and time available to them, this group represents a huge market for restaurants, hotels, airlines, and resorts (Shades of Grey, 1989, p. 65). Adults over 45 account for 57 percent of the $752 million in sales of walking shoes and 65 percent of the $282 million in sales of treadmills (Shades of Grey, 1989, p. 67). There have even been marketing firms created, such as LAVOA (Lifestyles and Values of Older Americans) of Annapolis, MD, and Life-span, based in New York, to address the impact of this aging trend.

Delivery systems ranging from small firms to corporate giants are beginning to retool to attract this target market. Grand Travel of Chevy Chase, MD, specializes in travel for grandparents and children with safaris to Kenya and other exotic vacations. Major resorts are already retooling for family vacation stays for the four-generation families they anticipate serving by the year 2000 (The Geezer Boom, 1989, p. 62). Many of the members of this generation are returning to college campuses for the nostalgia and access to learning and activity which accompany such areas.

The Marriott Corporation, in cooperation with the University of Virginia, is currently planning a retirement community to address this trend, which will be further heightened by the maturing of the baby boomers (Lewin, 1990, p. 1).

Consider a word of caution as this silver market trades in jogging for walking and work for hobbies. *Newsweek* suggests that "ever greyer results in even greater diversity" (The Geezer Boom, 1989, p. 62). In the past we have tended to lump all retired people into one category, referring to them as senior citizens or the elderly. Such generalizations will be replaced by more specific categories related to age, health, and wealth as well as recreational interests and lifestyles. In the not-so-distant future, leisure delivery systems will need to distinguish between those individuals 50+, the young-old, the old, and the oldest old, with further delineations based upon health and income.

Minorities

Minority population groups will continue to assume a higher percentage of the American population as we approach the 21st century. The Census Bureau numbers the black population at 30 million and the Hispanic population at 200 million (Leisure Industry Digest, 1989, p. 1). *American Demographics* projects that in the next 25 years, Hispanics will account for one fifth to one half of this country's growth, with Asian-Americans also developing a strong presence (Sneak Preview, 1989, p. 48).

While minority groups assimilate into the American culture, they continue to be attracted to their own cultural identity. The social and economic impact of such demographic changes will be substantial. Already Hispanic advertising is present in a number of major markets such as Los Angeles and Miami, and many American companies have adapted both their products and ad campaigns to reach this target market (How the Next Decade Will Differ, 1989, p. 144).

The growing importance of minority groups in America is underscored by the recent controversy linked to tobacco companies and distributors of alcohol, who have been sharply criticized for recent product developments and ad campaigns focused upon blacks as potential target markets for their products. While advocacy groups are attempting to curtail the target marketing approaches of these legal but possibly dangerous products, it does indicate the growing role of minority groups upon this country both socially and economically.

Minority groups make a excellent target market for parks, recreation, and leisure delivery systems. While assimilation into society often becomes a requirement of the work world, leisure time and recreational pursuits are excellent outlets for involvement with family, friends, and cultural activities.

Kids

In light of the shifting demographics reflecting the maturing of America, kids may seem like an unusual choice for a potentially profitable target market. While children have long been a primary target market of many public and nonprofit recreation delivery systems, their importance to all sectors of recreation and leisure will continue to grow in spite of the decline in the actual size of this population.

The impact of children as target market groups is changing in this country. The baby boomlet created by baby boomers becoming parents is somewhat responsible for this renewed interest and focus upon programs and services geared to babies, toddlers, and youth. Societal patterns such as divorce and dual-career couples further shape this trend as parents look for services to accommodate their needs for child care during nonschool time periods. According to the Census Bureau, by the year 2000, 70 percent of kids will be raised in households where both parents work, and the parents of the late-eighties baby boomlet will spare no expense in providing their offspring with the best of everything (The Nineteen Hotest Businesses, 1989, pp. 78-84).

The way children and teenagers are perceived in this country today is quite different than in the past. Kids have clout. In a recent survey conducted by the Roper Organization of working parents with children ages 7 to 17, "74 percent said that their children help decide family leisure activities and 52 percent indicated their influence related to choice of vacation destinations (Parents, 1990, p. 1D). The survey further revealed that the higher the parents' income and education level, the more influence children have upon these types of decisions (Parents, 1990, p. 1D).

While babies, toddlers, and young children are dependent upon their parents as sources for financing, teenagers often are not. Teenagers with more discretionary income of their own are a target market to be addressed. Despite a decline in the actual number of teenagers, teen spending is on the rise. This nation's 28 million teenagers spend $100 billion annually and Teenage Research Unlimited reveals that in addition to their own $100 billion, they spend another $150 billion making family purchases (Teen Scene, 1989, pp. 52-55).

Teenagers are a profitable target market for recreation and leisure agencies, since their predilection for fads encourages them to buy new things. However, this same predilection coupled with the importance of peer group influence should make leisure delivery systems examine carefully programs and services developed for this target market, since their preferences are often transitory in nature.

Societal changes such as divorce, dual career families, and the changing role of children make kids a viable target market for parks, recreation, and leisure. It is projected that in 1992 the decline in the birthrate will begin to rise increasingly minority driven, which will have a continued impact upon their selection as target market groups (Teen Scene, 1989, pp. 52-55).

Young Adults

A target market relatively new to our society is the extended adolescent/ young adult sometimes referred to as "twentysomething." There has been a sharp reversal in the ways Americans mature and enter adulthood. Many young adults are experiencing an extended adolescence, taking longer to go to college, establish careers, marry, and even leave the nest (Young Beyond Their Years, 1989, p. 54). This places them in an "in-between" state. They are too old to be considered teenagers, but have not yet assumed adult-like roles and behaviors.

American Demographics suggests that this extremely diverse group of individuals has created a new stage in adult development characterized by boomeranging or starting and stopping activity in all phases of their lives (Twenty Something, 1990, p. 1D). According to the Census Bureau, 54 percent of Americans aged 18 to 24 lived at home with their parents in 1988 (Twenty Something, 1990, p. 1D). This is an especially viable target market for leisure delivery systems. Members of this group, whose premature affluence is often due to jobs held as teenagers, are accustomed to discretionary income and continue to live at home in order to maintain their personal lifestyle and spending habits (Young Beyond Their Years, 1989, p. 57).

Fragmented Family Patterns

In the 1950s and 1960s, a family or household conjured up images of the Cleavers or the Nelsons. These families don't exist today, and the diversity of lifestyles produces some unusual patterns such as singles, childless couples, single parents, single mothers by choice, unmarried couples with or without children, dual-career families, stay-at-home mothers, house fathers, reconstituted families, gay and lesbian couples with or without children, grandparents raising children, and babies having babies (What Happened, 1989, pp. 10-12).

The societal changes of the past 20 years have naturally created a change in the family. The Census Bureau reports that household size has shrunk to 2.62 persons, and that people living alone in 1989 hit a record 22.7 million, or one-quarter of all households (What Happened, 1989, pp. 10-12). The array of alternatives for the new American family poses both a challenge and an opportunity for recreation delivery systems.

The nature of one's household has significant impact upon amounts of discretionary time and income as well as dictating interests and participation patterns. While attempting to meet the needs and interests of all these households would be difficult, the variations enable leisure delivery systems to subsegment their markets and design programs and services specifically geared to attracting one or more of these household groups.

Activity Profiles

Three of the more common areas of recreational activity are fitness, travel, and outdoor recreation. Interest and participation in each of these areas has been growing in the past few years. Due to specialization areas within both of these recreational outlets and the role played by lifestyle factors, it is of value to examine potential target market groups within each of these areas.

Exercise and fitness programs abound in this country. The innumerable options within this area indicate that peoples' perceptions and preferences for exercise and fitness activities (or lack of the same) vary extensively. A recent Louis Harris poll conducted for *Prevention* magazine found six basic types of potential target markets for fitness, as follows:

Healthy and Wealthy (25 percent)–middle-aged, college-educated, upper-income professionals who rate above average on diet and weight but below average on exercise; interested in improving;

Safe and Satisfied (7 percent)–below-average income and education who are fairly healthy with little desire to improve;

Sedentary but Striving (8 percent)–women, minorities, and blue-
collars who are poor exercisers and have weight problems with an
interest in improving;

Young and Reckless (38 percent)–generally under 35 with slightly
above average income and education along with poor eating and
exercise patterns;

Fat and Frustrated (7 percent)–tend to be older, female, minority
with less education who tend to be overweight but lack knowledge
and resources to improve; and

Confused but Indifferent (5 percent)–mostly white, blue-collar
males with below- average education and income who tend to be
overweight but don't care.
(Sterling, 1989, p. 1D)

An examination of these fitness profiles might help leisure delivery systems
to better modify programs and services to attract specific groups as well as
providing insights into nonuser groups as well.

An additional popular form of recreation is travel. Participation in
travel and travel-related expenditures have continued to grow at a fairly
rapid rate in the past decade. Delivery systems involved with travel or
resorts should be cognizant of the distinct types of leisure travelers.
According to a recent Gallup survey, there are five different types of
recreational travelers as follows:

Dreamers—are fascinated by travel and attach great importance to
the experience and meaning travel adds to their life;

Adventurers—are independent and confident seeking new experiences and valuing diversity in activities and culture;

Worriers—lack confidence in their ability to travel and the perceived stress of travel causes them to travel the least of all groups;

Economizers—seek travel as a break from routine and are looking for value rather than adventure or special attention; and

Indulgers—seek travel for pampering and special attention as opposed to the travel itself.
(Survey: Americans, 1989, p. T4)

These categorizations can be of value to travel, resort, and other leisure delivery systems. All five groups may travel to the same destination, but yet be seeking entirely different benefits and experiences. These differences need to be reflected in specific programs and services as well as in the packaging and promotion of travel.

Outdoor recreation is an increasingly popular activity. Based upon the report generated by the President's Commission on American Outdoors, Market Opinion Research Corporation identified five motivations for such participation. Five outdoor recreation activity profile types were then developed on the basis of this information. The five motivational groups are as follows:

Excitement—Seeking Competitives–young, upper-middle class; many singles; enjoy individual and team sports;

Get Away Actives—nearly all are baby boomers interested in experiencing nature and being alone through backpacking, hiking, and camping;

Fitness Driven—older and highest on socio-economic scale; participation relates to fitness, not socialization or excitement;

Health Conscious Sociables—one-third of American adults motivated by fitness and socialization; enjoy walking, picnicking, and outings; and

Unstressed and Unmotivateds—equal number of men and women; median age of 49; find few reasons to participate.
(Bryant, 1987, pp. 39-41)

Outdoor recreation encompasses a myriad of diverse activities from nature walks to sky diving. Attention to these five motivational types will enhance the marketing efforts of leisure delivery systems.

New Psychographics

The VALS (Values, Attitudes and Lifestyles) system of psychographics was created in 1978 by the Stanford Research Institute (SRI) and divided Americans into nine psychographic groups. These nine groups based upon a hierarchy of needs were detailed in an earlier chapter. Those nine profiles were determined on the basis of need-driven, outer-directed, or inner-directed approaches to life.

SRI has recently developed a new system referred to as VALS 2 to more accurately reflect the societal and demographic shifts of the last decade. VALS 2 identifies eight psychographic segments based upon two factors: "self" orientation and resources (Riche, 1989, pp. 24-25). "Self" orientation categories include principle-oriented, status-oriented, and action-oriented. Resources include such factors as income, education, intelligence and health ranging from minimal to abundant. Each of the three "self" orientations has two different segments based upon low versus high level of resources (see Figure 10.1, p. 242).

Strugglers appear at the bottom of the VALS 2 hierarchy and consist of an aging, need-driven group of Americans. *Actualizers* appear at the top of the hierarchy and include individuals with high levels of resources embracing any or all of the "self" orientations.

The principle-oriented segments are designated as *Fulfilleds* and *Believers*. These groups are guided by their perspective as to how the world is or should be. The Fulfilleds are the higher resource group and tend to be more mature and better educated than the Believers who have fewer resources and tend to be more conservative (Riche, 1989, p. 25).

Achievers and *Strivers* make up the status-oriented segments. Achievers are successful, work and family oriented, and politically conservative. While Strivers have fewer resources than the Achievers whom they emulate, they share similar values (Riche, 1989, p. 25).

The Action-oriented segments are designated as *Experiencers* and *Makers*. The Experiencers are younger with an abundance of energy directed towards physical and social activities with an emphasis upon the new. The Makers are action-oriented with fewer resources. They prefer the familiar and aren't especially attracted to material possessions (Riche, 1989, p. 25).

The original VALS system consisted of nine groups with several disproportionately large segments. In addition to providing more current information, VALS 2 is of greater value because the eight segments reflect a better percentage distribution (Riche, 1989, p. 26).

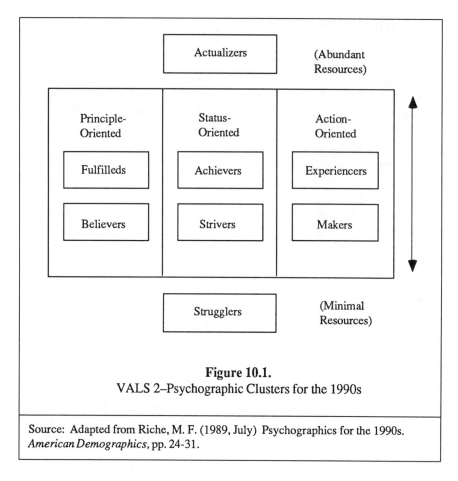

Figure 10.1.
VALS 2–Psychographic Clusters for the 1990s

Source: Adapted from Riche, M. F. (1989, July) Psychographics for the 1990s.
American Demographics, pp. 24-31.

The VALS 2 approach to psychographics separates potential target markets on the basis of their differences and then clusters them by their similarities (Riche, 1989, p. 27). Since recreation participation is a behavior influenced by people's values, attitudes, and lifestyles, this approach can significantly enhance the viability of leisure delivery systems.

New Clusters

The clustering of America or the use of geodemographic information to designate types of communities within our society were mentioned in previous chapters on target marketing. Neighborhood clusters have changed since the time Claritas Corporation developed the Prizm system.

Eight new clusters that emerged following the 1980 Census reflected a host of the demographic and societal changes of the seventies. The new clusters of the eighties were as follows:

Black Enterprise–black affluence created in upper-middle-class minority neighborhoods;

New Beginnings–single communities emerging in previously-blue-collar family areas;

Town & Gowns–college-educated baby boomers transforming once rural backwaters into sophisticated towns;

Gray Power–senior retirement communities;

Rank & File–declining number of young people living in industrial, urban neighborhoods;

New Melting Pot–growing influx of immigrants, many of them middle-class Asians and Latin Americans;

Single City Blues–lower-middle-class baby boomers in downscale urban areas; and

Golden Ponds–increase in middle-class retirees settling in rustic towns.
(Weiss, 1988, p. 242)

These clusters will continue to remain of interest and importance to leisure delivery systems since they represent emerging societal trends. Further examination of the values and lifestyles of these eight clusters could result in the selection of profitable target markets for an agency.

Since past findings reveal that 20 percent of this country's neighborhoods change every 10 years, it is anticipated that there will be eight new clusters emerging for the 1990s (Weiss, 1988, p. 259). The following represent the eight new cluster nicknames with trends projected for the future:

Young Rustics–Americans migrating from cities to exurban areas;

Boomlet Families–growth of suburban family neighborhoods;

Gentrification Chic–gentrifying inner cities become affluent;

Suburban Retirees–aging, empty-nesting suburbs become retirement areas;

New-Collar Condos–single townhouses and condos filled with new-collar service workers;

Minority Achievers–the nation's minority and immigrant groups rise to affluence;

Sunbelt Industries–manufacturing plants from the northeastern cities continue to migrate to small southern factory towns; and

Urban Independents–a wave of nontraditional households–stepfamilies, single-parent families, and unmarried couples move to quiet, city neighborhoods.

These projected neighborhood clusters for the 1990s reflect the latest demographic, societal, and economic trends of this country. The changing shape and style of our neighborhoods will substantially influence both the identification and selection of viable target markets for the 21st century.

Target marketing remains the foundation for the development of marketing plans for leisure delivery systems. Since this identification and selection of target market groups provides a basis for additional marketing activity, it is critical that leisure delivery systems monitor changes in target market composition and continue to search for ways to attract these viable target markets to their organizations (see Figure 10.2).

Summary

The process of marketing cannot exist in a vacuum and must continually be modified and adapted over time. Such adaptations and modifications will be shaped and influenced by changes within our world. Societal changes and technological changes produce prevailing trends and directions that influence recreation and leisure delivery systems and the marketing process.

DINKS	——	Double-Income, No Kids
BUMPIES	——	Black, Upwardly-Mobile Professionals
LUMPIES	——	Laid-back, Un-Motivated Professionals
WOOFS	——	Well-Off, Older Folks
YEEPIES	——	Young-Elderly, Energetic People into everything
20 SOMETHING	——	Young adults in extended adolesence
FLYERS	——	Fun-Loving Youth En Route to Success
SKIPPIES	——	School Kids with Income and Purchasing Power

Figure 10.2.
Acronyms for Target Market Groups

Current changes with particular impact upon parks and recreation include: shifting demographics, technological advances, and changes in values and attitudes. These changes need to be examined by delivery systems so that steps in the marketing process can be adapted and modified for continued effectiveness.

The aforementioned changes within society combine to produce changes in the way we live, work, and play. These changes result in the creation of new or somewhat different target market groups for parks and recreation. New target market groups with potential for such delivery systems are: baby boomers, minority groups, children, young adults, and new family/household groups. Other viable target markets include new clusters created through geodemographic research, and lifestyle profiles for speciality areas such as fitness, travel, and outdoor recreation.

An awareness and examination of current and projected changes within our society should be a priority for recreation and leisure delivery systems. This awareness of prevailing trends and directions should result in the identification and selection of new or modified target market groups for parks, recreation, and leisure.

Suggested Activities

1. Select a specific leisure delivery system. For that delivery system identify specific societal changes for that neighborhood or community.

2. Identify the current target market groups served by your delivery system. On the basis of current and projected trends and

directions, suggest ways in which these target market groups may change in the future. Examine how these changes will impact upon marketing mix variables.

3. Identify new or emerging target market groups and identify which of these target market groups may be potentially viable for your delivery system. Specify marketing strategies designed to attract these groups.

References

Bryant, B. E. (1987, March). Built for Excitement. *American Demographics,* pp. 39-41.

Farrell, C. (1989, October 16). The Age Wave—and How to Ride It. *Business Week,* p. 112.

The Geezer Boom. (1989, December). *Newsweek*—Special Edition, p. 62.

Godbey, Geoffrey. (1989). The Future of Leisure Services—Thriving on Change. State College, PA: Venture Publishing, Inc.

The Grey Boomers. (1990, February 6). *The Boston Globe*, p. 55.

How the Next Decade will Differ. (1989, September 25). *Business Week.*

Kelly, J. R. (1987). Recreation Trends—Towards the Year 2000 (p. 15). Champaign, IL: Management Learning Laboratories.

Leisure Industry Digest IX, October 1989, p. 1.

Lewin, T. (1990, February 19). Seniors Come Back to Campus Life. *Sarasota Herald Tribune,* p. 1.

Naisbitt and Aburdene. (1987). *Ten New Directions for the 1990's— Megatrends 2000.* New York: William Morrow and Company.

The Nineteen Hottest Businesses for the 1990s. (1989, December). *Entrepreneur,* pp. 78-84.

Parents Are Listening to Kids. (1990, January 24). *USA Today,* p. 1D.

Plummer, J. T. (1989, January-February). Changing Values. *The Futurist.*

Riche, M. F. (1989, July). Psychographics for the 1990s. *American Demographics,* pp. 24-31.

Russell, C. (1987). *100 Predictions for the Baby Boom—The Next 50 Years.* New York: Plenum Press.

Shades of Grey. (1989, December). *Entrepreneur.*

Sneak Preview. (1989, December). *Entrepreneur.*

Sterling, D. USA's Race for Health Leaves Most Gasping. (1989, August 22). *USA Today,* p. 1D.

Survey: Americans "Dreamers" as Vacationers. (1989, October 15). *Sunday Republican,* p. T4.

Teen Scene. (1989, December). *Entrepreneur,* pp. 52-55.

Twenty Something. (1990, February 2). *USA Today,* p. 1D.

Weiss, M. J. (1988). *The Clustering of America.* New York: Harper & Row.

What Happened to the Family. (1989, December). *Newsweek,* Special Issue, pp. 10-12.

Young Beyond Their Years. (1989, December). *Newsweek,* Special Issue.

Chapter Eleven

Marketing Opportunities and Strategies for Today and Tomorrow

Common Concerns for Parks, Recreation and Leisure Delivery Systems

- A large county park and recreation system reviews competition with private service providers and considers revising its role for the future.

- A mountain area summer resort catering to two-week, family vacations seeks to identify other marketing opportunities.

- An urban fitness club offering swimming, fitness, and racquet sports discusses a more specialized service approach.

- A suburban YMCA rich with traditional physical activity programs considers repositioning as a marketing strategy.

Marketing Opportunities

Every time period, whether it be a decade or an era, possesses its own particular set of circumstances that substantially shapes life during that period. The decade of the nineties and the dawning of the 21st century will be no different. There will be changes and circumstances acting in concert to determine the makeup of this future world.

Sociodemographic trends, economic conditions, and technological advances will all converge to shape the 21st century. Collectively, these trends and conditions will in turn present specific opportunities for park, recreation, and leisure delivery systems. Some of those opportunities to be explored in this section include: growth of the *experiential industry,* the *wellness* movement, *increases* in *travel,* and the rising importance of *convenience* and *specialization* to consumers.

Experiences

In 1980, Toffler in his book, *The Third Wave,* devoted a full chapter to the rising importance of experiences as part of society's future. Toffler maintained that under more affluent conditions, the economy would reorganize to deal with a new level of human needs for psychic gratification that he termed *psychologization* (1980, p. 195). He predicted the rise of the *experiential industries* encompassing pre-programmed experiences in the arts, recreation, and travel (p. 200). The plethora of experience-related recreation options available today, coupled with the proliferation of options within art and travel, reinforce his prediction.

Toffler identified two areas of the experiential industries: simulated environments and live environments. Simulated environments "offer a taste of adventure, danger, sexual titillation, or other pleasure without risk to a participant's real life or reputation" (Toffler, 1980, p. 202). Live environments include such experiences as safaris, gambling casinos, and travel. The recent increase in travel–particularly the adventure-oriented variety–as well as the trends within theme resorts and amusement parks, are examples of these categorizations.

Many organizations have capitalized upon this need for psychic gratification and have created marketing opportunities. The developers of shopping malls have plunged into the marketing of created environments. The New York City-based International Council of Shopping Centers reports that more than 126 million people visit the more than 30,000 malls monthly (Meet at the Mall, 1989, p. D1). Malls are adding cultural programs, festivals, and special events to create *experiences* to attract consumers. The West Edmonton Mall in Alberta, Canada has a World Waterpark where February shoppers can pretend it's July by splashing in warm waves. Shoppers also have access to a lagoon, water slides, and an ice rink, as well as an amusement park, 19 movie theaters, a chapel, and a bingo hall (Edmonton's Fantasyland, 1990, p. 7G).

Bars and restaurants have capitalized upon this marketing opportunity of experiences. Sports bars are a relative newcomer to the scene, creating an environment where fans gather to play and participate. The U. S. Navy's Morale, Welfare, and Recreation divisions have adopted such a concept at several of their clubs throughout the country. Bars often feature special theme nights or contests as a mechanism for luring patrons into their establishments. Restaurants have also taken advantage of this experience opportunity and have created specialized dining programs including Easter Egg Hunt brunches and dining tours of the French wine country.

Hotels and resorts are still another entry into the experiential industry. Hotels identifying low-occupancy patterns sponsor murder-mystery weekends, Scrabble® tournaments, or other activities to provide motivation for people to book space in their facilities. Some hotels have even taken this psychic gratification concept one step further and introduced what Toffler refers to as simulated environments. There are now several such establishments in the country that feature theme rooms. These theme rooms, ranging from the Arabian Nights to Victorian England, are designed to include motifs and furnishings appropriate for the theme and are often booked years in advance.

Resorts and amusement parks have responded to this trend as well. The construction of wave pools and water parks relates to this trend. Disney World in Florida has undergone substantial expansion to provide such experience options. The Disney organization has created Epcot Center, where visitors are immersed in the culture of other countries, as well as a typhoon lagoon where guests can swim alongside sharks. Their more recent development of Pleasure Island, a nightlife entertainment center, along with MGM studios, where guests can travel through scenes of great movies or star in scenes from TV, are additional examples of seizing the experiential opportunity (American Adventures, 1989, p. F9).

Amusement and theme parks continually scramble to compete. Universal Studios has added an earthquake simulation and a confrontation with King Kong to its tour, while Busch Gardens has created a water adventure safari (Get Ready, 1989, p. 12E). Amusement parks across the country continue to build bigger and more sophisticated roller coasters in an attempt to provide users with a thrilling experience.

Simulated environments are not the only options being created to profit from this growing desire for experiences. There is a plethora of real experiences being packaged and promoted for consumers. People who can afford to do so are being offered opportunities to fulfill dreams or have their fantasies come true. Consumers can now participate in major league baseball camps, cattle roundups, authentic car races, Mt. Everest climbs, or jams with musical greats (Silk, 1990, p. F1). Dream or fantasy experiences are now being made available to respond to this growth of the need for psychic gratifications.

Such adventure field trips are now prevalent. Learning and experience-oriented getaways are proliferating. There are tours and trips for people interested in learning, doing, or experiencing most anything. People can go to Mars with Isaac Asimov in a role-playing seminar or participate in a scientific experiment or an archaeological dig (Larsen, 1990, p. 97). People can learn to write a play, speak another language, or cook exotic foods. The options are nearly endless.

Travel

A major component of the experiential industries is travel. It is estimated that in the United States, travel generates approximately $318 billion annually (Marketing Experience, 1990, p. 1). Travel has become an essential component of the American lifestyle. A recent American Express survey revealed that Americans would forego luxuries before relinquishing travel plans (Marketing Experience, 1990, p. 1). It is estimated that travel will experience a 16 percent increase by the year 2000 due to baby boomers stimulating the market for less traditional vacations ranging from offbeat luxury to soft adventure (Marketing Experience, 1990, pp. 2-4).

The steady but significant growth of travel in recent years reflects changing demographics and societal trends such as the age wave, impact of stress in daily life, and the growth of psychic needs for experiences. Trends in travel are significantly influenced by societal trends. Recent changes in cruises serve as examples of such impacts. More than four million people will go on cruises in 1990 compared with 1.4 million in 1980, with the average age dropping from 65 to 45 over the same time period (Trick, 1990, p. 5D). The growing swell of passengers is credited to the introduction of innovative programs such as daycare and slumber parties for children, exotic destinations such as India and Africa, and shorter itineraries to adapt to busy schedules (Trick, 1990, p. 5D). The success of cruises is based upon the industry's ability to create marketing opportunities based upon societal changes.

Other marketing directions for the future of the travel industry include eco-tourism, soft adventure, and bed and breakfasts. Eco-tourism reflects an increased interest in nature and includes bird watchers, photographers, rock hounds, scuba divers, and spelunkers (Tourism with Purpose, 1989, p. 45). In 1989 soft adventures attracted more than three million people in 1989 who paid thousands of dollars each to risk getting wet, hungry, lost, or sick in search of exotic nature or cultural adventures (Tourism with Purpose, 1989, p. 45). Another travel option related to this growing desire for experience is the rise in popularity of bed and breakfasts. B & B's ranging from luxurious to very basic offer travelers an option for a different view of life in the country or region of the country where they are visiting.

Wellness

Another marketing opportunity for parks, recreation, and leisure is *wellness*. In recent years Americans have been obsessed with being thin, looking good, and maintaining a youthful appearance. However, this obsession has matured to a predilection for wellness. Wellness differs from just an interest in miracle diets, exercise plans, or plastic surgery. Wellness incorporates quality of life concerns related to all phases of existence (see Exhibits 11.1 and 11.2).

In 1989, Americans spent $16.3 billion on exercise footwear and apparel (Hot Businesses, 1989, p. 50). Recent legislation has banned cigarette smoking on all domestic airline flights under six hours. A substantial 89 percent of all adult Americans (158 million people) report experiencing high stress in their lives (Harris, 1987, p. 8). Sales of alcoholic beverages are on a long downhill slide due to concerns about weight and health. These reports reveal the need and interest on the part of Americans for a change in lifestyle.

Trend trackers predict that baby boomers will seek simpler, saner, more family-centered lives in the next decade, and the increasing moderation in alcohol and cigarette consumption coupled with the growing number of employees turning down transfers and promotions are indicative of this new lifestyle (Downey, 1990, p. G5). This tendency of Americans to address the quality of their lives has presented new opportunities for the service sector. A 400-franchise organization called Fit by Five specializing in children's fitness is currently in high demand (Hot Businesses, 1989, p. 78). The number of spa visitors seeking to restore physical, nutritional, and mental well-being and balance to their lives has increased between 8 to 10 percent annually since 1987 (Travelers Taking, 1989, p. F1).

The Foothills Metropolitan Recreation and Park District serving the suburban Lakewood region of highly urbanized Denver, CO, has repositioned its entire organization to focus upon wellness. The district wanted the concept to go beyond just not being sick and beyond emphasis upon just physical fitness so a six-dimensional approach to wellness was created that includes physical, spiritual, emotional, social, intellectual, and occupational wellness. This department's program brochure identifies and defines the organization's conception of wellness in each issue. In addition, the district's program and service offerings regularly promote the wellness benefits of each activity.

All phases of the leisure industry stand to benefit from acting upon this opportunity for wellness and quality of life as Americans seek better ways

Exhibit 11.1.
Use of Wellness as Marketing Opportunity

Foothills Metropolitan Recreation and
Park District, Lakewood, CO

WELLNESS-WHAT IS IT?

Wellness is a strange word that often lacks clear definition. To some people wellness is "not being sick" or may just mean "feeling well." To others it may indicate physical fitness and good health. Wellness, however, reaches beyond good health to include all aspects of our physical, mental, social, and spiritual well-being. How you spend your leisure time has a great deal to do with wellness. Relaxing and taking time for yourself is important to your personal health. An active wellness program serves to give you those opportunities and your recreation and park district offers a wide variety of programs to meet all your needs. Listed below are those areas important to each of us in achieving personal wellness.

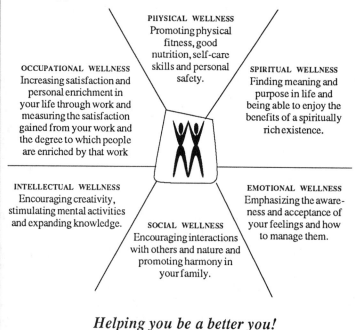

PHYSICAL WELLNESS
Promoting physical fitness, good nutrition, self-care skills and personal safety.

OCCUPATIONAL WELLNESS
Increasing satisfaction and personal enrichment in your life through work and measuring the satisfaction gained from your work and the degree to which people are enriched by that work

SPIRITUAL WELLNESS
Finding meaning and purpose in life and being able to enjoy the benefits of a spiritually rich existence.

INTELLECTUAL WELLNESS
Encouraging creativity, stimulating mental activities and expanding knowledge.

SOCIAL WELLNESS
Encouraging interactions with others and nature and promoting harmony in your family.

EMOTIONAL WELLNESS
Emphasizing the awareness and acceptance of your feelings and how to manage them.

Helping you be a better you!

COMMUNITY WELLNESS PROGRAM

Exhibit 11.2.
Use of Wellness for Art Class

Foothills Metropolitan Recreation and Park District, Lakewood, CO Winter/Spring Brochure 1989

FINE ARTS CO-OP

Set aside some time to enhance the harmony between your mind, hand and brush. Enjoy group comraderie as you work with fellow artists. Weekly critiques, problem solving tips and new techniques will be given by Washington Heights staff. It is mandatory to call in your lab reservation 48 hours in advance of class. Lunch break at noon.

FEE: $9.25D/$12.75DN per day

	Day	Time	Loc
Beginning FEB 22	WED	9:00 am-3:00 pm	WH

Relaxation is a big plus for joining an ART class. There is much satisfaction in finishing a beautiful work of art that you created from start to finish.

DRAWING AND PAINTING

The "emerging you" can draw and paint too—first drawing, then capture the memory with a variety of paint-along demonstrations and projects with emphasis on materials, color, value, and brushwork. Beginning supplies for drawing approximately $20; for painting, $60.

FEE: $20.23D/28.25ND (4 weeks)

Act. #	Session	Day	Session	Loc.
7204	1: JAN 24-FEB 14	TUE	1:00 pm-3:30 pm	WH
	2: FEB 28-MAR 21	THU	6:30 pm-9:00 pm	WH

to live. Leisure delivery systems can offer programs and services that capitalize upon these needs to quit smoking, reduce stress, or learn new physical activity skills. The organization can reposition itself as a center for life quality as opposed to just being a resort destination or a community center.

Personalization/Specialization/Convenience

All phases of the services industries will be influenced by the growing desire on the part of their customers for *personalization, specialization, and convenience (PSC)*. Americans are busy people. They feel as if they have less time and more things to do within that shrinking time framework. Convenience is important. They also feel as if they don't really belong or that they have little control over their lives. Personalization is a plus. The increasing evidence of fragmentation of interests and needs (as identified by Naisbitt in *Megatrends,* with his identification of a shift from *either/or* to *multiple options)* is still another factor to be addressed. Specialization is essential.

The combination of these three major forces within society is forcing all forms of the service sector to address the needs of consumers. VCRs and cable television allow couch potatoes to stay at home and watch the specific type of entertainment they desire. Leisure delivery systems must embrace this opportunity to remain viable in the future.

The opportunities within PSC are endless. Hotel chains have taken the lead in this area. Many major hotel chains have customized their facilities to address the specific needs of vacationers, business travelers, and even long-term business travelers. These organizations have recognized the importance of specialization. They have embraced the concept of convenience through express registration procedures and the provision of amenities such as bathrobes and hair dryers within guest rooms. To accommodate the preference for personalization, they have trained staff in specific techniques for making hotels seem like warmer and friendlier places.

Yes, the opportunities are endless, and they don't necessarily involve the extensive resources required in the hotel examples. Park, recreation, and leisure delivery systems have traditionally been organizations known for positive rapport with their consumers. Such delivery systems can further capitalize upon this strength by examining the peripheral "Ps" of the marketing mix. Small and relatively inexpensive techniques can be implemented to address PSC.

The 21st century will bring with it a myriad of changes, many of them unanticipated at this juncture. However, current trend projections include a plethora of changes and advances that bode well for the leisure industries. Such changes create extensive opportunities for delivery systems motivated to take advantage of them.

Marketing Techniques and Strategies

Societal changes and the subsequent emergence of new target market groups will substantially shape the marketing process for parks, recreation, and leisure. Specific marketing strategies and promotional techniques will need to be incorporated into the overall marketing approach in response to these changes. Included in this section are marketing strategies and marketing mix techniques, as well as promotional approaches designed to address these future changes.

Marketing Strategies

The single most important finding of the 1990 Census will reaffirm projected growth patterns and confirm a population growth rate of less than one percent a year and a rate of new household formations under two percent annually (Deveney and Francese, 1990, p. R29). This pattern, representing the lowest growth rate since the Depression, is no fluke, with even lower growth rates projected during the 1990s.

This represents a unique dilemma for recreation and leisure organizations facing growing competition in the experience industry in a no-growth market. It is predicted that in the 1990s there are two ways for service delivery systems to be weak. They can be weak by being too general or too big (Leisure Industry Digest, Feb. 1990, p. 4). There will be no market for products or services not targeted and personalized for a specific market segment.

The traditional mass-marketing strategy, besides being eroded by slow growth, has been fragmented by social changes into *micromarkets* or "many small pockets of different kinds of consumers with wildly different backgrounds, tastes, and needs" (Deveney and Francese, 1990, p. R29). These micromarkets or small pockets of consumers require a repositioning of leisure delivery systems in the form of a *niche* marketing strategy.

The shift to a niche strategy will be a requirement for organizations in the future. According to Joel Weiner, former senior vice-president of marketing at Kraft General Foods, "America is no longer a melting pot but a mosaic" (Deveney and Francese, 1990, p. R29). The presence of this mosaic compels leisure delivery systems to examine their target marketing strategies and through strategic planning identify programs and services that can be designed, adapted, and promoted to fulfill the needs of these small pockets of target market groups.

Public park and recreation departments have traditionally employed a mass-marketing approach seeking to provide areas, facilities, and programs for all residents within their jurisdiction. The fragmentation of consumer groups and preferences coupled with financial constraints may suggest a niche strategy for the future. The comprehensive resort providing golf, tennis, and swimming may narrow its approach to create a niche in one of these specialized areas.

Another marketing strategy appropriate for the experiential market place of the future is social marketing. *Social marketing* refers to the design and implementation of a marketing plan to increase the acceptability of a social cause or idea (Kotler, 1982, pp. 490-491). At one time this concept was considered to be exclusively for public or nonprofit agencies. They often used it for designing public awareness campaigns to promote social causes or to introduce behavior change such as fuel conservation or smoking cessation. Social marketing, distinguished by its emphasis upon so-called nontangible products such as ideas, attitudes, or lifestyle, is applicable for the experience industries.

Future participation in recreation and leisure activities will require the fulfillment of the public's need for experiences. Experiences are not the same as an activity but, rather, they consist of an idea. Consumers will be looking at resorts or cruises not as vacation options, but rather as an opportunity for escape, pampering, or new experience. Fitness clubs will not be sought as places to exercise, but rather as social experiences or outlets for restoring balance to one's life. It will become increasingly important for park, recreation, and leisure delivery systems to create an idea of what these experiences can offer and to communicate that idea effectively to their target market groups.

For instance, the National Recreation and Park Association has recently introduced a public service campaign that incorporates the social marketing approach. This campaign, "Exercise the Right Choice," attempts to position public park and recreation departments as a alternative for youngsters and drugs (see Exhibit 11.3).

A word of caution or restraint is required regarding social marketing. Social marketing concepts were originally developed to create positive social change. The opportunities generated for the experience industries may incorporate elements of this approach to marketing while neglecting positive social values and behaviors. The use of social marketing as a means

Exhibit 11.3.
Application of Social Marketing Approach

to profit while simultaneously encouraging negative behavior is not the intention of this approach. While it holds potential for all leisure delivery systems regardless of mission as a mechanism for attracting participants, the focus should be upon positive and socially acceptable behavior.

An additional marketing strategy in response to specialized target markets with potential for some park and recreation delivery systems is the *doublemint strategy*. This two-in-one tactic named after the ads for the gum of the same name is a strategy designed to add a whole new market to an existing one by adding a complementary service or product to the original location (Brown, 1989, p. 121).

While this may be an unusual way to think about a business, it is based upon the premise that by operating two businesses in one location, the organization simultaneously reduces overhead expenses while increasing revenue by giving people two reasons to make a stop at this one location. Many community centers house multiple public services such as visiting nurses, elderly services, and recreation. This illustrates an attempt by the public sector to implement this approach.

This same concept is now being applied to commercial recreation organizations as well. Bowling centers use adjacent space to add miniature golf. Some health and fitness clubs have introduced a restaurant/bar to their sites. The growth of competition in this low growth market of the future, along with emphasis upon cost effectiveness, make the doublemint strategy a consideration for the future.

An additional marketing strategy with potential for the future is *bottoms-up marketing,* conceived by Reis and Trout, who developed strategies for positioning. Bottoms-up marketing suggests that delivery systems focus upon *tactics* first, followed by *strategy.* Reis and Trout refer to tactics as being a competitive mental edge designed to identify better ways to attract and serve customers. They differentiate between the two terms by defining tactics as figuring out what the organization can do, as opposed to strategy, which focuses on what the organization would like to do (Reis and Trout, 1988, pp. 60-72).

Bottoms-up marketing addresses itself to what is possible for the organization and suggests that organizations need to find a tactic or competitive mental angle by finding a position to focus upon and then developing a strategy to create a vision to meet that position. The key players in this approach are the frontline service people who come into close contact with the customer and have the best likelihood of discovering appropriate tactics for the delivery system.

By using this approach, the recreator reverses the process by getting in touch with the marketplace, finding a competitive mental angle, and then being flexible enough to follow through with it. Tactics are external and reflected in the minds of the consumers and strategies are internal to the delivery system. In this future era of ever-growing competition and fragmentation of target markets in a no- or slow-growth period, bottoms-up marketing is a viable approach to be incorporated.

Marketing Mix Techniques

While marketing strategies generally relate to the overall management direction of an entire organization, there are specific marketing techniques related to marketing mix variables that will be helpful for the future. Some of these techniques include bundling of benefits, synchronization, convenience, and customer care.

Bundling of benefits is a concerted effort on the part of the delivery system to both identify specific benefits being sought by the users of a particular program or service, and to integrate those benefits into the marketing mix. While not an entirely new concept, it is rapidly receiving renewed attention. Recreation and leisure delivery systems are attempting to reach target market groups by arriving at the exact mix of benefits that will attract people to their programs or services.

Some leisure delivery systems have already implemented this practice. Many health clubs are now offering service packages that bring together various services offered by their organization such as fitness testing, medical testing, and nutritional counseling. Mecklenberg County Parks and Recreation Department in North Carolina noted the limited use of camping sites on weekends by their residents and attacked this lack of use by bundling benefits (What's Hot, 1989, p. 1). Now with one phone call, county residents can not only reserve a campsite for the weekend, but they can arrange for the rental of camping equipment and can even have their tent set up for them. It's made a substantial difference in usage rates. J. R.'s Festival Lakes located in the Washington, DC area clearly spells out the bundles of benefits offered to people planning group picnics or outings, as illustrated in Exhibit 11.4

This bundling of benefits approach can focus upon eliminating unwanted benefits for certain target market groups as well. Private country clubs have often used this approach. They make available full memberships

Exhibit 11.4.
Application of Bundling of Benefits Technique

Promotional Flyer from J. R.'s Festival Lakes

J. R.'s FESTIVAL LAKES

Takes The Headaches Out Of Picnic Planning

We Will . . . .

- **Plan** your event and menus with you
- **Arrange** your vendors and picnic give aways
- **Provide** a Chairman's Packet which includes:
  - Ideas for fun activities
  - Planning checklist
  - Art work and posters
    . . . for promoting your event
- **Conduct** personal tours or give group presentations
- **Provide** fun, facilities and equipment for:
  - Swimming
  - Fishing/paddle boating
  - Golf driving range
  - Softball, volleyball, badminton, horseshoes
- **Have** a friendly staff to cook and serve your sumptuous picnic feast
- **Host** a Chairpersons Day (your opportunity to see the facility, sample the food, and meet the vendors)

CALL (703) 821-1000
LET US MAKE YOUR EVENT PLANNING EASY

including use of all facilities as well as social memberships attractive to nongolfers who are primarily interested in the dining and clubroom facilities. Look for this unbundling approach to become more popular with consumers and more profitable for delivery systems in the future.

Convenience is clearly an issues for the nineties. Major surveys differ as to whether Americans have less or more leisure time, but they all seem to indicate that time is an increasingly precious commodity either in reality or perception. A recent study conducted by the United Way shows that Americans feel more rushed but concludes that much of this feeling is perceptual with people trying to fit all the things they need and want to do into a schedule (United Way, 1989-90, p. 4). The report maintains that the perception described about leisure time is actually due to an increase in activity during leisure (United Way, 1989-90, p. 4).

This emphasis upon convenience and time-saving measures may influence the policies and procedures aspects of the marketing mix as well as other variables. Mail registrations, credit card payments, and use of the FAX facilitate convenience. Providing users with complete information over the phone as well as ease of drop-off and delivery are all aspects to be addressed. All aspects of the marketing mix variables for a program or service should be examined and modified with an eye towards making usage more convenient for the participant.

This technique can be used in conjunction with bundling of benefits in many instances. Summer day camp programs for children that include transportation in the camp fee may be better received by dual-career couples than less expensive alternatives without transportation, due to the convenience. Convenience is the key to future success. People feel pressured to make the most of their time. Organizations that ignore this high priority run the risk of losing clientele.

Synchronization is another technique that refers to this important element of time. However, this use of time can refer to the delivery system's identification of off-season or nontraditional participation times and the subsequent development of programs or services to be planned for these time periods. Off-season rates at resorts, year-round programming at ski areas, and use of early morning, lunchtime, or weekend scheduling are all examples of use of this technique by leisure delivery systems.

The other application of synchronization involves time usage patterns of participants. Getaway weekend packages and mini-courses capitalize on changing time usage patterns. Some fitness centers are now offering and promoting 20-minute workout programs to attract people who feel as if they don't have sufficient time to exercise.

Synchronization and convenience are closely related. These two marketing mix techniques focus upon time. Peoples' use of time and perception of this time are critical considerations for the future.

Customer care is clearly a competitive edge of the future. This technique relates to the PSC (personalization, specialization, and convenience) previously cited. People today want exactly what they want in a time framework that is convenient for them, as well as wanting personal attention. Marriott's Desert Springs Resort and Spa in Palm Desert, CA offers 19 guest guarantees, including a free half-hour tennis lesson if the guest is unable to find a playing partner in 30 minutes. Poolside amenities include chilled, bottled drinking water as well as attendants who provide sunscreen lotion to sunseekers who don't want to get into the pool.

This list of the modifications made to marketing mix variables designed to enhance customer care is virtually endless. Such modifications can be costly or relatively inexpensive. However, with the increase of competition within leisure services, most experts believe that customer care is truly the definitive difference for future success.

The aforementioned marketing techniques relate to modifications or adaptations to marketing mix variables. While the applications of these techniques will vary for individual organizations, a review of these suggestions may prove helpful for providing future directions for a park, recreation, or leisure delivery system.

Promotional Techniques

As target markets change and technology advances, promotional techniques and strategies will naturally undergo changes as well. In the recent past, national companies relied upon ads on network television to promote goods and services to a few dominant market groups. However, the onset of cable television service has seriously eroded into network TV viewership, along with the fragmentation of target market groups making this approach less effective for the future.

There are a number of new promotional options with promise for the nineties. One such technique is the introduction of personalized or customized ads. As of January 1990, such magazines as *Time, Sports Illustrated,* and *People* featured ads personalized with the names of their subscribers (Jacobson, 1990, pp. C1-5). Magazines as promotion will become a key tool. The lifestyle profiles of magazine subscribers and readers are well-defined and present a cost-effective mechanism for advertisers to customize ads to reach specific lifestyle groups. Several top business magazines such as *Forbes, Business Week,* and *Inc.* have created *lifestyle magazines* that are mailed free to subscribers and supported wholly by advertising revenues (Leisure Industry Digest, Jan. 1990, p. 4). Other magazines are modifying specific topics or focus of articles based upon their knowledge of the subscriber.

Park, recreation, and leisure delivery systems can address this personalization and customization in a number of ways. The 1990 Census data make lifestyle data tied to geographic parameters more widely available. Organizations can generate mailing lists and then customize their promotional materials for specific target market groups. For instance, a resort can design distinct brochures for different target market groups and then mail them accordingly to appropriate zip codes or neighborhoods. Public or nonprofit organizations without the resources to undertake three separate brochures could consider flyers with different headlines or pictures that would better relate to specific target market groups.

Computerized printing programs can be used to personalize promotional materials. Newsletters featuring the names and activities of members can be inexpensively created and mailed. Names of household members can be inserted into promotional pieces. The advances in computer technology lend themselves to incorporation by leisure delivery systems as a mechanism for personalizing promotion.

Event sponsorship is another promotional technique being utilized by advertisers to reach specific, niche market segments. Many companies have identified the interest in experiences as a way to promote their organization or their product. Miller Brewing Company sponsored a free concert tour that visited 11 cities with strong Hispanic markets in an attempt to reach this target market group (Leisure Industry Digest, 1989, p. 2). Event sponsorship is a natural for public park and recreation departments with access to a number of target market groups as well as the capacity for organizing and implementing such specialized events.

Although event sponsorship has increased over the past few years, it is still in its infancy. The potential for this approach to simultaneously provide experiences while reaching specific target market groups may prove to be both an effective and cost-efficient technique for promotion.

Soft ads or the use of computer or video technology is yet another promotional option with promise for the nineties. The use of computerized programs to assist people in selecting the appropriate recreation program with specific options or video guides to overview recreation experiences, resorts, or travel destinations will all be key promotional techniques.

The public and nonprofit sectors of the industry can capitalize upon this approach by utilizing existing public access cable television stations to visually acquaint target market members with leisure options and experiences available to them. The commercial sector might make use of this trend by joining the other for-profit organizations by creating *infomercials,* the 30- to 90-minute programs designed for cable stations actually promoting a product, program, or service in the guise of a televised program.

Societal changes will also influence approaches to advertising and promotion that will change the tone and focus of such promotions. Two such approaches are gender-blending and use of nostalgia. *Gender-blending* refers to cross-sex marketing or promotion. A product or service that was once sold to one sex is now promoted to both gender groups. Economic and social forces change traditional gender roles and so advertisers are aiming food and personal care products at men and automobiles and alcoholic beverages at women (Elliot, 1989, p. 5B).

These same social and economic changes carry over into leisure experiences. Women are now members of softball leagues and men enroll in cooking classes. This shift in preferences for leisure experiences will continue. Along with that shift is the need for leisure delivery systems to incorporate gender-blending into their promotional campaigns.

The use of *nostalgia* is an effective technique for advertisers hoping to incorporate the youthful memories and emotions of baby boomers. The use of once-popular music and the re-creation of scenes and experiences from youth and teen years are featured in ads as a means for attracting this target market group. There are a number of applications in use by leisure delivery systems as organizations change the names of programs or incorporate appropriate slogans in promotional materials to attract this target market group and their children.

One of the challenges that will increase in the future is the ability of promotion to actually receive the attention of the target markets. In this society where people are bombarded with several types of media bearing thousands of messages on a daily basis, it will continue to be a challenge to be heard or stand out. The escalating cost of such promotional efforts only heightens this challenge.

One such approach to this challenge is *streetfighting,* masterminded by Jeff Slutsky, of the Retail Marketing Institute of Fort Wayne, IN. Slutsky, who specializes in low-cost, creative approaches to attract attention for organizations, defines streetfighting as "out-thinking as opposed to out-spending your competition" (Slutsky, 1984, p. 5). Some of Slutsky's low-cost approaches included an ice cream giveaway for an appliance dealer to curtail further customer comparison shopping; prepaying parking meters accompanied by a flyer; and the creation of a false sense of urgency for reservations at a restaurant.

His entire focus is to find an effective way to gain the attention of potential customers but to do so in a manner that is inexpensive for the organization. Slutsky makes the most of every opportunity. He uses free raffles as a means for drawing people into an establishment while simultaneously using the entry forms to pinpoint geographic and lifestyle characteristics of target markets.

An additional technique used by Slutsky is cross-promotion. *Cross-promotion* involves using the customers of an existing and noncompeting organization as a potential source of new customers for one's own business (Slutsky, 1984, p. 101). For instance, the owner of a fitness center might approach the management of a nearby tennis center and propose offering a free month's fitness membership to any of their current users. Conducted at no expense to its own organization, the tennis center was able to offer an additional free benefit to their tennis players and the owner of the fitness center was able to conduct a low-cost promotion to attract new members to his establishment.

This type of promotional technique is well-suited for park, recreation, and leisure delivery systems. Since the programs and services offered by these organizations are perceived as being desirable and pleasurable, they would most likely be well-received by other types of establishments with an existing user base. This technique tends to be low-cost, since it generally involves only the printing costs associated with the free membership offer or discount and is distributed through existing channels by the cooperating organization.

An additional technique being used extensively by numerous types of organizations is the creation of loyalty programs. Airlines were among the first to seize this opportunity for establishing programs for frequent users of their services and were quickly followed by car rentals, hotels, and even bookstores. The purpose of these frequent-user programs is to foster loyalty among current users and to establish incentives that will encourage continued participation by user groups. The Broward County, Florida Parks and Recreation Division sponsors an incentive program for frequent hikers. Residents who participate in six or more nature walks during the year receive a hiking staff. Each succeeding year they receive a dated emblem to add to the walking stick. Anticipate seeing more of this type of promotional activity in the future as organizations struggle to maintain market share in this low growth period.

Promotion will remain a challenge for the future. As target market groups become more fragmented and while the cost of advertising continues to climb, it will become increasingly more difficult to get the message out to members of one's target markets. The use of computerized technology as well as integration of creative and timely approaches are necessary for organizations to remain competitive.

Summary

Although every new decade or century heralds the onset of changes and new directions, the 21st century holds the potential for significant shifts in the ways we live, work, and play. Many of the trends, changes, and conditions create unique and highly profitable marketing opportunities for parks, recreation, and leisure. Among those opportunities are the preference for experiences, wellness, travel, and the emphasis upon personalization, specialization, and convenience.

These marketing opportunities will influence and shape all phases of the marketing process for parks, recreation, and leisure. Marketing strategies to be explored and considered by these delivery systems include niche marketing, social marketing, the doublemint strategy, and bottoms-up marketing. In addition to overall marketing strategies, there are specific techniques related to marketing mix variables that will be useful in the future. Some of these techniques include bundling of benefits, convenience, synchronographics, and customer care.

Naturally, these marketing strategies and techniques coupled with societal changes and technological advances will change advertising and promotion. Such techniques with potential for future use by leisure delivery systems include personalized and customized ads, event sponsorship, soft ads, gender-blending, use of nostalgia, streetfighting, cross-promotion, and loyalty programs.

The new century offers a host of opportunities for parks, recreation, and leisure. This era of opportunity will become real for those organizations that identify such opportunities and then modify or adapt marketing strategies to seize those opportunities.

Suggested Activities

1. For the generic field of leisure, brainstorm a list of possible marketing opportunities for the 21st century.

2. For a specific leisure delivery system, attempt to identify both current and long-term opportunities. Suggest strategies for both categories.

3. Conduct a marketing audit of the programs and services offered by a leisure delivery system. Identify modifications to be made on the basis of bundling of benefits and PSC.

4. Review the current target market strategies of a delivery sys tem. Create niche strategies where appropriate and suggest implementation approaches.

5. Examine the current promotional materials of a delivery system. Identify areas where new promotional techniques could be introduced.

References

American Adventures. (1989, January 29). *Hartford Courant,* p. F9.

Brown, P. E. (1989, March). The Doublemint Strategy. *Inc.,* p. 121.

Deveney and Francese. (1990, March 9). Shrinking Markets—Finding a Niche May Be the Key to Survival. *Wall Street Journal,* p. R29.

Downey, M. (1990, March 4). "Fast-Track Generation Swerving Toward the Exit Ramp. *Sunday Republican,* p. G5.

Edmonton's Fantasyland Is a Dream World Hotel. (1990, February 25) *Sarasota-Herald Tribune,* p. 7G.

Elliot, S. Changing Times for Ads. (1989, August 7). *USA Today,* p. 5B.

Get Ready for New Ways to Be Taken for a Ride. (1989, March 12). *USA Today*, p. 12E.

Harris, L. (1987). *Inside America* (p. 8). New York, NY: Vintage Books.

Hot Businesses for the 90s. (1989, December). *Entrepreneur.*

Jacobson, D. (1990, January 3). Technology Helps Magazines Track Target Audiences. *Hartford Courant*, p. C1-5.

Kotler, P. (1982). *Marketing for Nonprofit Organizations* (2nd ed.) (pp. 490-491). Englewood Cliffs, NJ: Prentice-Hall.

Larsen, C. (1990, February). Field Trips. *Travel and Leisure*, p. 97.

Leisure Industry Digest IX, August/September 1989, p. 2.

Leisure Industry Digest X, January 1990, p. 4.

Leisure Industry Digest X, February, 1990, p. 4.

Marketing Experience Travels in the 1990s. (1990, January). *Travel and Tourism Executive Report X*.

Meet at the Mall. (1989, November 19). *The Sunday Republican*, p. D1.

Reis and Trout. (1988). *Bottom Up Marketing* (pp. 60-72). New York, NY: McGraw-Hill.

Silk, S. (1990, March 4). The Daydreams of a Lifetime. *Hartford Courant*, p. F1.

Slutsky, J. (1984). Streetfighting: Low Cost Advertising/Promotion for Your Business. Englewood Cliffs, NJ: Prentice-Hall, p. 5.

Toffler, A. (1980). *The Third Wave*. New York, NY: William Morrow and Company.

Tourism with Purpose. (1989, November/December). *CLIPS (Congressional Institute for the Future)*, p. 45.

Travelers Taking Adventure and Shorter Trips. (1989, January 29). *Hartford Courant*, p. F1.

Trick, D. R. (1990, March 5). Cruise Business is Shipshape. *USA Today*, p. 5D.

United Way Report Shows Sweeping Change for the Decade. (1989-90, Winter). *What's New-A Newsletter of Emerging Trends and Issues, 11*, (4), p. 4.

What's Hot—What's Not. (1989, July). *PIN (Programmers Information Network) 1* (3), 1.

BOOKS FROM VENTURE PUBLISHING

Acquiring Parks and Recreation Facilities through Mandatory Dedication:
A Comprehensive Guide,
by Ronald A. Kaiser and James D. Mertes

Adventure Education,
edited by John C. Miles and Simon Priest

Amenity Resource Valuation: Integrating Economics with Other Disciplines,
edited by George L. Peterson, B.L. Driver and Robin Gregory

Behavior Modification in Therapeutic Recreation: An Introductory Learning
Manual,
by John Dattilo and William D. Murphy

Benefits of Leisure,
edited by B. L. Driver, Perry J. Brown and George L. Peterson

Beyond the Bake Sale—A Fund Raising Handbook for Public Agencies,
by Bill Moskin

The Community Tourism Industry Imperative—The Necessity,
The Opportunities, Its Potential,
by Uel Blank

Dimensions of Choice: A Qualitative Approach to Recreation, Parks,
and Leisure Research,
by Karla A. Henderson, Ph.D.

Doing More With Less in the Delivery of Recreation and Park Services:
A Book of Case Studies,
by John Crompton

Evaluation of Therapeutic Recreation Through Quality Assurance,
edited by Bob Riley

The Evolution of Leisure: Historical and Philosophical Perspectives,
by Thomas Goodale and Geoffrey Godbey

The Future of Leisure Services: Thriving on Change,
by Geoffrey Godbey

Gifts to Share—A Gifts Catalogue How-To Manual for Public Agencies,
by Lori Harder and Bill Moskin

Great Special Events and Activities,
by Annie Morton, Angie Prosser and Sue Spangler

Leadership and Administration of Outdoor Pursuits,
by Phyllis Ford and James Blanchard

The Leisure Diagnostic Battery: Users Manual and Sample Forms,
by Peter Witt and Gary Ellis

Leisure Diagnostic Battery Computer Software,
by Gary Ellis and Peter Witt

Leisure Education: A Manual of Activities and Resources,
by Norma J. Stumbo and Steven R. Thompson

Leisure Education: Program Materials for Persons with Developmental
Disabilities,
by Kenneth F. Joswiak

Leisure in Your Life: An Exploration, Third Edition
by Geoffrey Godbey

A Leisure of One's Own: A Feminist Perspective on Women's Leisure,
by Karla Henderson, M. Deborah Bialeschki, Susan M. Shaw
and Valeria J. Freysinger

Outdoor Recreation Management: Theory and Application,
Revised and Enlarged, by Alan Jubenville, Ben Twight and
Robert H. Becker

Planning Parks for People, by John Hultsman,
Richard L. Cottrell and Wendy Zales Hultsman

Playing, Living, Learning: A Worldwide Perspective on Children's
Opportunities to Play,
by Cor Westland and Jane Knight

Private and Commercial Recreation,
edited by Arlin Epperson

The Process of Recreation Programming: Theory and Technique, Third Edition
by Patricia Farrell and Herberta M. Lundegren

Quality Management Applications for Therapeutic Recreation,
edited by Bob Riley

Recreation and Leisure: An Introductory Handbook,
edited by Alan Graefe and Stan Parker

Recreation Economic Decisions: Comparing Benefits and Costs,
by Richard G. Walsh

Recreation Programming And Activities For Older Adult,s
by Jerold E. Elliott and Judith A. Sorg-Elliott

Risk Management in Therapeutic Recreation: A Component of Quality
Assurance,
by Judy Voelkl

Schole VI: A Journal of Leisure Studies and Recreation Education,

A Social History of Leisure Since 1600,
by Gary Cross

Sports and Recreation for the Disabled—A Resource Manual,
by Michael J. Paciorek and Jeffery A. Jones

A Study Guide for National Certification in Therapeutic Recreation,
by Gerald O'Morrow and Ron Reynolds

Therapeutic Recreation Protocol for Treatment of Substance Addictions,
by Rozanne W. Faulkner

Understanding Leisure and Recreation: Mapping the Past, Charting the Future,
edited by Edgar L. Jackson and Thomas L. Burton

Wilderness in America: Personal Perspectives,
edited by Daniel L. Dustin

Venture Publishing, Inc
1999 Cato Avenue, State College, PA 16801